Enactments

EDITED BY CAROL MARTIN AND RICHARD SCHECHNER

To perform is to imagine, represent, live and enact present circumstances, past events and future possibilities. Performance takes place across a very broad range of venues from city streets to the countryside, in theatres and in offices, on battlefields and in hospital operating rooms. The genres of performance are many, from the arts to the myriad performances of everyday life, from courtrooms to legislative chambers, from theatres to wars to circuses.

ENACTMENTS will encompass performance in as many of its aspects and realities as there are authors able to write about them.

ENACTMENTS will include active scholarship, readable thought and engaged analysis across the broad spectrum of performance studies.

T0385027

CRUCIBLE BODIES

POSTWAR JAPANESE PERFORMANCE
FROM BRECHT TO THE NEW MILLENNIUM

Tadashi Uchino

LONDON NEW YORK CALCUTTA

Seagull Books 2009

© Seagull Books 2009

Cover image: Hiropon, 1997. Oil paint, acrylic, fibreglass and iron. 223.5 x 104 x 122 cm. Courtesy Galerie Emmanuel Perrotin. © 1997 Takashi Murakami/ Kaikai Kiki Co., Ltd. All Rights Reserved.

Cover design: Sunandini Banerjee

ISBN-13 (HB) 978 1 9054 2 272 2
ISBN-13 (PB) 978 1 9054 2 274 6
ISSN   1751 0864

British Library Cataloguing-in-Publication Data
A catalogue record for this book is available from the British Library

Typeset by Seagull Books, Calcutta, India

Printed and bound in India at Rockwel Offset, Calcutta

CONTENTS

ACKNOWLEDGEMENTS

Part of the Introduction has appeared in *Half a Century of Japanese Theatre*: *1990s Part III* (Tokyo: Kinokuniya, 2007), as 'Introduction: Japan's "Ill-Fated" Theatre Culture', pp. 1–14.

Chapter 1: 'Political Displacements: Towards Historicizing Brecht in Japan, 1932–1998' has been published in Carol Martin and Henry Bial (eds) *Brecht Sourcebook* (New York: Routledge, 2000), pp. 185–205. The first version of this article was presented at the International Brecht Conference, New York University, October 1998.

Chapter 2: 'Images of Armageddon: Japan's 1980s' Theatre Culture' was first published in *TDR* 44(1) (2000): 85–96. The original Japanese version of this article appeared as '80 Nendai Engeki to Armageddon Genso' ('1980 Theatre and Armageddon Fantasy') in *Theatre Arts* 4 (1996): 77–86.

Interlude 1: ' "Beauty" in Modern and Postmodern Japan' was first published in Wu Hung and Ackbar Abbas (eds), *About Beauty* (Berlin: House of World Cultures, 2005), pp. 209–217.

Chapter 3: 'Deconstructing "Japaneseness": Towards Articulating Locality and Hybridity in Contemporary Japanese Performance' was first published in Rachel Fensham and Peter Eckersall (eds), *Dis/Orientations—Cultural Praxis in Theatre*: *Asia, Pacific, Australia* (Clayton, Australia: Center for Drama and Theatre Studies, Monash University, 1999), pp. 35–53. The first version of this article was presented as a keynote address at the Australian Drama Studies Association Annual Meeting, Monash University, Melbourne, Australia, July 1997.

Chapter 4: 'Playing Betwixt and Between: Intercultural Performance in the Age of Globalization' was first published in Bjern Tasmussen and Anna-Lena Ostern (eds), *Playing Betwixt and Between*: *The IDEA Dialogues 2001* (Bergen: IDEA Publications and IDEA World Congress, 2002), pp. 67–76. The original version of this article was presented as a keynote address at the IDEA Fourth World Congress, Bergen, Norway, July 2001.

The original version of Interlude 2 was read at 'Body and Ancient Greek Drama', an international symposium organized by the Desmi Center for Ancient Greek Drama and the Municipality of Elfisina, Elfisina, Greece, October 2004.

Chapter 5: 'Pop, Postmodernism, and Junk: Murakami Takashi and "J" Theatre' was first published in *Dokkyo International Review*, 16 (2003): 115–29. The first version of this article—'Super-flat Japan: Thinking about Bodies in Contemporary "J" Performances' was read at the Asian Contemporary Theatre Conference, Esplanade, Singapore, October 2002, and subsequently published *Coping with the Contemporary: Selves, Identity and Community* (Singapore: Esplanade, 2004), pp. 43–56. The revised version was read at the Dokkyo International Forum, at a panel entitled 'East Asian Cultural Flow: Performative Inventions and Imagining East Asia', December 2002.

Chapter 6: 'Globality's Children: The "Child's" Body as a Strategy of Flatness in Performance' was first published in *TDR* 50(1) (2006): 57–66. The original version of this article was presented at the 10th Performance Studies International Conference, Singapore Management University, June 2004.

The original version of Interlude 3 was read at an international sympo-sium at Laokoon Festival, Kampnagel, Germany, August 2003.

Chapter 7: 'Zapping/Mapping "J" Theatre' was first published in *Performance Paradigm* 2 (2006) [www.performanceparadigm.net/articles/article-mapping-zapping.html] and later published in Edward Scheer and Peter Eckersall (eds), *The Ends of the 60s: Performance, Media and Contemporary Culture* (Sydney: Faculty of Arts and Social Sciences, UNSW and Performance Paradigm, 2006), pp. 79–86. The original version was read at the Asialink Annual Forum, 'Sun Rising: Japanese Culture Today', Sidney Myer Asia Center, University of Melbourne, July 2005.

Chapter 8: The original Japanese version was published as '"J-to-iu Basho" de Rekishi wo "Undo" suru koto'—9.11 iko no Miyazawa Akio wo Megutte' ('Undoing History in the "J" Locality: On Miyazawa Akio after 9/11') in *Eureka* (Miyazawa Akio Special Issue) (2006): 72–85.

The original version of the Epilogue—'From Interculturalism to Con-fusion: Thinking through Possible Forms of Theatre in the Age of Globality'—was read at 'Making Tradition, Remaking Tradition', an international seminar for Theater Utsav, Ninth Bharat Rang Mahotsav, National School of Drama, New Delhi, India, January 2007.

AUTHOR'S NOTE: *Throughout this book, Japanese names have been spelled in the Japanese order—surname (family name) first, given name last.*

Crucible Bodies is a collection of essays about bodies-in-performance I have witnessed over the last 10 years, mostly in Tokyo. The title also has personal meaning as my graduation thesis in theatre studies was on Arthur Miller in 1981, though it was not on *The Crucible* but *Death of a Salesman*. The notion of 'crucible' was suggested by Carol Martin (a great supporter of this book project and a General Editor of this series) who rightly pointed out that Japan has been in a social, cultural, political and historical flux during the post-War years. This flux is evident not only through its performances of existential and metaphorical bodies within theatrical frames but also in the unveiling of the ontological status of my body which, in a dialectical relation to my brain, inevitably circumscribes what the readers of this book will encounter in the following pages.

In this introduction, I will be telling two stories (almost) simultaneously: my own (hi)story and what I call an 'ill-fated' history of Japan's theatre culture. Through an exploration of these two seemingly unrelated discursive sites, I hope you will begin to understand how the notion of crucible bodies can be made to operate in quite an unexpected way.

ENTERING THE BATTLEFIELD (1): THE ORIGIN

I still remember an interview with the staff members of the Department of English Literature in the Graduate School of Humanities at the University of Tokyo in 1981. Not entirely sure of what I was doing, I found myself sitting for the entrance exam for the Graduate School. The late Prof. Takahashi Yasunari (1932–2002) helped me out when one of the professors asked me why I had written a thesis on Arthur Miller; in his opinion, Miller was a second-rate playwright and not worth studying at the graduate level. I should have studied Chekhov or Ibsen instead, if I was interested in modern realist theatre (though he knew perfectly well that I read neither Russian nor Norwegian). While I groped for an answer to this inexplicable question, Prof. Yasunari spoke up on my behalf, 'It's a tough question to answer, I know, but I have a different one for you. The study of theatre is something that includes many unexpected intellectual challenges. It's much more than just reading literary texts, consulting *The Oxford English Dictionary* and learning the classic languages of Greek and Latin. Are you ready for it?'

I don't remember what I said to him then but I do remember what followed. After one of his graduate seminars on the plays of Harold Pinter, Prof. Yasunari asked me to meet him. 'What are you doing this summer vacation?' he enquired. 'Nothing much. Probably working at a preparatory school for high school kids, teaching English,' I answered. 'Do you know Suzuki Tadashi?' was his next question.

I'm afraid that was a time when I did not know Suzuki Tadashi; my knowledge of theatre was very limited, raised as I had been in the provincial city of Hiroshima. Even after entering a university in Tokyo, I was not attracted to theatre, simply because theatre-going was not part of everyday life for most Japanese and I was no exception. In fact, many of us had a decisive reason to dislike theatre: our experience of it had been a visit to our high school from one of those amateur Shingeki companies who put up an (unbelievably naive) morality play. We were, by then, accustomed to being entertained by TV shows and 'cool' Hollywood films. Live theatre was thus rightly considered to be a puritanical device to 'preach' moral lessons to students.

This was during the 1970s, and I had no clue about events in Tokyo. I was born in Kyoto in 1957 and moved to Hiroshima at the age of 10. My father had lived in the US and our home was imbued with a distinctly 'American' feel; he liked American TV shows and films and we lived a fairly Westernized life. After moving to the more provincial city of Hiroshima, that sense of elitism, fuelled by Westernized values, 'alienated' me from my immediate environment. I had always felt that I did not necessarily belong to any particular sociocultural configuration; I was always negotiating the spaces between different poles of value systems—the provincial versus the urban, the elitist versus the democratic, the Japanese versus the Western (American) and the traditional versus the modern.

In terms of theatre, though, I came to acquire a somewhat different background. I spent a year in the US as an exchange student in Barrington, Rhode Island, in 1974 and 1975. At the high school I attended, there was a tradition of foreign students participating in the theatre arts club. It was, according to the school authorities, a better way for the foreigners to know more people and pick up more English. I participated in several productions, although I never landed a major role because of my accent. Dopey in a Christmas production of *Snow White* for children was as close as I could get to a 'big' part. Dopey was almost always on stage, but never spoke until the very last moment of the play. What an appropriate role for a foreign-exchange student to play! Towards the end of the school year, we went on a day trip to watch *Grease* on Broadway—my first visit to New York City.

In a typically East Coast liberal curriculum, the high school instructor used 'American' texts such as Melville's 'Bartleby, the Scrivener', Thoreau's *Walden* and Miller's *The Crucible* while teaching the American Studies class. This was 1974, when Nixon's impeachment and the end of the Vietnam War were burning issues and I was living with a Jewish family in a quiet, New England, mostly white, rich town. In most cases, such an environment would be enough to 'Americanize' a 'poor' boy from a Far Eastern country. I, however, am not too sure. My one-year stay in this liberal East Coast atmosphere gave me enough confidence as a person but, at the same time, inculcated a more complex and ambivalent feeling towards America and things American. What I felt was not necessarily nationalistic pride but more an existential habit, as it were; I constantly displaced myself from what seemed to be the dominant sociocultural configuration and its practical manifestations within which I was supposed to completely contain myself and feel secure. I didn't know why but it certainly gave me a sense of identity and intellectual pride by always putting myself outside the dominant and the mainstream. I therefore acquired the habit of being self-reflexive and critical even when everyone else around me seemed to be very much 'in' it.

AN 'ILL-FATED' HISTORY OF JAPAN'S THEATRE CULTURE (1): THE ORIGIN

As I write this introduction in September 2006, Japan's contemporary theatre culture should be proud of its incredible number of productions although, naturally, most of them are concentrated in urban areas, especially in the capital city of Tokyo. Not unlike Broadway or the West End, Tokyo is filled with enough playwrights, directors, actors, producers and theatre-goers to comprise an established theatre industry. In terms of the specific genre of 'Little Theatre', according to a very interesting personal survey conducted during 2005, there were 2,038 performances done by 1,639 theatre groups.[1] This survey included those productions that were qualified by the following conditions: performed within the metropolitan area of Tokyo and running for seven days or less, and tickets priced under 5,000 yen (approximately 43 US dollars). These conditions ensured that the productions came under the rubric of the ambiguously defined 'Little Theatre', and it is hard to know whether or not they were commercially feasible. Living in Tokyo, especially in the last five years or so, one does have an undeniable sense of the growing domain of the theatre industry, with theatre culture gradually recognized as an integral part of the social life of the urban middle-class. From the glossy commercial theatres of Ginza and Shibuya to the literally little theatres in Shinjuku and Shimo-kitazawa,[2] there is something to watch every day of the year.

Despite this impression of Tokyo as a theatre city, we have to be cautious in understanding theatre culture's sociopolitical positioning within Japan's cultural history. Just as we must not lose sight of theatre culture's 'ill-fated' deployment within the matrix of Japan's modernizing and nation-building, so must we not assume that there was a similar 'fortunate' linear progression of history as there was in many Western nation-states whose sociopolitical systems and institutions Japan aspired to during its nation-building process. Because of diverse political reasons and historical conditions which I do not here have the space to articulate, theatre culture was never a part of the national project of modernization nor was it a component of Westernization in Japan (except, perhaps, in a negative way which resulted in some traditional forms being regarded as objects of drastic reformation, as we will soon discuss). For a long time, Japan had no national theatre, nor any public theatres, and theatre was not part of public education. The aesthetic genres chosen to help establish and consolidate 'structures of feeling' (Raymond Williams)[3] for the elite and the middle class were music, visual arts and literature. Before World War II, the educational institutions contributing to the national project of identity-construction were the Tokyo School of Music and the Tokyo School of Fine Art. These came together after the War to form the Tokyo University of Fine Arts and, until very recently, theatre was never a part of its curriculum.[4] In contrast, literature departments following Euro-American models were installed in many national and private universities.

Thus, theatre was not a part of the knowledge required of Japan's cultural elite or middle class in the post-War democratizing years. It naturally followed that no form of public subsidy was available at either the national or the local level. In other Asian countries, because of their experiences of colonization, traditional performance genres could sometimes be (and are still) privileged. In Japan, however, at the dawn of modernization in the late nineteenth century, traditional performance genres, especially Kabuki, were condemned as 'old', 'feudal' or 'vulgar'. This attitude caused the rise of several 'new' theatre movements which in turn contributed to the establishment of the generic notion of Shingeki.[5] Kabuki was the main target of reform during the nineteenth century in terms of content and there were several attempts at 'modernizing' the genre—for example, with the so-called 'Theatre Reformation Movement'. There were even some attempts at establishing a 'modern' national theatre (1873–74, 1886 and 1906).[6] But all these efforts failed while each 'old' or 'feudal' form of theatre, faced with the danger of extinction, discovered its own way of survival.

Shingeki, on the other hand, as a generic term, usually connotes modern theatre, in which the term 'modern' is almost always equated with things Western. Typical of this ideology was the Tsukiji Sho-gek-ijo (Little Theatre),[7] established in 1924 by Osanai Kaoru (1881–1928) and Yoshi Hijikata (1898–1959) who infamously announced that they would produce only Western plays in translation. Though theirs was the first and sincere attempt to transplant the then-fashionable Little

Theatre Movement in the West, it took another 40 years for Japan to have its own version of little theatre movement, usually referred to as Angura Theatre Movement.[8] This dichotomy and/or the dialectical relations between the modern (new and progressive) as the West and the old (traditional and conservative) as Japan did lend a certain degree of creative and political energy to Japan's theatre culture, but the state itself, for most of its modernizing history, seldom felt a necessity to appropriate either form into its national projects, unlike visual art, music and literature. The only exception seems to be during the pre-World War II years when the militarist government banned all leftist Shingeki practices[9] and thereby, paradoxically, both acknowledged *and* denied Shingeki's sociopolitical influences.

Thus, at least from an external perspective, just as we may observe various 'ill-fated' moments and instances in the history of Japan's theatre culture, we may also notice what can only be described as outrageous outbursts and breakthroughs. The sense of both unpredictability *and* historical irresponsibility became trademarks of Japan's theatre culture though it was never able nor allowed to constitute an integral part of the national imagination; it remained as a kind of distilled reflective/refractive mirror site of the ongoing historical process of social, economic and political relations to which personal and/or collective anxieties and desires were added, uncensored, aestheticized, (mis)articulated and privatized or, sometimes, collectivized.

Noi Sawaragi, visual art critic, refers to the failure of constructing a definable public genre of 'visual art' in the post-War discursive space:

> There, the power relations between not only high art and subculture but also every other genre, from manga, figurines, and graphic design to contemporary art, are at par with each other, and no one genre is privileged in terms of its value. And as if responding to this 'thorough lack of depth', every work of art is reduced/retreated to a glittering slick surface, and in reality, there is no difference between two- and three-dimensionality. The disappearance of depth, the lack of thickness is a kind of *mise en abyme* of the psychic structure of pseudo-society. Hence visual art does not constitute 'history' but refracts its simulation. In this formation, no one takes respon-

sibility, bygones are left to be bygones. Today is today, and tomorrow is another day. As is typically shown by Chappies drawn by Groovevision, in this kind of space, people without any difference in features, height, and taste propagate themselves as interchangeable and characterless beings, by living in the same kind of house, watching the same kind of TV shows, listening to the same kind of music, wearing the same kind of clothes, and speaking in the same kind of voice and tone[10] (2001: 97–8).[11]

If we changed the passage to 'Japan did not and will not constitute "theatre",' I would surely have to agree with the rest of what Sawaragi says. And that is exactly what I mean by theatre culture's 'ill-fated' history in Japan.

ENTERING THE BATTLEFIELD (2): THE APPRENTICESHIP

'Mr Suzuki [Tadashi] is looking for an interpreter,' Prof. Yasunari said, smiling his very gentle smile. 'He is directing Euripides' *The Bacchae*, mixing American actors with his own.' That was five years after Suzuki moved his centre of activity from Tokyo to the remote village of Toga in Toyama Prefecture in 1977. As I have mentioned, I did not know who Suzuki was nor what he was doing. The Japanese theatre I knew at the time was limited to some Shingeki and to Noda Hideki; Noda was still a student at our university and I had seen his work on campus. I was told to meet Suzuki at the coffee shop inside Imperial Theatre where he was directing Stephen Sondheim's *Sweeney Todd*. I did, and took the job.

That assignment launched my involvement in the practical theatre world. I spent one month at Toga Village, attending every rehearsal and welcoming American actors from the Graduate Acting Programme at the University of Wisconsin, Milwaukee. Then, in 1982, Suzuki asked me to accompany him on a US tour with his company. Waseda Sho-gekijo (Waseda Little Theatre) performed the legendary *The Trojan Women* in St Louis and Chicago. In New York, Suzuki performed *The Trojan Women* at the Japan Society and *The Bacchae* at La Mama. For a bilingual production of *The Bacchae*, I sat every night in the front row as a prompter, as neither Shiraishi Kayoko (playing

Dionysius and Agave in Japanese) nor Tom Hewitt (playing Pentheus in English) could understand what the other was saying. Of course, they understood each other through physical contact but accidents could have occurred. During the stay, there was an academic conference on Suzuki's work hosted by the Japan Society, which Richard Schechner and the late Victor Turner attended. I did not know their names then nor about 'performance studies', which was still in the process of consolidating itself as an academic discipline.

Suzuki was preparing an International Theatre Festival for the summer of 1982 at Toga, and I was deeply involved in the preparations. The first Toga International Theatre Festival was a historical event with Suzuki personally organizing it and inviting both traditional forms (Noh, Royal Masked Dance of Bhutan and others) and the avant-garde (Tadeusz Kantor, Robert Wilson, Meredith Monk, Terayama Shuji, Ota Shogo and others), along with a site-specific performance by John Fox's Welfare State International from the UK. I felt I was being exposed to the entire world of post-War avant-garde all at once, both in the West and in Japan, along with some traditional forms I had not been interested in until then (see Chapter 2).

After working at Toga for a while, I wrote a Master's thesis on Eugene O'Neill and very luckily got a tenured position in 1984 at Okayama University. As theatre culture is almost exclusively limited to Tokyo, I was forced to be away from the practical theatre world again, though I came to learn about the organizational power of Shingeki during my six-year residence (1984–89) in that city. Shingeki established the so-called *roen* ('theatre for workers') system after the War, a network of volunteer 'theatre appreciation' organizations for Shingeki with a nation-wide subscription system, with each local sector loosely connected with the others. At the Okayama Shimin Gekijo (Okayama Civic Theatre), you could become a member if you gathered at least three people to form a group. You paid an annual subscription fee, and you could watch five or six productions a year. It was a volunteer organization so you were asked to help out with one of the productions (working at the theatre, ushering, taking care of artists during their stay and so on). Each year, participating companies published a thick volume containing detailed information on the works they could bring to local cities. The members had the right to vote and decide which productions they wanted to see.

In the meantime, Tokyo was in the midst of the 'Little Theatre boom'. I still don't know what it was like even though I write about it quite often, simply because I was not there during most of the 1980s. There was a decisive difference in the cultural climate between what was happening in Tokyo and in Okayama. In Okayama, for instance, Okayama Shimin Gekijo decided to invite Noda Hideki and his company. Not entirely sure that Noda would draw an audience, his performance was assigned a much smaller theatre (the regular performances usually took place in a huge public multipurpose hall with a capacity of almost 1,800). Noda, who had been performing in a steamy small space on the university campus in Tokyo during my university days, suddenly became a cultural icon. The small theatre in Okayama was filled with more young people than usual, making me aware of a decisive gap between the traditional Shingeki and the contemporary 'Little Theatre' that was becoming popular and recognized as a legitimate theatre practice in Tokyo.

AN 'ILL-FATED' HISTORY OF JAPAN'S THEATRE CULTURE (2): THE APPRENTICESHIP
At the root of this 'ill fate' and the consequential bizarre nature of Japan's theatre culture lies the problem of theatre-making as a private/privatized practice. Nevertheless, theoretically, theatre has to be an open medium in which anyone can participate in order to suggest the possibility of achieving a certain degree of influence.

Open participation is key in the development of the genre of 'Angura Little Theatre' in the post-War years. Angura has been loosely used over the last 40 years or so, and, as Shingeki was used in opposition to Kyugeki (Old Theatre) of Kabuki and Noh, Angura has been and is still sometimes used in opposition to Shingeki. At the beginning, Angura was called Angura-engeki—'Underground Theatre', an abbreviated nickname given to underground theatre practices that emerged as a movement during the latter part of the 1960s. The 1960s were a decade of rapid economic growth, led by the Liberal Democratic Party, and this growth, so visibly achieved in the physical reconstruction of larger cities, was accompanied by a sense of growing national pride;

economic prosperity seemed to guarantee the return of a 'great' nation after the devastating effects of losing the War and of the ensuing occupation by US forces. For people living in that decade, though the term can only be used metaphorically as Japan has never been officially colonized, it was a 'postcolonial' moment with political, economic and cultural independence from the US's domineering influences avidly sought after in many fields, including the cultural.

The name Angura was also used because many experimental performances were taking place, quite literally, 'underground'—in the basements of newly built buildings in Tokyo—and because the Angura imagination was understood as 'underground' with its theatrical and performance ideas fundamentally opposed to dominant middle-class values. Idiosyncratic figures such as Terayama Shuji (1935–83), Kara Juro (1940–), Suzuki Tadashi (1939–), Sato Makoto (1943–) and, somewhat later, Ota Shogo (1939–2007) emerged. Hijikata Tatsumi (1928–86), one of the originators of Butoh, was also a part of the movement. Angura is characterized by its use of the aesthetics and the politics of both Western avant-gardism (high modernism) and Japanese traditional forms (Kabuki and Noh) through collectively created physical performances which resist, interrogate and, in most cases, nullify dominant middle-class values.

Most of Angura's participants were university graduates (or dropouts), despite the fact that almost none of them officially studied theatre as an academic discipline at the university. Angura writings and performances embraced an imaginary bond with those excluded from the then-emerging sociopolitical space usually referred to as an ideological closure of 'post-War democracy', an official and authenticated version of democracy which the US occupational forces had brought to Japan and which was later implemented by Japanese themselves.

The emergence of the first generation of Angura artists was deemed scandalous—some of them were intentionally so, in their public disturbance of society—and their activity was reported by the mass media not necessarily in the 'art' section but in the 'news'. In terms of practising resistance to and subverting mainstream values in the public domain, however, their scope of influence was necessarily limited; society was not changed because of their work nor did it ever acknowledge their existence as a vital and indispensable part of culture or politics. Angura was considered a direct expression of the *zeitgeist* of the 1968 generation, in which real politics and aesthetics overlapped and were sometimes confused. Angura, and the youth culture of which it was a part, was, at most, tolerated by the urban middle class as a pattern of behaviour that the participants were expected to 'grow out of'. As the movement itself can only be represented by charismatic male figures, i.e. exceptional artistic geniuses of patriarchal relations, Angura Theatre at this stage was obviously a private/privatized practice that reflected the gender hierarchies present in society as a whole. Certainly, the theatre was historically important: practitioners sought new kinds of theatre space (for instance, they performed in tents), abandoned the then-dominant psychological realism and its linear narrative structure, centralized the actor's body in their performance and attracted younger audiences. By consciously positioning themselves at the periphery of civil society, they intended to maintain the image of transgression and subversion, however romantic their intentions may seem now. That is why they kept asking the essential question, 'What is theatre?', both in their performance practices and in their discursive outputs.

ENTERING THE BATTLEFIELD (3): OPENING UP

The real break for me came when I was able to get a Fulbright Grant to study in a graduate degree programme in the US in 1986, at a time when I was not really sure about whether I wanted to continue my study in literary circles. Deconstruction was becoming a 'fad' in Japan while drama studies or theatre studies, because of the historically determined positioning of theatre culture in Japan, was always kept at the periphery of literary studies. My reason for studying at the Department of Performance Studies at New York University was accidental. Yale University was considered to be at the cutting edge of critical theory but it did not accept my application which, naturally, was to be able to continue studying the plays of Eugene O'Neill. A few other English departments did not accept me either and so I chose New York University. The Department of Performance Studies was in the process of forming the discipline itself. Richard Schechner, Barbara Kirshenblatt-Gimblett, Brooks McNamara, Michael Kirby and Marcia Siegel were all part of it. Peggy Phelan joined the faculty that same academic year.

The MA Programme was for two years and we had to write a Master's thesis. I had a serious problem at first in coming to terms with the material. In those days, most students had a social science background whereas mine was purely English literary studies. It was 'between theatre and anthropology' (see Schechner 1982), that most of the classes were aimed at. In one of the assigned reading materials, I came across the word 'performativity', the meaning of which I could not find in my English–Japanese dictionary. I was perhaps a little more privileged than the others because I already had a tenured position at a Japanese university; if I could not adjust to my new intellectual environment, I could always return. The first semester was hell and, even though I was living in New York, I had no time to watch any performances. I even lost a considerable amount of weight.

What encouraged me to go on, at least for another semester, was my advisor Schechner's comment on my term paper: he said he would consider it for publication in *TDR*. The paper was on Suzuki Tadashi, about whom I had first-hand knowledge. I could not fulfil Schechner's request but I published the Japanese version after I came back to Japan and it became one of my first published works (Uchino 1988). And, of course, I did become a contributing editor for *TDR* after about 10 years. My strangely fortunate and long-lasting tie with *TDR*, therefore, started in 1986 when I took Schechner's course. I also have to thank Phillip Zarrilli, then Acting Chair of the Department, who carefully introduced incoming students, including myself, into the discipline of performance studies through an introductory course called 'Issues and Methods in Performance Studies'.

I somehow got through all the other courses and the next semester went unexpectedly well. I had some time to watch performances in New York, and the time soon came to consider the extending of the grant for another year. I was willing to continue but unfortunately Okayama University did not approve my extension. As I did not have the courage to give up my tenured position, I reluctantly went back to Japan in the summer of 1987.

Looking back at my first exposure to performance studies in 1986 and 1987, I admit I was not mature enough, intellectually, to take in everything that was taught there. Nor was I sure of which academic direction I would take after returning to Japan. What was certain was that I could no longer remain in the very conservative study of American theatre as a literary genre—I had to find a way out. My accumulation of both articulated and unarticulated knowledge during my time at New York University led me to think of ways in which performance studies could be 'useful' in Japanese intellectual and academic contexts.

AN 'ILL-FATED' HISTORY OF JAPAN'S THEATRE CULTURE (3): OPENING UP

When Angura was in full bloom with its first generation of practitioners, Japan was undergoing a phase of rapid economic growth that, by the end of the decade, created a completely new sociopolitical configuration. As Japan achieved economic triumph, the season of political revolt (and its aesthetic expression) was obviously over. Everyone was (or, at least, was supposed to be) a middle-class member of the established civil society of the post-War democracy. The middle-class class-consciousness was firmly established and came to be widely accepted among Japanese nationals during the 1970s. This imaginary category of identity would remain intact until the beginning of the 1990s.

The second and third generations of Angura practitioners, which emerged during the 1970s and the 1980s, had to work within this milieu of civil society and its middle-class conformism. They also had to face the historical given that their theatre could only be practiced in a private/privatized environment. Because of this, however, the aesthetics of Angura (named by theatre critic Nishido Kojin 'the Angura paradigm'[12]), through mostly personal means of transmission, were eventually naturalized and internalized in the creative imaginations of younger Little Theatre practitioners. Because of the privatized nature of their practice, what they had to face during the 1970s was not the pressure of institutionalization and appropriation from the mainstream cultural system but issues of market-creation and survival within late-capitalist social relations. This tendency continued with the emergence of the third generation of Angura during the 1980s, a decade characterized by the 'bubble economy'. The third generation of practitioners succeeded in becoming much more visible than the previous two, a phenomenon which the mass media labelled the 'Little Theatre boom'. Some of the exponents of this 'boom' were Noda Hideki (1955–), Kokami Shoji (1958–) and Kawamura Takeshi (1959–). Female Little Theatre practitioners such as Kisaragi Koharu (1956–2000), Kishida Rio (1950–2003) and Watanabe Eriko (1956–) also emerged. Some of them, after gaining recognition in their field, worked in television and film. Hence, during that decade, the expression 'Angura Little Theatre' gradually lost its Angura: the sympathy towards the 'underground' of the previous generation was almost non-existent. At the same time, in the 1980s' theatre culture, Angura experienced an enormous amount of popularization—although not necessarily democratization—and came to be recognized by much larger sections of society. 'Little Theatre' was now a distinctive genre, with some of the more popular practitioners already performing in fairly large theatres. From a theoretical point of view, their theatre practice, however, shared much the same aesthetic assumptions as explored by the previous generations in terms of dramaturgy, acting style and methods of using the performance space. As a result, except for a few, none of them discussed their work in terms of interpreting dramatic texts. It was as if the question 'What is theatre?' had already been answered.

The 1980s' theatre culture, especially in Euro-American contexts, is usually characterized by its (re)politicization. American theatre culture, because of the Reaganite neo-liberal conservatism and the AIDS crisis, witnessed newly formed cultural fronts opening up the possibility of thinking about the productive relationship between art practice and activism, and artists, intellectuals and activists. This process in the US was undoubtedly assisted by the proliferation of post-structural discourses, from feminist to postcolonial theories. In Japan's 1980s' theatre, however, we saw no such politicization, perhaps because there was (and still is) no feminist theatre in Japan, though feminism itself found its way into Japan's sociopolitical sphere and was (and still is) very influential.[13] For the first generation of Angura practitioners, there was at least an aesthetic and political tension between Angura and preceding Shingeki practices, and they had accepted both Western modernism (Brecht and Artaud among others) and Japan's traditional forms as their frame of reference. When the third generation emerged, its frame of reference suddenly seemed to experience a geographical and historical contraction, becoming almost solely restricted to domestic subcultural genres [manga, anime (see Chapter 3, NOTE 6), television and B movies], perhaps because its practice found a domestic market and Japan had become a (seemingly) self-sufficient economic giant. There was no longer the need to look outwards (geographical extension) or backwards (historical extension) in order to be embraced by this market. This then was the decisive phenomenon that helped create the cultural seclusion of the nation. In the meantime, 'Little Theatre' without the title of Angura remained private/privatized but found its own market value in the 'bubble economy'—the proper and the only possible ontological status within the late-capitalist social relations, considering there still was no public funding available to make Little Theatre practices 'official', 'public' and/or 'national'.

ENTERING THE BATTLEFIELD (4): MATURING YEARS

I stayed at Okayama University until 1989, when I took another tenured position at Meiji University, a huge private institution in Tokyo. My link with Japan's practical theatre world had been almost severed, and it was by pure accident that I came back to it. I met Nishido Kojin—a theatre critic who remembered me from when I had worked at the Toga Festival—at a performance, and I asked him a rather silly question: 'Is there anything interesting happening in Tokyo?' 'I will not answer that kind of question now. But I will send you an article in which I speak of why I will not answer it,' he said and later, sent me a critical magazine he was editing which contained an article by him, criticizing exactly the question I had asked. According to Nishido, 'interesting' was becoming the only norm in theatre criticism and thereby harming the prospects of theatre culture; theatre was not a commodity for sale. In return, I sent him some of my own articles, including my piece on Suzuki Tadashi. He liked what I was writing and invited me to contribute a theatre review in *Tosho Shinbun* (Book Review Press), a book-review weekly. My debut as a theatre critic thus occurred in February 1990 with a piece on Richard Foreman's *Lava* which I had watched in New York.

Nishido was (and still is) a conscientious critic and scholar whose sympathy lies not with the mainstream but with those on the periphery. He was the only person I knew who was trying to theorize Japan's theatre culture in the 1980s, on the basis of the revolutionary break that Angura Theatre had introduced.

Nishido is the one who invited me into the battlefield of theatre criticism in Japan, where journalism is the dominant force and academism or academic thinking has no power. Not only letting me write a review, Nishido also asked me to join several interesting projects: one, to publish a new theatre magazine and the other, the Heiner Müller Project (see Chapter 3). Nishido invited three other critics to launch a small theatre magazine and in July 1992, the first issue of *MUNKS* was published (*MUNKS* stands for the first initial of each critic: Matsui Kentaro, Uchino Tadashi, Nishido Kojin, Kan Takayuki and Saeki Ryuko.) Most of the articles I wrote for *MUNKS* were published in my first book, *Melodrama no Gyakushu* (*The Melodramatic Revenge*), in 1996. Kan and Saeki were both very active critics for Angura and the magazine's political stance was very clear: to find viable languages to historicize Angura and to critique the 1980s' 'Little Theatre boom'. During the three very intensive years at *MUNKS*, we met very often, discussing various issues till late at night: it was, for me, a training school to learn about Angura, the subsequent history of the Little Theatre and the Japanese avant-garde. I learned a lot from Kan and Saeki who had worked through the fervent years of Angura but, at the same time, I was not too sure about how I should theorize more recent theatre practices other than condemning them as 'stupid' and 'a sell-out' from the Angura perspective. It was obvious that Japan had entered its postmodern stage, and I was reluctant to articulate contemporary Japanese performances using Euro-American critical languages.

In 1995, Nishido and I left *MUNKS*, as ideological differences were becoming visible between its participants, and joined Ootori Hidenaga in launching yet another new theatre magazine—*Theatre Arts*—published by the International Association of Theatre Critics (Tokyo section). Ootori, initially a Russian literary scholar, had returned from studying in the US. Thoroughly familiar with modernist discursive and performance traditions, he was exposed to the newly forming political languages of theatre and performance during the 1980s. His intention was to find a way to talk about Japan's contemporary performance, making references to Euro-American modernist and postmodern theories and performance practices. For instance, we translated Judith Butler's 'Performative Act and Gender Constitution' (1988) for the magazine's third issue in 1995 and it was, as far as I know, the first translation in Japan of any of Butler's work. For the first issue, we asked Dumb Type to create a performance score for their legendary *S/N* (1995) (see Interlude 1 and Chapter 3).

There was always a strong demand to 'popularize' both the discourse and the subject matter of the magazine from many quarters according to which Ootori was too avant-garde and too radical. Considering the 1990s' mainstream theatre practices and the surrounding 'petit-nationalist sentiments' (see Kayama 2002), the magazine was destined to fail in terms of sales. Ootori resigned as editor after eight issues and continued his admirably disciplined editorship with *Performing Arts* in 2001.

In the meantime, I took another tenured position in 1992 at the University of Tokyo. It was not, however, with the Faculty of English Literature but with the College of Arts and Sciences (the Department I belong to was to be renamed the Department of Interdisciplinary Cultural Studies in 1993). The University of Tokyo has a unique structure—in our department, all professors taught at all three levels of the educational programme: the general education programme for all of the first- and second-year students, specialized fields for some of the third- and fourth-year students, and at the graduate level. My teaching load was typically four English-language courses, one specialized class for the third and fourth years and one graduate seminar. Teaching across the curriculum and so many courses at the same time is unthinkable not only in other countries but also in other universities in Japan. I became intensely busy but, at the same time, because of its liberal and intellectual environment, I was able to experience a renewed sense of academic life which ultimately made it possible for me to publish my second book in 2001, *Melodrama kara Performance he* (*From Melodrama to Performance*) on American performance culture in the twentieth century, which was also my Ph.D. dissertation.

AN 'ILL-FATED' HISTORY OF JAPAN'S THEATRE CULTURE (3): MATURING YEARS

In 1989, the cold war came to an end unexpectedly and, quite incidentally, Emperor Hirohito died. The Japanese government started to prepare the first public subsidy system for various genres of cultural practices. In 1990, the first subsidies were distributed under the name of the Japan Arts Fund (the literal translation of the Japanese original is Art and Culture Development Fund). Despite nobody asking for it, the government suddenly turned its attention to the genre of 'Little Theatre' with its own private/privatized history of development, although the subsidy, of course, was not only for 'Little Theatre' but for other theatrical genres as well, including Shingeki and traditional forms, in addition to music, visual art and film. Over the first 10 years, some 400–500 million yen was doled out annually to various performing arts genres. In 1996, another subsidy fund called the Performing Arts Project Development Fund was established. By fiscal year 2006, the former Fund's performing arts budget was about 5.8 billion yen and the latter's about 3.1 billion yen (at approximately 117 yen to 1 US dollar). A little less than 9 billion yen was thus distributed as public funding. Subsidy budgetary matters for both genres are handled by the Japan Arts Council, an independent administrative institution, supervised by the Agency for Cultural Affairs, which organizationally belongs to the Ministry of Education, Culture, Sports, Science and Technology. The Agency itself has a different funding system called Arts Plan 21, established in 1996, of which the above-mentioned Performing Arts Project Development Fund constitutes a part. Art Plan 21, which is now called New Century Arts Plan, has become more influential as the budget is larger than the previous funding system.

In 1993, quite accidentally, just after the time when public funding became available, the 'bubble economy' burst, and Japan entered a long period of recession. (In reality, between 1990 and 1991, the economy was already on the decline, but the collapse of the 'bubble economy' became widely recognized in 1993.) Some Little Theatre practices, as mentioned earlier, were becoming marketable, and, accordingly, a certain amount of private subsidy was becoming available. Because of the economic collapse, however, the Little Theatre practitioners had paradoxically turned to the public funding system unlike other sections of society that witnessed a strong shift from the public to the private, in accordance with what was happening elsewhere in the world, especially in the US or the UK, a phenomenon usually understood as 'the end of the welfare state'. But Little Theatre practitioners who had sought to survive by becoming popular in the market during the 1980s now had to depend upon the public funding system rather than on throwing themselves into the game of 'the survival of the fittest' as in the recession period.

The 1990s can thus be characterized as a decade when contemporary theatre practice genres, including 'Little Theatre', were finally recognized and legitimized by the nation. Many public theatres opened not only in Tokyo but also in other parts of Japan. The symbol of this national legitimization of contemporary theatre was the opening of the New National Theatre, Tokyo, in 1997 for opera, ballet, dance and contemporary theatre, with three theatre spaces installed within a huge complex. The national legitimization of performing arts, however, did not necessarily mean their 'officialization'—their deployment within the national cultural space—and because of the obvious issue of economic recession and governmental budgetary cuts, the New National Theatre has neither its own theatre company nor its own orchestra. It is also heavily dependent on ticket revenues for budgets, unlike European models, thus making its management systems more like those of American regional theatres. Theatre productions staged at the New National, therefore, eventually had to adopt the star system as the norm.[14] It is a national institution but, in terms of its finance, the productions have to be commercially feasible 'within reason'. It may sound outrageous from the European viewpoint, but not necessarily so if we look at how American regional theatres are run. The New National can produce only more or less conservative theatre works with well-known stars in order to secure sufficient ticket sales. Other newly opened public theatres have taken up similar managing principles, so the productions we see in those public venues are not so different from those produced in purely commercial venues and, of course, the same actors appear in both.[15]

The theatre culture of the 1990s was heavily influenced by such global phenomena as the end of the cold war and the ensuing American pronouncement of the forced construction of a 'New World Order', and by such local phenomena as the burst of the 'bubble economy' in 1993, the Great Hanshin Awaji Earthquake and the Sarin Gas Attack on the Tokyo subway by Aum Shinri-kyo cult members, both in 1995. While the Japanese government began to adopt neo-liberal policies more openly, the ideological shift from 'disciplinary power' to 'surveillance power' was starting to affect Japan's sociopolitical configurations, including Foucauldian bio-political power relations. Most obvious was the (seemingly) deliberate heightening of the sense of security, campaigned for by some conservative cultural producers, mass media and politicians, especially after 1995, which gave rise to neo-nationalistic sentiments among the younger generation. Kayama Rika, a practising psychiatrist and cultural critic, termed this tendency 'the petit-nationalist syndrome'.[16] Society as a whole became radically conservative in response to the 'bubble'—festive but empty— sentiments of the previous decade. The post-War democratic ideology, equivalent to the liberal humanism in the West, was losing its grip on the younger members of the population. Nationalism was revisited, manifesting itself within discourses of historical revisionism towards the latter half of the decade, as if to make sure that Japan was 'still' a great nation even though the long-lasting recession looked endless for some. The reason Kayama used the word 'petit' is that the nationalism was not necessarily connected to traditional right-wing ultra-nationalists and their radical militant xenophobic ideology but was adopted as an easy and even nonchalant identity category, a very loose kind of 'Japanese' self-image. It was, in other words, deployed as a cultural and political device to construct a sense of identity at the moment of the postmodern loss of a stable sense of the self. 'Petit', therefore, connotes a transitory and temporary kind of nationalism, though Kayama herself fears its accidental tie-up with more dangerous kinds of ultra-nationalism. The reason why people suddenly discovered the nation as an object of identification, therefore, can only be explained by the new conditions imposed by the historical process usually called 'globalization', in which the category of the local is always interpellated against that of the global.

Within such sociopolitical configurations, Japan's 1990s' theatre culture took a peculiar turn as is evident in the emergence of 'Quiet Theatre' (*shizukana engeki*). This movement was led by the playwright-director Hirata Oriza (1962–), who calls his theatre 'contemporary colloquial theatre' (*gendai kogo engeki*) and who discards what Nishido has called 'the Angura paradigm'—the creations of previous generations of Little Theatre practitioners (see Chapter 6, NOTE 7). From a historical perspective, Hirata's theatre appears to be a return to psychological realism, though Hirata himself claims that he has finally invented a true and authentic Japanese realist theatre. His plays depict, in a very detailed and meticulous fashion, how (usually contemporary) Japanese speak and behave with each other; all theatrical effects, including showy lighting and sound effects, have been done away with.

Hirata's influence was widespread and many playwrights followed or tried to expand his mode. It is also important to note that as public funding became available, Quiet Theatre and its variations spread to regions beyond Tokyo. Three plays included in the collection of plays that this Introduction was first written for[17] were written by playwrights working in regions other than the capital; both Fukatsu Atsushi (1967–) and Tsuchida Hideo (1967–) work in the Kansai region, the western part of the Japanese mainland that includes Osaka and Kyoto, and Hasegawa Koji (1956–), though his Hirosaki Gekijo (Hiroskai Theatre) was established in 1978, works in Hirosaki, a northern city in Aomori Prefecture in the Tohoku region. Theirs are not necessarily plays of 'local colour' but the readers will find a strong degree of resonance with Hirata's 'contemporary colloquial theatre'.

The declining popularity of the post-War democratic ideology resulted in another trend in 1990s' theatre culture. Along with Nagai Ai (1951–) and Sakate Yoji (1962–), there emerged a group of conscientious theatre practitioners who kept problematizing, each in her/his own way, 'petit-nationalist' sentiments, and who continued examining the manner in which government policies were becoming more and more neo-liberalist and how that in turn affected people's lives. Many of them, however, were not interested either in the formal aspects of theatrical representation or in theatrical experimentation. Their work was conservative in its dramaturgical method and comprised a traditional linear plot through which a liberal-humanist social and/or political critique was delivered to the audience. Both the emergence of Quiet Theatre and the visible proliferation of the theatre of social critique, however, do have a certain degree of ideological resonance with what I have already described as the legitimization and recognition of theatre culture by the national state during the 1990s. Both seemed to fulfil the role of a 'healthy' theatre culture as expected by the state: they invented a new 'Japanese', i.e. 'national', theatrical mode (Quiet Theatre) and fuelled a spirit of criticism (theatre of social critique), required for the construction of a neo-liberal civil society. In this sense, whether or not they liked it, both could only be understood as being inevitably and contextually incorporated within the scope of Kayama's 'petit-nationalist syndrome'.

In the meantime, as an extension of the 1980s' Little Theatre, practitioners emerged who did not want to accept the role that the state began to assign to theatre culture. Figures such as Matsuo Suzuki (1961–) and Keralino Sandorovich (1963–) stuck to the private/privatized nature of Little Theatre and its market value established during the 1980s by their predecessors, and achieved great commercial and popular success. Their theatre can also be called conscientious as they implicitly and explicitly claim that, without depending on public subsidies, they have created and sensitized a large enough audience for their work to be able to continue creating their work on their own terms. From an 'official' theatre culture perspective (which came to be, quite accidentally, substantiated only during the decade), their work is very popular because they are subcultural products, i.e. meaningless entertainment. When we look at their works more seriously, however, there is more to them than perhaps the formalist plays of Quiet Theatre. From the perspective of theatrical history, theirs is a conscious attempt at updating Nishido Kojin's Angura paradigm, however 'popularized', i.e. degraded, it may seem to be. In resisting both Quiet Theatre and the theatre of social critique, theirs is noisy, 'irresponsible' and playful theatre which, indeed, Angura Little Theatre was all about at its inception in the 1960s.

A TEMPORAL CONCLUSION: INTO THE TWENTY-FIRST CENTURY

Theatre culture, it seems now, was not able to respond adequately to 9/11, or, more precisely, to what was so publicly and globally revealed through the incident. Metaphorically speaking, Little Theatre practitioners were too busy writing applications to get public funding. Instead, there was a shift of interest to the emerging genre of contemporary dance in which the body and its movements/gestures is a major concern. A great number of interesting young choreographers and individual dancers emerged at the beginning of the twenty-first century while, after the national legitimization of theatre culture during the last decade, we witnessed only the continuation of the trends described so far. Dance appears to be a genre that quickly adapted and responded to the fast-changing sociocultural landscape of the post-9/11 post-political/ideological milieu, while theatre culture as a whole seems to be entering a phase of cultural amnesia and complacency. As I observed at the beginning of this Introduction, the number of productions has continued to increase. We have a wide range of Little Theatre practices now, as if we are in a kind of Angura Little Theatre museum; Suzuki Tadashi is still creating new work and Kara Juro is still performing in the tent, while exponents of each generation of Little Theatre are still working in different contexts. There are even so-called neo-Angura performances (created by young practitioners interested in reviving the Angura paradigm) and other, and younger versions of Quiet Theatre and so on. But it does not follow that Little Theatre practitioners in the new millennium are interested in exploring, experimenting or critiquing. There are always some exceptions but at the moment we are, quietly and carefully, watching and measuring the degree of impact of Japan's national legitimization of theatre culture in the last decade within the context of the post-9/11 ideological space, without being overwhelmed by the number of Little Theatre productions.

For one year between 1997 and 1998, I had another Fulbright (Research) Grant to go back to the Department of Performance Studiers at NYU. The structure of the department had changed and new professors such as José Muñoz were part of the faculty. As a visiting scholar in the Department, I participated in some courses that interested me but the main purpose of my stay was to observe the changes that had taken place in the cultural and political climate over the preceding 10 years. The heat, as it were, of the late 1980s' 'politicized' New York seemed to have subsided, and a 'there-is-nothing-new' kind of cynicism pervaded people's minds and the cultural scene in general. Performance studies as a discipline was firmly delineated, but its ambiguous relationship with cultural studies had become an important issue which, at least for me, has yet to be settled. This was before 9/11, however, when all those subsumed, concealed and interpenetrating layers of 'the structure of feelings' were still trying to manifest themselves through various performative forms. In short, it was the beginning of the unfolding of the post-political, post-theoretical landscape which we would have to face more openly after 9/11.

After returning to Japan, I joined Ootori at his *Theatre Arts* magazine as a seasonal review writer. 'A seasonal review' is a 30-page (in Japanese), rather long article discussing important performances that the reviewer has watched over a period of about three months. For five years, between 2001 and 2006, I wrote about Japan's theatre culture, experiencing the life of a professional theatre critic. At the same time, it became almost customary to give lectures on Japan's performance culture at academic conferences and theatre festivals abroad, simply because I was one of the very few Japanese critics who could lecture in English. Most of the essays included in this volume were initially written for such occasions. At the same time, I began to be involved in various intercultural projects, especially ones involving other Asian artists, about which I will write in the near future (a part is included in this volume as the Epilogue).

Yet another important factor for the last five years or so was that I became a board member of the Saison Foundation in 1999. The Foundation, established in 1988, was then the only funding organization that devoted its grants to the performing arts, giving financial help to emerging young artists at a time when there was no public funding. It is careful in giving out grants—some are given to individuals or groups for three consecutive years and it carefully monitors the grantees' development as artists, giving not only financial but also artistic and administrative support. It is a small organization and thus its work is flexible and useful. My involvement with the Foundation made me look at Japan's performing culture more realistically, and I was forced to redefine my critical position. I lost interest in watching mainstream performances after being disappointed every single time, and shifted my attention to a younger generation of artists whom the Foundation may have found interesting and/or important, and I began to rearticulate and reformulate my discursive languages towards them. That is to say, considering the fact that we live in a post-political age and in the historical environments that I have been delineating thus far, I can only speak for the future, having decided to devote myself to two projects: one, to historicize Japan's theatre culture, and the other, to encourage a younger generation of artists who I think have both artistic and intellectual potential.

My field of vision has thus kept expanding and I am still not sure where I belong. At the moment, I am publishing this book in English and another in Japanese, which is a collection of reviews and articles written during the 10 years since the publication of my first book in Japanese (see Uchino 1996). These books settle some accounts for my most recent past as a scholar and critic, and I am thinking about where to go for the next 10 years; it seems that mobility is what I like and that is precisely what Prof. Takahashi wanted to warn me about when he asked me, 'Are you ready for it?' 'Mobility' is and can only be the norm for those who deal with the transient currency of performance and the performative in our current globalized 'Empire'.

Notes

1   See numberten.seesaa.net/article/15748469.html (last access date 25 August 2006). The definition and historical configuration of Little Theatre as a genre are complicated. We will return to this issue later in this Introduction.

2   Tokyo has no theatre district, unlike New York or London. Shimo-kitazawa is perhaps an exception because there are several small theatres in a rather small area. But six of them are owned by one person, Honda Tadao, a former actor who opened Za Suzunari Theatre with 200 seats in 1981, followed by Honda Theatre in 1982 with nearly 400 seats, opening the way for Shimo-kitazawa to become a Mecca for Little Theatre practitioners during the 1980s.

3   I will not cite a specific page for this famous notion which Raymond Williams developed and used in many places.

4   In 1999, the Tokyo University of Fine Arts initiated a new under-graduate and graduate programme, the Department of Inter Media Art, within the Faculty of Fine Arts, in which some performing arts courses are taught.

5   Shingeki literally means 'new theatre', the word coined in the nine-teenth century, as opposed to the traditional forms such as Kabuki and Noh, identified as Kyugeki (old theatre). See the start of Chapter 1 and NOTES 2 and 3, for more detailed discussion of the notion of Shingeki.

6   Sho-gekijo was the name used to describe the emergence of a radi-cal 'underground' or 'small' theatre in the 1960s in Japan. Critics have noted the increased popularity of this style of performance and, during the 1980s, variations of Sho-gekijo became so popular that the term 'Sho-gekijo boom' was coined to describe both the popu-larity of the movement and its increasing accommodation of, and links with, corporate and late-capitalist culture in Japan. The boom phase of Sho-gekijo will be dealt with in detail later in Chapter 2.

7   Those incidents are adequately described under the entries Shingeki, Kokuritsu Gekijo (National Theatre) and Engeki Kairyo Undo (Theatre Reformation Movement) in Heibon-sha's *Daihyakka Jiten* (*World Encyclopaedia*). I have referred to the digital version pub-lished in 2004.

8   There is an ongoing controversy about the definition and use of the terms Angura (Underground Theatre) and 'Little Theatre'. Angura usually refers to a wide variety of radically new theatre practices

emerging in the late 1960s and the term 'Little Theatre Movement' came to be widely used in the 1980s, as the newer generations of theatre practitioners lost the sense of being 'underground' though still performing in small theatres. The 'Little Theatre Movement' as a whole is supposed to include Angura Theatre but some critics do not agree. Newer practitioners and practices, they claim, lost the sense of being a movement, when they were no longer underground.

9   Shingeki was very closely connected to several social movements during the depression of the 1930s. In 1940, therefore, most Shingeki companies were disbanded under order of the authorities.

10 Geisai, as in the title of Sawaragi's article is an art festival organized by Murakami Takashi to recognize new talent.

11 Note that all translations of quotes in this volume are the author's unless otherwise mentioned.

12 Used by Nishido in his *Engeki Shiso no Boken* (*The Adventures of Theatrical Philosophy*) (1987).

13 Feminism found its way into Japan's cultural, social and political fabric mainly through two academic venues: literary studies and sociology, and eventually established strong ties with activists in Japan. On the other hand, theatre culture, both Shingeki and Little Theatre, was very slow or, rather, did not respond at all. It does not necessarily mean practitioners were not dealing with feminist issues but that when they did, it was at quite an unconscious level. The notion of 'gender', in my experience, came to be popularized only in the latter half of the 1990s.

14 At the beginning, the New National Theatre, Tokyo, did not consciously adopt the star system. As was always the case with the history of Japan's theatre culture, it looked at the models of continental Europe. There has been a strong public image, sustained for a long time, that Europe represents high art, of which theatre culture is a part, whereas America represents popular and commercial culture, in which no 'real' theatre culture grows. It is of course a 'correct' understanding to a certain degree but actually running a theatre is a completely different matter. Realizing that, the New National seems to have had to turn to the star system soon after its opening.

15 I am not sure whether or not it is a conscious choice, but most public theatres seem to have turned to the UK for their model. In the UK, as is well known, the boundary between public and commercial theatres is not so clearly defined as in continental Europe or the US.

Accordingly, on many occasions, we see half-commercial productions staged in Japan's public theatres. In this sense, they can best be characterized as semi-privatized public theatres. The only exception is Suzuki Tadashi's Shizuoka Geijutsu Gekijo (Shizuoka Art Theatre) in Shizuoka Prefecture, which strictly follows the continental European model, with its own theatre company and technical and administrative staff. Suzuki first started this kind of experiment at Mito in Ibaragi Prefecture in 1990, where he was an artistic director until 1995. In Shizuoka, Suzuki has been very active since 1997 as an artistic director in establishing the European model public theatre. Suzuki stepped down from his artistic directorship in 2007, and Miyagi Satoshi (1959–), from the younger generation of Little Theatre practitioners, has taken over.

16 Kayama wrote a book-length study of this syndrome in 2002, entitled *Petit-nationalism Shoko-gun—Wakamono-tachi no Nipponism* (The Petit-Nationalist Sentiments—Nipponism among the Youth), published by Chuo Koron Shin-sha. Nippon is the Japanese word for Japan, but she wrote Nipponism, derived from Nippon, not with Chinese characters as is usually the custom but with Katakana, a writing system usually used to transliterate foreign words. Nippon here suggests a hybrid and fluid ontological status of Japan(ese) between traditional Japan and Westernized Japan.

17 The collection of plays was published by Japan Playwrights Association (2007).

PROLOGUE: SEPTEMBER 1998, TOKYO, JAPAN

SCENE: The Playhouse, a middle-sized theatre within the New National Theatre Complex, that opened in the fall of 1997. The production: *Buddha*, a play with music. Originally published as a manga (comic strip) epic by Tezuka Osamu, adapted for stage by Sato Makoto, directed by Kuriyama Tamiya.[1]

CHARACTERS: Playwright and director Sato Makoto (1942–). Founding member of Black Tent Theatre Company, Sato was theoretically influenced by Brecht in the 1960s and 1970s and is now the artistic director of Setagaya Public Theatre. Tezuka Osamu (1928–89), the most representative and influential manga master after World War II, known for establishing manga as a 'serious' art form with such influential works as *Tetsuwan Atom* (Iron-armed Atom, 1951–81) and *Jungle Taitei* (The Emperor of the Jungle, 1950–54). Kuriyama Tamiya (1953–), member of the emerging generation of Shingeki directors, known for his technical mastery of stagecraft and, later, the second artistic director of the New National. And, of course, the New National Theatre Complex with three theatres within its oppressive modern architecture but no resident opera, dance or theatre companies. Although built with taxpayers' money, the operating budget is designed to come from commercial tenants (and ticket sales) who rent the space in the adjoining high-rise, Opera City.

SYNOPSIS: The New National Theatre, Sato Makoto, Tezuka Osamu and Kuriyama Tamiya. The production of *Buddha* at the New National Theatre is a curious and even impressive site to begin thinking about Brecht in Japan. There is a complex set of contexts and issues in the subject of this chapter that are almost accidentally present in this single production.

In 1998, Brecht's centennial year, commemorative celebrations are supposed to have taken place all over the world. There is, however, very little 'celebration' in Japan, except perhaps within academic circles associated with Brecht or Germany. In the world of theatre, only two companies devote themselves to producing Brecht's plays: the Tokyo Engeki Shudan (TES; Tokyo Theatre Ensemble) and Doro Theatre Company. Both considered Shingeki companies, the one professional, the other amateur, they are the only ones 'celebrating' Brecht's centennial in any substantial way. Other major theatre venues, commercial or experimental, have taken little notice of Brecht, his works, his theatrical techniques.

In an article titled 'Brecht Seitan Hyaku-shunen—Gendaisei Minaosu Engekijin' ('Brecht's Centennial—Theatre People are Rethinking Brecht's Contemporaneity') that appeared in *Nihon Keizai Shinbun* (The Japan Economic Newspaper) Kono Takashi, one of the editors of the paper, attempts to explain Brecht: 'Brecht criticized established theatre practices and proposed new ideas that included a so-called alienation effect in which allegorization of social contradictions make the audience think there is something wrong. He advocated a dialectical theatre in which characters' good and evil can be seen as social constructions' (1998: 40). After his short but adequate summary, Kono quotes Sato Makoto: 'It's almost impossible to find anybody who was not influenced by Brecht,' and follows it up with a comment by theatre critic Nishido Kojin, '[the] Little Theatre Movement has unconsciously embodied Brecht's theatre theories, including the A-effect.' Sato is quoted again: 'Brecht became classic too early for Japan's theatre culture. But if new translations of Brecht's plays became available and a younger director were to direct one of them without any preconceptions, we may able to change the fixed image of Brecht in this country' (see Kono 1998).

Although Sato is well known for his innovative direction of Brecht's plays in the 1970s, he did not do a production of Brecht in 1998. Instead, he directs *Woyzeck* with Black Tent Theatre Company at his Setagaya Public Theatre in September 1998, in addition to writing the script for *Buddha*. 'Little Theatre practitioners', who have, according to Nishido, supposedly embodied Brecht's theories, seem not to care that 1998 is Brecht's centennial. In short, nobody is thinking seriously about Brecht on his 100th birthday when it would be, in fact, commercially and/or critically feasible to 'do' so.

Instead, we have a typically apolitical and ahistorical theatrical extravaganza called *Buddha* at Japan's newest National Theatre complex, featuring Takashima Masanobu, one of the most famous TV stars of this decade, as Buddha. It is not impossible, however, to hear the death rattle of Brecht in Japan in this apparently un-Brechtian performance. Tezuka's original manga consists of 7 parts and 69 chapters or episodes. Published in 14 volumes in his *Collected Manga Works*, Tezuka wrote this epic over 12 years (1972–83) in order to retell the story of Buddha, making full use of his capacity to secularize and popularize in the easily accessible manga form the sacred and historical texts which depict Buddha's life and his teachings. Full of youthful and romantic adventures, it is, as Tezuka himself asserts in an afterword, a 'fictionalized' version, thus making the work a typical 'Tezuka SF' manga (1984: 5).

I do not want to argue either the 'authenticity' of Tezuka's understanding of Buddha's life or philosophy or his appropriation of it. I merely want to note that Tezuka's version is a straightforward negotiation between the complete canonical texts of Buddhism in Japan and his own post-War liberal-humanist 'popularization'. Using numerous references to contemporary sociocultural icons, images and concrete events, Tezuka tells the story of a suffering individual who later becomes one of the most influential religious figures in world history. In his usual entertaining and pedagogical manner, Tezuka is successful in doubling two completely separate historical processes: those of ancient India and of post-War Japan. The suffering of people, chaotic power relations and class struggles in ancient India are given narrative life in such a manner that people living in Japan, with their memories of World War II and its devastation, including the nuclear holocaust, post-War chaos and eventual revivification from material and spiritual defeat, can easily and immediately understand and identify with it.

In staging *Buddha*, as if to respond to its essentially allegorical nature and structure, Sato introduces or, rather, appropriates Brecht's characters into his production, namely, the three gods from *The Good Person of Szechwan* who are supposed to function as narrators, leaders of the chorus and, sometimes, enact some of the characters in the play.

Although Sato uses some Brechtian 'songs', *Buddha* is a straightforward play in which the action is depicted through dialogue. But two of the main characters who, curiously enough, are both female, are played by actors well known for their roles in recent popular musicals.

The chorus is present on stage most of the time, sometimes singing, occasionally dancing. After Brecht, *Buddha* is not called a musical but 'a play with music'. The intention is to refer to Brecht's influence (especially *The Threepenny Opera*) rather than to that of American musical theatre.

Inclusion of such Brechtian characters and techniques, of course, does not guarantee any Brechtian effect. What is strangely sad about this production is its aesthetic mediocrity. I say strangely sad because this production was meant to offer an apolitical aesthetic experience to the audience but it failed to do so quite miserably despite the gigantic budget provided to the director, Kuriyama. There is a huge river (with real water) visibly running upstage; fire, smoke-machine effects and an unnecessarily large chorus with many dancers—47 names are listed in the programme. But it all adds up to nothing more than mediocre, even downright bad, theatre. The representation of 'Indian-ness' is so amateur and 'innocent' that even Indians may find it difficult to criticize the production as a 'misrepresentation' of 'Indian-ness'.

The most disturbing thing about *Buddha* is that it lacks a sense of history both in Sato's script and in Kuriyama's staging. Brecht is thus radically decontextualized and demeaned in the production. The question we should ask, therefore, is: why has such a bad production, with techniques drawn from Brecht, been presented at the New National Theatre, a venue designated for 'representative' cultural products? Productions at this theatre are supposed to have something to do with contemporary methods of constructing Japan's national identity. Is this supposed to be some sort of non-commercial 'national' and/or 'official' 'popular' culture? Is this meant to be one of the end products of the'democratization' of high culture in this country? Why is political and historical consciousness omitted from this particular production? Why do even aesthetics have no place in it? What does Brecht in Japan mean in this context?

ACT I: MARCH 1932, TOKYO, JAPAN

SCENE: The Production of *The Beggar's Play* by TES.

CHARACTERS: Senda Koreya (1904–94), actor, director and, later, one of the most influential Shingeki practitioners, especially during and after World War II. Also a major force in introducing Brecht's work in Japan. He organized the production of *The Beggar's Play* soon after his return from a four-year spell in Germany, and at a time when many Shingeki theatre practitioners were faced with the possibility of a ban by the military government because of the leftist proletariat theatre movement before the War. Although Shingeki was understood by the Japanese government to be a leftist movement, there was, in fact, a political split among Shingeki practitioners. Since its inception at the end of the nineteenth century, the movement's political sympathies have been continuously changing.[2]

SYNOPSIS: Senda Koreya, after participating in the foundation of Tsukiji Sho-gekijo in 1924, the first 'official' Shingeki company founded by Osanai Kaoru, grew weary of the company's mainstream, apolitical and elitist attitudes. Senda left Japan for Germany in 1927. At the time, he considered himself to be a radical Marxist theatre practitioner travelling to Germany to study the workers' theatre movement. According to Ozasa Yoshio, a theatre historian who describes Senda's adventurous stay in Germany in detail, Senda was, during his first few years in Berlin, more an observer; much later, he became closely connected with those involved with the German Workers' Theatre Association (ATBD) (Ozasa 1990: 570–2). Senda also participated in the first meeting of the International Workers' Theatre Association (IATB), held in 1930 in Moscow. Consequently, Senda became active in agitprop theatre in Germany. He returned to Japan to establish a Far Eastern division of IATB in 1931 (ibid.: 577).

While in Germany, Senda did see some of Brecht's work (*Man is Man*, *The Threepenny Opera*, *The Decision*) and, although he never managed to meet him, was 'very impressed by his work' (ibid.: 570). Senda later recollected that he considered Brecht 'a slightly leftist bourgeois artist' (1976: 17–18), who had nothing to do with what he and his German friends were doing. *The Threepenny Opera*, however, seems an exception to his general assessment of Brecht at the time: Senda was 'mindblown and very surprised' by it (ibid.: 19).

When Senda went back to Japan, the Japan Proletariat Theatre Coalition (PROT) was dominating the leftist Shingeki scene. Curiously enough, at the time of his return, Senda did not join the association; instead, he established the agitprop theatre group Tokyo Proletariat Engei Shudan (Tokyo Proletariat Popular Entertainment Ensemble) which was later renamed Mezamashi Tai (Troupe for Uprising). Senda made his directorial debut with a work titled *Blue Uniforms* in February, 1932 that demonstrated 'how an agitprop theatre company could be collectively organized with small scenes, narration, chants and songs and how professionals, amateurs and audiences could be interconnected, and how political and economic issues could be dealt with' (Senda 1975: 232).

At the same time, Senda was involved in establishing the theatre collective called Tokyo Engeki Shudan. Yet, government officials were ever eager to eliminate the leftist movement. When Japan invaded Manchuria in 1931, the start of the endless invasion of Asia that continued until the end of the War in 1945, many leftist Shingeki practitioners began to have an extremely difficult time.

Several Shingeki groups like Tsukiji-za (Tsukiji Theatre Company) and Theatre Comedie were more interested in transplanting European psychological realism than in leftist theatre. In fact, before the unexpected death of Osanai Kaoru in 1929 and when it had to be disbanded, Tsukiji Sho-gekijo produced 127 productions of which only 27 were written by native Japanese playwrights. It was only after this company fell apart that some newly established companies, and the publication of some theatre magazines like *Gekisaku* (Playwriting, 1932–40), expressed an eagerness to nurture native playwrights, among who Kishida Kunio (1890–1954) grew to be a major voice. Though difficult to produce plays because of the War, the 1930s is considered to have been the time when 'native' playwriting reached its apex in the pre-War period (Ibaragi 1973: 82–8).[3]

The 1930s were also a time when diverse kinds of popular entertainment flourished, many genres of which had actually been established in the preceding decades during the Taisho era (1912–26), the first phase of Japan's democratization. Takarazuka, the all-female review, was founded in 1914. Other popular forms like Kei Engeki (Light Theatre), revues and talkies were attracting large audiences and producing popular stars. Still newer forms of popular culture emerged in the early Showa period (1930s)[4] and were characterized as 'Ero (erotic), Gro (grotesque), Nonsense'—Japan's version of decadent culture and degraded aesthetics. This particular image of the 1930s would be taken up in the post-1960s era by theatre practitioners such as Sato Makoto and Inoue Hisashi (1934–), both of whom were heavily influenced by Brecht's theatre practice and writings.

In the meantime, Senda chose to produce *The Threepenny Opera* as the first production of TES with the intention of creating a site where cultural producers from a wide spectrum of practices, including Shingeki, could come together. TES was established, according to Ozasa (1990: 597), for four reasons: to bring together Shingeki practitioners, including fragmented members of PROT who were hostile to each other because of their ideological and/or personal differences; to experiment with new theatrical forms including music, dance and cinema; to create opportunities for Shingeki practitioners who were suffering economically; to appear in radio programmes and movies; and to create a space where interaction between Shingeki practitioners and those working in other genres—commercial theatre, Kabuki, musical revues and cinema—could come together to discover a new 'popular' theatrical form.

I quote Ozasa at length, despite the fact that TES did not last even a year, because the reasons for establishing TES later became the *raison d'etre* of Shingeki practice, even after the War. The search for a new popular theatrical form became a kind of dogma for Shingeki practitioners, especially after the War, and this dogma was used on many occasions. Brecht was tactfully appropriated whenever Shingeki prac-titioners performatively and discursively referred to 'a new popular theatrical form'. It is interesting to note, therefore, that Brecht's play was chosen at this particular historical conjuncture as a site for many forms of performance, including popular entertainment; performers in the production were Senda's close associates, some from PROT, Tsukiji-za, Theatre Comedie and Asakusa Kei Engeki (Asakusa Light Theatre).

Brecht in Japan was, however, doomed from the beginning. As Senda recollects, 'Kurt Weill's score was easily available, but the script for *The Threepenny Opera* was not published [in Germany], and we didn't have time to acquire the unpublished script used for its production in Germany' (1975: 237). As a result, Senda had to 'reconstruct' the script from memory and Bapst's movie version. He set the play '[i]n Tokyo at the early years of Meiji period and tried to incorporate Weill's music as much as possible' (ibid.: 238):

> Considering we had to create scenes for those participating in the production, we 'faked' something like a script. We could not call it Brecht's *The Threepenny Opera*. Because opera was not popular, it could not become the object of parody as in the original. So we decided to call it *The Beggar's Play*, freely adapted by the Dramaturgy Department of TES (ibid.).

The Beggar's Play was performed at the Shin Kabuki-za (New Kabuki Theatre) in Shinjuku, Tokyo, at the end of March 1932.

It is difficult to know what the production looked like from the reviews of the day. Although it included a few popular stars like Enomoto Kenichi (nicknamed Enoken) from Kei Engeki and Tsukigata Ryunosuke, a movie star, it was not a great success. More interesting, however, is the fact that the first production of Brecht in Japan was intentionally distorted for external political reasons: Senda, as a young radical artist, was apparently in a hurry to establish TES as a major force in the cultural circles of the day. It is clear that he saw the possibility of 'new popular theatrical form' in *The Threepenny Opera*, he even envisioned it as the beginning of 'organizing a united front' of cultural producers against the fascist government (Senda 1985: 409), but he was not able to pursue this goal substantially. In fact, after this first Japanese version, it took 21 years for Senda to return to Brecht. In 1940, all the Shingeki companies, except the Bungaku-za Theatre Company (Literary Theatre), were forced to disband by an official order from the government, and Senda was subsequently imprisoned on several occasions.

ACT II: MAY 1953, TOKYO, JAPAN

SCENE: The production of *Fear and Misery of the Third Reich* by Haiyu-za Training School.

CHARACTERS: Senda Koreya and Haiyu-za Theatre Company.

SYNOPSIS: Brecht was rediscovered in Japan quite accidentally after the War in 1953. Senda was involved in establishing a new Shingeki company called Haiyu-za (Actor's Theatre) in 1944, although he was prohibited by officials from appearing in public during the War years. Along with Bungaku-za (the only theatre company not ordered to be disbanded in 1940), Haiyu-za would become a major force in re-establishing a modern theatre tradition during the post-War period.

The seven years from 1945 to 1952 were a decisive period for Shingeki practitioners. Their new beginning was based upon what they thought they had achieved before the War; and, although they wanted liberation from fascist domination, post-War everyday reality was extremely chaotic. They were, however, quick to recover and to start a so-called Shingeki Joint Production which took place in December 1945. That they chose to perform Chekhov's *The Cherry Orchard*, one of Shingeki's favourites in the pre-War period, was symbolic in many ways and indicated the direction, both theoretically and practically, of New Shingeki.

From the beginning of Tsukiji Sho-gekijo in 1924, Stanislavsky and the Moscow Art Theatre were considered a kind of 'master' model. For Shingeki practice, as I mentioned earlier, there were public and private struggles over which brand of modern European theatre practice it should model itself on. Some emphasized the coalition with labour and other social movements and some others were in search of the equivalent of a playwright's theatre. In the 1930s, when a modified version of Soviet socialist realism was adapted as the official aesthetic by mainstream Shingeki practitioners, some representative works in the vein of Japan's version of realistic theatre were produced. These later overshadowed the way Shingeki practitioners chose to proceed after the War, which manifested itself in the joint production of *The Cherry Orchard*.[5]

Senda was at the centre of Haiyu-za revitalizing the Shingeki practice after the War and survived a complex relationship with the Japan Communist Party and its cultural policies. The Party re-established itself immediately after the War and was eager to engage leftist Shingeki practitioners in disseminating Marxist ideology among the masses. Senda successfully negotiated with the General Headquarters (GHQ) of the US occupational forces in Tokyo. In fact, it was GHQ who summoned Senda and Shingeki practitioners in October 1945 and told them to 'fight against the old' and establish a 'democratic' theatre tradition (Senda 1980a: 353). By tactfully negotiating with both the Communist Party and GHQ, Senda continued his radical project of establishing a leftist modern theatre tradition in Japan. For Senda, this meant developing a European-style theatre production system.[6] Senda wanted Haiyu-za to grow into a European-style theatre company, with its own space and training school, supported by patrons and diverse kinds of audience organizations. Before acquiring a theatre for Haiyu-za in the heart of Tokyo, Senda helped organize its training school in 1951 and, for its second batch of graduates, decided to produce Brecht's *Fear and Misery of the Third Reich* because he accidentally came across the text in a bookstore in Kyoto. Senda 'chose the text not for its content but for its many scenes and characters which were quite convenient for the kind of production [he] wanted to do' (1985: 409): he wanted every graduating student to participate in the production and *The Third Reich* was the kind of play that would make that possible.

Senda's ideological ambiguities would later be critically interrogated by many (Kan 1981a: 73–5), because 1950 was the year when the Red purge policy of GHQ began to dominate political and cultural life. The fact that most members of Haiyu-za were not purged does not prove much. More importantly, political theatre activities usually referred to as *jiritsu engeki* (independent theatre), consisting of amateurs' and activists' theatre practices within actual working environments, were systematically banned and erased by GHQ and the Japanese government throughout the next decade. This drastic change in the policy of the occupational forces occurred because of the Korean War. Most Shingeki practitioners had to come to terms with the fact that liberation from the fascist government by the US forces meant another kind of governmental control. Hence, pre-War social and cultural structures and power relations (and actual political figures) were, for the most part, kept 'alive', especially the continuation of the emperor system by GHQ[7]—to give stability to Japan as a newly appointed ally of the US. It was as if the social structure and agencies did not change at all but were simply given different names.

Senda's main objective in those years was to 'popularize' and 'professionalize' Shingeki theatre practice (1980b: 333–6). By 'popularize' Senda meant that he would solicit the help of providers/creators of professional cultural products for what he called 'mature adult' audiences. He worked hard to organize the 'unenlightened' masses into appreciative 'adults', as he was intent on providing good non-commercial theatre to the people. Senda was an 'old leftist' theatre practitioner and, to that extent, political, and his political project did have a certain validity and relevance at least in the first decade after the War. Yet Senda wanted to establish a Western dramatic tradition in Japan in which Western modern drama was produced in what he thought to be authentic and even traditional ways, employing the Stanislavsky style of psychological realism.

In the programme note for his production of *The Third Reich* (1953), Senda writes:

> We decided to work on Brecht's *Fear and Misery of the Third Reich* not because we wanted to show an example of 'Epic Theatre', or a 'Learning Play'. I am now seriously spending most of my time studying 'dramatic theatre' and 'empathetic' acting techniques. Therefore students who will be performing in this production are those who have been educated in that line of theory (1976: 141).

According to Senda, Brecht's theory was the antithesis of the dominant Western dramatic tradition. As there was no such tradition in Japan, one had to be established before it could be criticized or overcome. Here, we can observe the often-mentioned schizophrenic effect of the modernization of Japan, where Stanislavsky and Brecht were introduced almost simultaneously and as if they were not in contradiction.

Senda was very cautious about introducing Brecht even after this production, because 'popularization' and 'professionalization' of Haiyu-za, as already mentioned, was his first concern and Brecht's theatrical ideas were too 'unfamiliar' (see Senda 1985: 411). Senda did continue to direct Brecht's plays although not with Haiyu-za. The first production of Haiyu-za's Brecht had to wait until 1961 when Senda directed *The Good Person of Szechwan*. This was after Shingeki practitioners actively protested the signing of the Japan–US Security Treaty in 1960.

ACT III: TOKYO, OCTOBER 1968, SHINJUKU, JAPAN

SCENE: The Shinjuku Riot by students at Shinjuku Station on International Students' Day.

CHARACTERS: Brecht in Japan, Senda Koreya, Inoue Hisashi and Angura Theatre practitioners, including Sato Makoto and the Black Tent.

SYNOPSIS: After the initial problematic introductions of his work by Senda, Brecht was more widely disseminated in the 1960s. Senda had been translating Brecht's plays since 1953 and these were later collected and published along with Brecht's stagings, as *Collected Plays by Bertolt Brecht* (5 VOLS; see Senda 1961–62). Brecht's theoretical writings were slower to appear in translation, the first appearing in 1953, translated by Komiya Kozo. But it was not until Senda published *Can the Present-day World Be Reproduced by Means of Theatre: Brecht's Theatre Theories* (1962) that an 'authoritative' translation of Brecht's theories appeared in Japan. With this book, Brecht became one of the most widely read authors, not only by theatre practitioners but also by political activists, philosophers, literary figures and other cultural producers.

In this context, it becomes very difficult to follow the whole spectrum of Brecht's influence in Japan. The main threads are: Senda's
introduction of Brecht, mainly to Shingeki practice, and the more subtle and complicated influence of Brecht on Angura Theatre practice
and its practitioners.

Although 1960s' Japanese theatrical history is currently remembered for and mostly discussed in terms of the rise of the Angura
Theatre Movement, Shingeki was still very active all through the
decade. The failure of direct political activism against the Japan–US
Security Treaty in 1960 brought about a deep change in Japan's political climate. There was widespread disillusionment with the idealistic
notion of socialist revolution and this took the form of a hegemonic
struggle between the Old Left and the New, especially over organizing
an effective resistance against the renewed imperialistic alliance
between Japan and the US. While prolific productions of the democratization narrative and of the 'modernization theory' were carried on by
the authorities and the dominant cultural producers in many spheres,
including academia and popular media, Japan as a whole was experiencing drastic social and economic changes. People became 'tamed' citizens or *shomin*, a word which came to mean, at least in some quarters,
the newly emerging bourgeois class especially in cities like Tokyo. The
1960s was also when Japan's postcolonial and post-War national identity was established, mainly through the process of economic growth
(the Income-doubling Project by the ruling Liberal Democratic Party),
and manifested through mainstream cultural products, such as commercial films and television dramas, which tended to emphasize
Japan's cultural 'tradition'.

Interestingly enough, Shingeki never became a mainstream cultural product. Major Shingeki practitioners were seldom interested in
newly discovered and/or invented Japanese 'tradition'; most of them
were still stuck to the idea of 'Japanizing' what they had decided was
Western modern theatre tradition. For Senda and his followers, at
least, Brecht and Brechtian theory was still something to 'study' rather
than to 'appropriate'. Senda established a 'Brecht Study Group' within Haiyu-za in 1963 that would be reorganized into his 'Brecht's
Group' in the next decade and which continued to exist from 1974 to

about 1990. Therefore, Brecht's name was gradually becoming almost inseparable from Senda's in the 1960s and, in 1968, as if to prove his status as the only Brechtian in Japan, Senda was invited to represent Japan in 'Brecht Dialogue 1968' in East Berlin. Brecht, therefore, continued to be perversely canonized by Senda and other Shingeki practitioners; he became classic, as Sato mentions in 1998, but not necessarily in a straightforward fashion. Brecht in Japan, as far as Senda was concerned, had and has always been displaced from mainstream Shingeki practice, as if to say Brecht is what Senda really wanted to do but had to wait till the audience become more 'mature'.

Ironically enough, this perverse way of canonizing Brecht—by displacing him from mainstream Shingeki practice, which continued to identify itself against mainstream cultural producers and their products—made it possible for him to be taken up by some newer generations of Shingeki practitioners. Playwrights of the post-War generation, such as Fukuda Yoshiyuki (1931–) and Miyamoto Ken (1926–88), turned against their predecessors, including Senda, and started to write plays overtly that were more subtle and self-reflexive in their notion of the political, using Brechtian epic theatre style and allegorical structure. Brecht in Japan, i.e. Brecht as a displaced political playwright and theatre theorist of the 'alienation effect', now began to have a stronger impact on Japan's theatre culture than Senda's faithful introduction of his work. Diverse contemporary theatre practices included the emergence and rise of various kinds of contemporary 'popular' theatre within and around Shingeki and the other new trend that would later be categorized as the Angura Theatre Movement. The former would accumulate in the person and work of Inoue Hisashi, one of the most popular playwrights in post-War Japan and a professed supporter of the Japan Communist Party, whose more recent work (*Kamiya-cho Sakura Hotel*) was chosen, quite ironically for some, to be produced at the opening of the New National Theatre in 1997.[8] The latter would culminate in the work of Sato Makoto.

One of the formalistic characteristics of Inoue's line of playwriting is the concept of the musical play as a serious but 'popular' art form, in opposition to other forms of commercial 'popular' entertainment, such as imported and appropriated versions of American musical theatre. Inoue has a concrete image of whom he writes for and with: *shomin* of Japan. *Shomin* can be translated as 'commoners' but it can be more precisely defined as follows:

> It [*shomin*] refers to common masses. The notion of *shomin* is different from that of citizen or people in that the latter are conscious of their political position and their class under particular historical conditions. It is also different from the notion of unorganized masses in an industrialized society, or 'common people', who are identified by anthropology as those who retain traditional lifestyles and an indigenous culture. In short, *shomin* are 'people who are unconsciously immersed in the conventional value system' (Hidaka Rokuro). But the notion of *shomin* emerges, in such expression as *shomin kankaku* (*shomin*'s sensibilities), when intellectual discourses or governmental policies are felt to be so far away from the actual, in order to criticize those from a perspective of *seikatsu-sha* (actually living people). Because they are *shomin*, leading their own 'small' lives, without any recognizable social, financial, political status, they could have an actual meaning on such occasions (N.A. 1988).

The *shomin* class became the dominant agency for the ideology of post-War democracy towards the end of the 1960s while Shingeki still stuck to the notion of *taishu*—the unorganized masses in industrialized Japan—as the target audience that it would 'educate' and 'enlighten'. Inoue's innovation—appropriating Brecht to devise his version of 'popular theatre' in Japan—stemmed from the Shingeki tradition and from his experience as a writer in mass media. Most of his plays, including many of his music theatre works, have allegorical narratives, decisive humour, sentimental 'good' scenes and mild political messages. It is not accidental that *Yabuhara Kengyo* (1973), arguably his most Brechtian play, won great critical acclaim. As this play abundantly demonstrates, Inoue was apparently against art theatre, political theatre and commercial 'popular' theatre all at once and wanted to provide *shomin* with what they thought they wanted. He was never avant-garde or politically active or commercially popular but kept to a middle ground, as if to assert that that is the only site where the 'true' notion of the popular can be constructed. Being mediocre, being in-between has, perhaps, been his strength all these years. As the first playwright to be presented at the New National Theatre in 1997, his 'triumph' was echoed in the curious mediocrity of the production of *Buddha*, a play with music. The politics of Brecht in Japan has produced some very un-Brechtian results; his notion of the 'popular' without any ideological echoes found the easiest and fastest way into Japan's theatre culture.

We are, however, still in 1968, when the *shomin* class is still almost invisible and Brecht in Japan is in the first phase of diverse appropriations by other theatre practitioners, most notably of the Angura Theatre, who made themselves quite visible by the end of the 1960s. Brecht, of course, was not their only reference; there was Artaud—*The Theatre and Its Double* was already translated in 1965 as were works by Sartre and Beckett. Just as the Tsukiji Sho-gekijo practitioners were faced with diverse 'choices' at the beginning of their existence in 1924—decontextualized and dehistoricized names, 'isms' and writings were simultaneously imported—so also Angura Theatre practitioners, in an attempt to articulate their cultural and political positions, had to negotiate their theoretical, political, aesthetic, collective and personal concerns through layers and layers of information in the form of translations, journalistic and academic writings and so on. For Angura Theatre practitioners, immediacy of information was most important and the context in which ideas were imported and appropriated did have a serious effect on their understanding and use.

Brecht's name, then, was conceptualized as a kind of absolute canonical text in Japan's theatre culture by the middle of the 1960s, because, as we have seen, his name had become inseparable from Senda's theatre practice. Brecht's political and aesthetic implications were considered authoritative and thus out-of-date by the time major Angura Theatre practitioners began to make themselves visible. Kara Juro (1940–) formed his Jyokyo Gekijo (Situation Theatre) in 1963, and, as the name of his company indicates, his frame of reference was decisively Sartre and existentialist philosophy and aesthetics. Suzuki Tadashi (1939–) started his career during his university days in the early 1960s by directing some of Sartre's plays, and participated in the formation of Waseda Sho-gekijo in 1967 with Betsuyaku Minoru (1937–), a playwright writing in the Beckettian absurdist tradition. It is more difficult to locate Terayama Shuji's (1935–83) sources of reference, but Brecht was not obviously one of them; in fact, he would later explicate his own theatre theory, as Nakajima Hiroaki (1997) brilliantly demonstrates, *against* Brecht or, at least, against what Terayama thought Brecht stood for.

Significantly, most initial Angura practices were not overtly political; politics was notably outside their performance spaces, especially towards the end of the 1960s, with the renewal of the Japan–US Security Treaty approaching in 1970, with Japan's direct and indirect involvement with the Vietnam War. This time, however, the ontological formation of political activism was completely different from that of the previous decade, as the notion of an orthodox Marxist revolution by the underprivileged masses had become archaic. In 1960, the revolt was initiated by labour unions and university student organizations, but the Shinjuku Riot in 1968 was not really an organized one. It was an accidental and spontaneous eruption of the unorganized energy of university students, more a cultural than a political event and so full of contradictions that its political content could not be easily articulated. As Kan Takayuki appropriately describes, the riot made 'the political a festive event' (1981a: 189), by which he meant that the notion of the political was drastically challenged at the end of the 1960s, after tremendous economic growth had been achieved.

It is interesting, therefore, that Kan, a major theorist and practitioner of Angura Theatre, sees the appropriation of Brecht as a significant factor in this whole process. While referring to Sartre as the most important figure in the configuration of politics and aesthetics in Angura Theatre practice during the early 1960s, Kan includes Brecht as another important influence:

> Komiya Kozo's translation of Brecht's *Theatre Theories* was such a bad translation that one third of the whole book was almost incomprehensible; nonetheless, we attempted to read from that bad translation what Brecht's critical theory was and what his alienation theory meant. There was a lot to learn from his alienation theory in terms of a general notion of the critical mind and how we should relate theory to praxis. But this was not enough to teach us a valid methodology for changing the the-

atrical language and the relationship between language and the body. . . . I must say our understanding of Brecht remained in the sphere of intellectual 'recognition'. But it was important for us that it reached the sphere of the level of physical expression (1981b: 176–7).

Angura Theatre practitioners were more interested in Brecht as a theorist than as a playwright. They were not naive enough to believe that they could 'transplant' the Brechtian theory, whatever its meaning. Brecht was rather a resource for devising their own theories, from which they would go on to generate their respective theatrical performances. Kan's passage can be read as a confession of their failure to translate Brechtian theory, including its political aspect, into performance.

The notion of 'alienation', nevertheless, did become a key concept for Angura theorists and practitioners, including Kan. The meaning of 'alienation' differs from one to the other. Yet none of them seems to have included its most important aspect, since for them it mostly seems to have remained within the realm of aesthetics and was used for what was understood to be its shock value. Many Angura Theatre practitioners sought to revolutionize theatrical language, especially physical language, as the most effective means for the A-effect. At first, very political in its aesthetic and historical implications, this newly devised theatrical language later became stabilized and its political implications were lost by the 1970s. In other words, most Angura practitioners were not able to respond to the symbolic event of the Shinjuku Riot in 1968, in which the old notion of the political was drastically challenged. Both Angura practitioners and the Shinjuku Riot were political only because of their positions within the historical process. Around 1968, with a radical paradigmatic shift in theatre practices, the political began to be gradually displaced from Japan's theatre practices, which was nevertheless part of a political–cultural process. During that process, the political Brecht was consensually erased from Japan's cultural memory and we were given Brecht, the great playwright.

EPILOGUE: JUNE 1969, TOKYO, JAPAN

SCENE: Jiyu Gekijo (Theatre of Liberty) and Rokugatsu Gekijo (Theatre of June) decide to jointly form the Engeki Center 68/69, which later became Center 68/71 (1971) and, still later, Black Tent Theatre Company (1990).

CHARACTERS: Sato Makoto and members of Black Tent Theatre Company. While most Angura companies (Suzuki's Waseda Sho-gekijo, Kara's Red Tent, etc.) were led by charismatic patriarchal figures, and their collectivity, consciously or not, almost always replicated Japan's typical familial structure, Black Tent was, and still is, a theatre collective, faithfully reflecting the ideals of post-War democracy. Its structure is quite close to that of the European public-theatre system, although it does not have an artistic director and was not publicly funded until the late 1980s. Sato Makoto is undoubtedly a major figure in the collective, but also notable are Saito Haruhiko (actor), Yamamoto Kiyokazu and Kato Tadashi (directors), and Tsuno Kaitaro, Saeki Ryuko and David Goodman (dramaturges). Sato is a graduate from the Haiyu-za Training School, which Senda established, and most of the other practitioners are also from the Shingeki tradition. Tsuno Kaitaro was then a member of Shin Nihon Bungaku (Alternative Japanese Literature), an important cultural site for both the Old Left and the New, in which Brecht was often discussed and written about since the beginning of the 1960s. Saeki, now a professor of French Literature at Gakushuin University, is an expert on French theatre. In short, most members belong to the cultural elite, and are well informed about contemporary Euro-American theatre practices and theories and leftist political and cultural theories.

SYNOPSIS: The Black Tent Theatre Company, during the late 1960s and early 1970s, maintained the many facets of Brecht that we have been discussing. They were very conscious of their position within Japan's theatre culture, and, as displaced successors of pre- and post-War Shingeki practice, they tried to reinvent and reinscribe Brecht in Japan, negotiating Senda's Brecht, Inoue's 'popularization' of Brecht and other Angura practices, including those inspired by Artaud and the Absurd.

The Company's slogan was 'Theatre for Revolution' and, in 1969, it issued a manifesto entitled 'Communication Project No. 1', in which it promised to organize its theatre practice into a radical social movement, a process that included the notion of the Base Theatre, a permanent theatre space, with a repertory system, in Tokyo; the Migrating Theatre, a mobile theatre practice performing and sometimes conducting workshops all over Japan; and publication and pedagogy. Accordingly, it started to perform its works all over Japan in its 'black tent'. Its work was meant to be a serious response to what was happening in Europe and the US around 1968. It naturally did not mean a socialist revolution when it put 'Theatre for Revolution' in its slogan. Rather, it was concerned with revolutionizing and/or transforming the sociopolitical status quo through cultural experiences, by establishing hybrid sites for resistance against dominant cultural practices. In 1968, Japan, however, was situated at a historical conjuncture that signalled the completion of the postcolonial moment and the process of reconstructing and restructuring national identity. In cultural practices, what H. D. Harootunian calls the 'National Poetics', had by then become the dominant ideological device to 'eliminate the realm of criticism that once belonged to the space of culture' (1993: 215–16).

In light of the concept of 'National Poetics', the Black Tent's political project was destined to fail. Its conscious strategy of decentralization through diasporic journeys, therefore, was understood more often than not as the romantic political gesture of cultural elites. Before the project faded away, it provided the last vital moment for Brecht in Japan's theatre culture. Most notably, Sato's plays are rich examples of this; in his five serial plays with *Nezumi Kozo Jirokichi* (1969–71) as a protagonist–anti-hero—Jirokichi is a mythic robber in the Edo period, a chivalrous robber who robs the rich for the poor, and a transformation of Mack the Knife in *The Threepenny Opera*—and in his three serial plays entitled *Comedies: The World of Showa Trilogy* (1972–79), Sato and members of the Black Tent explored the possibility of historicizing twentieth-century Japan, by appropriating many aspects of Brecht's work. *Abe Sada Diaries of Showa* (1973) is the first play in *The World of Showa Trilogy*, and in it Sato uses only Weill's music for *The Threepenny Opera*, itself a very political gesture and perhaps most representative of Sato's reinvention of hybridized Brecht in Japan. Sato attempts to articulate the historical process by which the possibility of revolution has been systematically erased from Japan's public imagination. In devising an overtly allegorical narrative and using the epic theatre format, Sato transforms the actual 1930s' historical figure of Abe Sada, known for having cut off her lover's penis, into the symbolic by portraying the *shomin* class as representative of the status quo while embodying the possibility of female sexual transgression. The real protagonist in this play, however, is a Showa Emperor who is drastically demeaned and reduced into the timid leader of a small closed community. He is the one suffering from a castration complex/fantasy (the possibility of which is demonstrated by Abe Sada) and, fearing that his penis will be cut off by the people in the community, he declares martial law. Revolution is impending all through the play but it never happens and the Emperor enjoys a natural death at the end, some 15 years later.

As I have shown, a political and cultural revolution was forever emerging all through the 1960s, but it never 'happened'. Sato's *Abe Sada* is an allegory of the 1960s. It is significant that Brecht in Japan revealed himself in such a manner; he was exceptionally successful in inscribing himself within Sato's text, although he has to be (re)discovered, as I have been attempting to do, from a Harootunian 'National Poetics' which urges us to forget and erase—to forget and erase the fact that history is wilfully forgotten and cultural memory can be systematically and consensually erased.

Black Tent returned to Brecht in its 'Brecht Renaissance' Project between 1989 and 1993. In the intervening years, as if to correspond to Japan's neo-colonial economic invasion of other Asian countries, the Black Tent turned to Asia, via Brecht and Augusto Boal, and via their respective transplantation and appropriation by some Asian theatre practices. Notions of workshop and pedagogy, accordingly, have become more important in the Black Tent's theatre practice as well as the forming of alliances with other Asian theatre practitioners and practices. Its political project, however, has not been visible in Japan's theatre culture because of its subtlety, its political ambiguities and its apparent lack of recognition of specific historicity(ies) that each Asian country was then staging.

When Black Tent came back to Brecht in the late 1980s, he was considered by some to be a 'classic' playwright, almost enjoying the same status as Shakespeare. Other theatre practitioners in Japan were more interested in producing Brecht's plays rather than in using Brecht to reconfigure their theory and praxis. The younger generation of spectators either had never heard of Brecht or had only a very fixed image of him. Trapped between these radically demarcated positions and statuses within Japan's theatre culture, Brecht had to start 'proving himself' after more than 50 years of his existence in Japan. Brecht's theatrical identity was, at times, fatally associated with those who tried to stage his plays. Ironically, the potential of his political perspective was mostly lost or was not even a subject for radical theatre practitioners in Japan. Even after Brecht's centennial year, it is very difficult to feel his presence, ghostly or not, where I come from.

Notes

1   While I was writing this article, Kuriyama Tamiya was appointed the next artistic director of the New National Theatre, starting in 2000. He served as artistic director for two terms, between 2000 and 2006. In 2007, Uyama Hitoshi (1953–), also from a Shingeki tradition, took over. In the meantime, Sato Makoto served as artistic director of the Setagaya Public Theatre between 1997 and 2002, and was succeeded by Nomura Mansai (1966–), a Kyogen actor.

2   Shingeki is, at best, an ambiguous term. By definition, it is supposed to refer to all theatre practices which have nothing to do with traditional theatrical forms. In a more exclusive usage, it refers to modern theatre practices which were heavily influenced by equivalents in Western (mostly European) theatre. Companies such as Bungei Kyokai (Literary Association, 1906–13) and Jiyu Gekijo (Theatre of Liberty, 1909–19) are considered pioneers but, in my conception, Tsukiji Sho-gekijo was the first serious and influential attempt to transplant modern Western theatre practices in Japan, including their production system, acting style, aesthetic and political concerns.

3   In pre-War Shingeki practices, there was a conflict between politics and aesthetics. Tsukiji Sho-gekijo, for instance, was considered more aesthetic than political (which is why Senda left the company for Germany). As we will later see, while both positions were hypotheti-

cally integrated into one under the name of 'socialist realism' during the 1930s, this radical binary operated in both Shingeki practice and its theory even in the post-War period. It is usually understood that pioneering Shingeki practitioners on both sides tried to imitate Western modern theatre practices: they wanted to look 'as if' they were 'Westerners' by using wigs and false noses. It may sound ridiculous now, but if you are familiar with Japan's traditional theatre culture, Shingeki's way of imitating 'Westerners' was such a fictional, even fantastic 'as if' style that it was not far from the exaggerated make-up and gestures of Kabuki. I, therefore, suspect that Shingeki's acting style might have an 'alienation effect', as not so many audiences at the time were familiar with how 'Westerners' looked and behaved. It may be more appropriate to understand Shingeki's way of 'imitating' Western acting style as a hybridizing project of juxtaposing (essentialized) Japanese bodies with (idealized/exoticized) Western looks, gestures and behaviours. The same kind of theoretical enquiry should be made into how the 'native' playwrights appropriated what they claimed to be the dramaturgy of Western psychological realism.

4   Japan's system for designating eras by years is called *gengo*, After the Meiji period, it was decided that *gengo* would be according to the life of the emperor. When one emperor dies, new *gengo* are designated with the enthronement of the next. Thus, in the years covered in this chapter, Japan has had Meiji (1868–1912), Taisho (1912–26), Showa (1926–89) and Heisei (1989–), with four emperors. It is now customary to prefix emperor names with *gengo* such as Meiji Emperor or Showa Emperor.

5   This joint production was possible by referring to the 'origin' of Shingeki. By referring to the pre-revolution rather than the post-revolution Moscow Art Theatre (Chekhov and Stanislavsky) as their 'origin' and theoretical model, post-War Shingeki practitioners, consciously or not, confessed their ideological ambiguities. *The Cherry Orchard* was chosen as an obviously apolitical piece of work which different Shingeki practitioners with different ideological backgrounds could agree on producing.

6   You may detect a certain degree of politically charged rhetoric in Senda's way of positioning himself within Japan's theatre culture. In his case, especially after the War, his politics were not so much about the Marxist revolution but a gradual democratization of the country.

He did not want to mingle with the Communist Party or with GHQ. GHQ, accordingly, did not consider him to be 'dangerous' to their policy in post-War Japan but, rather, to be a potential cultural agency for democratizing Japan.

7   The Emperor denied his divine lineage on 1 January 1946, and this was to later save him from being accused of his wartime responsibility. In the subsequent restructuring of Japan's social and political system, the 'definition' that the Emperor is just a 'regular' human being was appropriated, as is clearly stated in the Japanese Constitution, to reintroduce many pre-War 'elements' (social institutions, personnel and so on).

8   It may sound confusing. How is it possible that a play written by a professed supporter of the Japan Communist Party is chosen to be performed for the opening of the New National Theatre? First of all, the Japan Communist Party is a legitimate political organization, and anyone has a constitutional right to support it. Second and more importantly, Inoue has long been thought to be an anti-emperor-system writer; this new play, according to theatre critic Nishido Kojin, was apparently written to 'cunningly evade the issue of Showa Emperor's war responsibility' (1998: 27) although it pretends to take up that very issue. The New National Theatre is the place, as Nishido also points out, where the emperor's family is supposed to have all the rights to visit, and Inoue, despite being given a chance to raise the issue of wartime responsibility, was unable to face the challenge.

The end of Japan's 'bubble economy' around 1993 resulted in a new version of neo-nationalism. Cultural producers had been desperately attempting to create a narrative connecting the failure of Japan's once invincible economic power to its unexpected downfall. Was it US-manufactured global capitalism that undermined 'our' healthy desire for prosperity? Or was it some deep-rooted 'national' character flaw that ended 'our' own global economic hegemony? From daily talk shows on TV to serious literary magazines, these questions are discussed and debated every day in the interest of redefining Japan's 'national' character and what 'we, the Japanese' should do at this critical stage of Japan's modern history.[1]

Yet, in the process of redefining Japan's 'national' character, it is what I call the 'Aum-esque' that is eliminated from Japan's discursive space. I say 'eliminated' because the Aum-esque is surreptitiously implied by both the political Right and the Left. Those who are familiar with the Aum Shinri-kyo's (Aum Truth Cult)[2] terrorist gas attack in 1995 may be surprised to hear this, for more effort has been spent on trying to 'explain' the Aum phenomenon than on discussing the disastrous outcome of the Hanshin-Awaji earthquake earlier in 1995. As if there was nothing to explain about the earthquake because it was a 'natural' phenomenon while what the Aum attempted to 'achieve' through their poison gas attack needed elaboration.

Towards this end, a recurring Japanese narrative relying on the idealization of a homogeneous Japanese identity has been resurrected in which the dichotomy of 'outside' and 'inside' is unanimously employed so that Aum cult members and their actions are regarded as those of exceptionally sick outsiders with criminal minds. The Aum-esque has thus been successfully 'bracketed' within Japan's cultural memory.

Within the narrative of Japan's new national character, the Aum-esque is fully understood and, therefore, already vanquished.

The same kind of manipulative displacement of Japan's cultural past can be detected in the construction of the narrative of 1980s' theatre culture. Mainstream theatre journalism has taken up the notion of *shizukana engeki* or Quiet Theatre as the representative style for the 1990s. Major critics unanimously praise *shizukana engeki* practitioner Hirata Oriza as a major artistic voice in 'post-bubble' Japan.[3] Politically conservative and artistically innovative, *shizukana engeki* practices have been successful in drawing unreasonably emphatic media coverage and younger audiences. This success, however, is predicated on conservative journalists who designated 1980s' theatre culture as 'not Quiet Theatre' through a strategy of not articulating the difference by not mentioning, nor making any reference to, 1980s' theatre culture. Thus, in affirming the *shizukana engeki* practices of the 1990s as better and more appropriate, Japan's theatre culture of the 1980s, as well as the Aum-esque, has become something 'fully' understood and, therefore, already overcome.

Historically speaking, 1982, when the first Toga International Arts Festival was held, was an important point of departure for theatre culture. As the festival was a rare occasion for post-War avant-garde theatre artists from both the East and the West to present their work, it was an important point of departure for Japan's theatre. Audiences, including myself, were very excited by the sumptuous display of diverse and provocative visions, and were led to imagine theatre arts in the future tense. For critics like me, at least, the festival signalled the coming of an age of truly intercultural theatre. The festival was organized by Suzuki Tadashi, the director of Suzuki Company of Toga (SCOT), and prominent European and American avant-garde artists such as Robert Wilson, Meredith Monk (both from the US), John Fox (from the UK) and Tadeusz Kantor (from Poland), along with Terayama Shuji and Ota Shogo. It was the first international festival in which mostly avant-garde theatrical works were presented to Japanese audiences.

Looking back, however, I cannot help but feel that we should have felt a certain fear instead of an aesthetic pleasure at the contradictions of post-World War II world theatre. Watching, for instance, Kantor's radically contradictory, performative and reflexive commentary on the nature of representation and on the incongruities between memory and 'lived' experiences in *The Dead Class*, we should have seen the limits of representation and the impossibility of theatre as a political practice.

Our 'innocent' acceptance of Western aesthetic avant-garde theatre traditions as 'our own' during the 1980s gave us a theatre dominated by notions of universality. But this was, in fact, a perverse manifestation of a localized/Japanized version of postmodernism. Ahistorical and unproblematized, 'imported', radical theatre practices became yet another 'brand' to be eagerly consumed by the Japanese middle class. 'Native' theatre practitioners, consciously or not, began investing in a cultural relativism that allowed them to follow their immediate and comprehensible impulses without facing what was 'other' and therefore incomprehensible. Under the guise of postmodern universality, contemporary Japanese theatre was able to be unselfconsciously xenophobic.

Within these closed-circuit theatrical and discursive practices, references to that which lay outside Japan, to 'otherness', were repressed in favour of postmodernist notions such as surplus consumption, simulacra, play of visualities and 'surface', as if these ideas contained a priori 'universal' applications. In short, in the very gesture of opening up towards the 'other' and the 'foreign' instigated by the Toga Festival, Japan's 1980s' theatre culture closed down around itself.

As the Aum Shinri-kyo incidents became known to the Japanese public in 1995, many people associated the cult with 1980s' theatre culture usually referred to as Sho-gekijo. This resonance was a result of the Aum Shinri-kyo's strategies for attracting its cult believers by exploiting the sensitivities of the 1980s' youth with apocalyptic dogmas and teachings that propagated images of the end of the world. Asahara Shoko, the Aum leader who was deemed the second Christ, was to save the world after Armageddon. The Aum's political and religious campaigns used many theatrical and performative techniques considered unique to 1980s' theatre culture. Their outrageously kitsch and cheap costumes, and unprofessional yet 'sincere' energetic acting style in pseudo-Broadway song-and-dance street performances, seemed to be replicas of the 'Little Theatre' of the preceding decade. Yasumi Akihito, theatre critic, wrote: 'the Aum is a grand repetition of the theatre culture of the 1980s' (1995b: 167). Referring to the Aum cult, he defines the theatre culture of the 1980s as 'young people's theatre' talking about 'the end of the world' as if within 'the premises of the nuclear shelter' (ibid.). Yasumi had already written: 'The "here and now" that was "rediscovered" during the Sho-gekijo boom[4] was theoretically secured by the kind of closure that makes it possible to accumulate scattered memories in the ongoing process of oblivion, as if carefully observing the "outside" from within a nuclear shelter in order to make sure that the world "outside" has certainly ended' (1995a: 160). In the subcultural genres of the 1980s, including Sho-gekijo, everybody was concerned with describing the end of the world and post-Armageddon (i.e. nuclear holocaust) dystopia. Within this world of 'euphoric nothingness', in which traditional value systems were declared dead, there was only one transcendental 'truth': 'people will die, everyone will die and there is no exception' (Yasumi 1995b: 167).

According to Yasumi, the lesson to be learned from the theatre culture of the 1980s and the Aum is that 'poor strategies such as parody or pastiche do not constitute a viable site of resistance against the invisible space of power,' and 'those who feel alienated from Japan's power system eventually construct its mirror image in their own organizations' (see Yasumi 1995b). Power relations within the Aum mirrored Japan as a nation-state—it had an organization very similar to the Japanese system of government with its own bureaucracy and its own version of a Ministry of Finance. Asahara was the emperor, the transcendental being.

THE RETURN OF THE 'THEATRE OF THE PRIVATE'

Theatre culture of the 1980s also contained the return of what I call the 'theatre of the private'. Because I have discussed the term elsewhere (see Uchino 1996), I want to give here only a loose definition of the term. 'Theatre of the private' is a Japanese form of melodrama in which an unarticulated subjectivity, neither singular nor collective, dominates the theatrical space, including the audience. This is not a theatre of Cartesian subjects but of pre-modern undifferentiated selves in which spectators are supposed to contribute a full range of sentiments. 'Theatre of the private' presupposes the existence of a community of sentiments, one in which members are neither connected nor defined by ideology, language, law or contract but only by and through shared sentiments.

Historically speaking, much of Japan's theatrical representation, as I have argued elsewhere, can be understood as 'theatre of the private', including Noh, Kabuki and Shingeki. It has been given different names but it continues to dominate Japan's theatre culture. The only notable exception is the Angura of the 1960s, in which clearly definable Cartesian selves were the dominant form of theatrical representation. Angura's desperate attempt to establish a Western modern theatre tradition in Japan was however doomed to fail and, in the 1980s, the 'theatre of the private' returned with dazzling speed and spectacular quality, amply demonstrated by, for example, Noda Hideki, a playwright/actor/director who was an exponent of the Sho-gekijo boom. Despite the naivete of its contents, his flashy, fast-paced spectacles, in which young actors ran around and jumped about, were regarded as something truly new. The 1980s' 'theatre of the private' was, accordingly, also called 'young people's theatre' and, as Kazama Ken acutely observed, it became as popular as Kabuki had been during the Edo period (1992: 133).

Both the practitioners and audiences of the 'theatre of the private' comprised young people—mostly city dwellers, many of them university students, occupying the middle ground of the social structure, positioned between two areas of adult supervision: between their high school years and their life as business persons. As students, under strict school supervision, they were urged to study hard so that they could win the race to enter one of the better universities. As working men and women, under strict corporate supervision, they were urged to win the race in the capitalist economy. Stranded between these inevitable socialized states, young people seemingly have, or had, for a brief moment, a liminal space and time after one and before another.

What made the return of 'theatre of the private' possible in the 1980s? Theatre, during this time, suddenly started to engage with the subject of 'nuclear holocaust' and/or 'the end of the world'. References to the apocalyptic dominated visual and thematic representations of the 'theatre of the private'. Critics consider Kitamura So's *Hogi-uta* (*A Celebration Song*, 1980) one of the most representative and influential plays of this period. The text starts with a simple and drastic stage direction: 'The nuclear war has ended. A local city in the Kansai area. A road among the ruins. Smell of burning air [. . .]' (Kitamura 1982: 7).

Other Sho-gekijo practitioners such as Kokami Shoji of The Third Stage and Kawamura Takeshi of Daisan (Third) Erotica were known for setting most of their plays in the near post-Armageddon future. Sho-gekijo theatre practices had a strong affinity to other subcultural genres of the same decade. For instance, *Akira*, an epic manga written by Otomo Katsuhiro, later made into an animated movie, was serialized in a weekly manga magazine (*Young Magazine*) for young adults published by Kodan-sha between 1982 and 1990 (later, *Akira* was published independently in six volumes between 1984 and 1993). Like Kitamura's play, Akira's story begins when the world ends in 1982 because of World War III. In relation to these kinds of subcultural representations, Sho-gekijo practitioners, some would argue, chose images of the apocalyptic as an appropriate, though cheap, metaphor for the world they were forced to live in; the world in which, to quote Yasumi again, 'euphoric nothingness' was the only shared and shareable sentiment, where 'traditional value systems are declared dead' (Yasumi 1995b: 167). It is tempting to interpret the themes of 1980s' theatre culture as such; the apocalyptic is an easy metaphor for 'childish' theatre practitioners who cannot face the real world.

'THE END OF THE WORLD' AND THE THEATRE OF THE 1980S

Interestingly enough, most of the cultural representations of the end of the world, from Kitamura's *Hogi-uta* to *Akira*, do not explain how the world actually ended. In the case of *Hogi-uta*, Kitamura only tells us that there was a devastating nuclear war. In the case of *Akira*, Otomo tells us it was World War III. These representations of the end of the world are more concerned with trying to reconstruct the world amid the ruins of war than with any actual historical reality.

In his influential sociological study of the 1980s' subcultures and their relation to the Aum Shinri-kyo, entitled *Owari naki Nichijo o Ikiyo* (*Live and Endure a Neverending Everyday Life*, 1995), Miyadai Shinji asserts that the subculture of this period wanted to evoke a sense of community after Armageddon. In this, Miyadai sees two contradicting impulses: 'to face the reality that whatever happens in everyday life will continue on forever', and 'to end the world in order to imagine a renewed sense of community' (ibid.: 86). This latter impulse was appropriated by Asahara Shoko to attract adherents and he and the Aum would later take the idea from the virtual/cultural space of theatre and manga into the real space of a Tokyo subway where, on 20 March 1995, they implemented a gas attack that killed 11 and injured more than 5,000 people.

More importantly, however, what Miyadai posits as two contradictory ontological questions do in fact coexist in Sho-gekijo practices and its significant works. Kitamura's play *Hogi-uta* is constructed around three figures: Gesaku, a middle-aged popular entertainer; Kyoko, a young female stripper; and Yasuo, a magician and Christ-like character. A definite mirroring of Beckett's *Waiting for Godot*, 'Nothing happens' in *Hogi-uta*, and we do not find out anything about the characters. Despite the apparent similarity, there are very important differences between *Hogi-uta* and *Godot*, the most obvious being the fact that, unlike in *Godot*, there is a God or, at least, a Christ-figure although he cannot 'save the world' or do anything about what has happened or is happening; he is simply a very sensitive and helpless 'guy'. The setting itself is more concrete than Beckett's abstract universe and the characters often refer to various lights in the sky—from far-away nuclear missiles—as 'fireworks', though we do not know whether they are the only survivors of the nuclear holocaust.[5]

The message is very clear: even if a nuclear holocaust devastates Japan, some people will survive and will have to live Miyadai's everlasting everyday life. What will they do after the holocaust? The characters in the play converse meaninglessly, eat and entertain each other by enacting some of the scenes that Gesaku and Kyoko used to play, while Yasuo preaches his Christian beliefs. They are not allowed to kill each other or themselves and must carry on living until they die. In the process of this non-linear narrative, a sense of community is discreetly created between the characters and, perhaps, the audience. The characters mention the devastation all over Japan and the world: 'Mt Fuji is half blown away' (Kitamura 1982: 11), yet the annihilated landscape is never seen and there is no visible chaotic confusion of any kind. Even the nuclear missiles are, for them, 'fireworks'; far away and not affecting them. Their world is metatheatrically secured by what Yasumi calls a 'closure'; they are 'carefully observing the outside from within the nuclear shelter in order to make sure that the world outside has certainly ended' (Yasumi 1995a: 160). Inhabitants of the shelter are expected to acquire a sense of community—a community of shared sentiments. Towards the end of the play, it starts to snow and everything is eventually covered in white. Yasuo declares he will go to Jerusalem. The other two may or may not follow him. The world inside the theatre has virtually been made into a nuclear shelter, while the world outside remains uncertain.

A COMMUNITY OF SENTIMENTS

A similar evocation of shared sentiments and a sentimental plea for the construction of a new sense of community is unashamedly expressed by Kokami Shoji at the beginning of his 1984 play *Asahi no Yona Yuhi o Tsurete* (*With a Rising Sun which Looks Like a Setting Sun*) in the chorus's opening song (see Figure 1):

> With a rising sun which looks like a setting sun
> I keep standing
> Without connecting with each other
> Without flowing into each other
> Like a flashing star.
> For standing alone is painful
> For standing alone is enjoyable.
> With a rising sun which looks like a setting sun
> I am alone.
> For I cannot stand being alone.
> For I cannot do anything alone.
> To admit that I am alone
> Is to join hands with many people.
> To join hands with many people
> Is a very, very sad thing to do.
> With a rising sun which looks like a setting sun
> Like a star in a winter sky
> I am alone (1991: 11).

FIGURE 1: *ASAHI NO YONA YUHI O TSURETE (WITH A RISING SUN WHICH LOOKS LIKE A SETTING SUN)*, 1984. PHOTOGRAPH COURTESY OF THE THIRD STAGE.

Or, as Kawamura Takeshi of Daisan (Third) Erotica wrote:

> The myth, however, has completely collapsed. After its col-
> lapse, we started to weave our own narrative without the pro-
> tection of myth, without any fantasy of 'faraway' and without
> any confidence in ourselves. Is it even possible to write a
> 'story' which resists 'history'? If it is possible, how is it possi-
> ble? This is the place. This is the place into which we may
> have been thrown whether or not we like it. It is a place of tab-
> ula rasa (1984: 277–8).

Kokami's melodramatic plea for 'shared sentiments' in a community
where everyone is 'alone' is also a declaration of the lack of history.
This same historical deprivation is manifested in Kawamura's passage
as 'tabula rasa'. Kokami's easy metaphor of 'a rising sun which looks
like a setting sun' is like a common déjà vu; in the repetition of history
there is nothing new, only the endless cycle of dailyness.

In this shared sense of the deprivation of historical memory, sentimental as it may sound, we are logically led to interrogate these representations of the end of the world. Is it really the end of the world? Is
it really set in the near future? Especially now, after the Aum, after the

collapse of the 'bubble economy', representations of the end of the world cannot be read at face value. In other words, it is possible to read these representations of the end of the world as a desperate and largely unconscious attempt to historicize the dehistoricized present that the Sho-gekijo practitioners found themselves in during the 1980s.

When we read his words now or look at Kitamura's landscape and characters, we are struck by the fact that the play could have been written right after the War. Kitamura's image of three 'bums' strolling through the ruins does not make us think of an upcoming Armageddon or a Beckettian metaphysical post-human landscape but, rather, of the ruins of war in post-World War II literature and popular culture.

Was Kitamura then talking about Hiroshima and Nagasaki? Not necessarily. His representations of the end of the world can and should be read as constitutive of a viable site of resistance against the 'ongoing process of oblivion', as Yasumi puts it (1995a: 160), within the ideology of post-War democracy which incessantly asks us to 'forget' and deprives us of history and historical memories. What are we being asked to 'forget'? Is it, to use Carol Gluck's words, 'the memory of the Empire' (1995: 4), the process of modernization in Japan after the Meiji restoration, which led to World War II and the Nanjing Massacre?

The revisionist neo-nationalist narrative of the 1990s does not include this 'memory of the Empire'. World War II and the Nanjing Massacre are 'exceptions' to the successful modernization of Japan. Similarly, 1980s' theatre culture is excluded from the narrative of theatre history and theory, just as the Aum is excluded from historical memory. These phenomena have been explained away, so they are not part of our cultural memory of either the remote or the recent past.

It is this urge to erase history, I would propose, that all the cultural producers at the end of the millennium have to resist. Both 1980s' theatre culture and the Aum still offer critical insight into this particular historical crossroad.

Notes

1   In the past decade or so, there has been much reinterpretation of
    World War II. Many want to revise a 'self-torturing sense of history'
    which, they claim, has afflicted 'our' national pride and sense of
    identity since 1945. This assertion is, in part, a reaction to a new con-
    sciousness of 'comfort-women'—Korean women forced into prostitu-
    tion by the Japanese army during the War. These women, all very old
    now, finally agreed to testify.

    A heated debate occurred between revisionists and liberals con-
    cerning how the history of Japan's involvement with World War II
    should be written in school textbooks. Revisionists argue that the
    Nanjing Massacre and 'comfort women' issues are not 'proven' histor-
    ical facts, hence school textbooks should not mention them. The
    debate continues in various fields. Kobayashi Yoshinori, a popular
    manga writer, is a major revisionist voice in this debate, and a series of
    his manga discussing these issues has become a bestseller.

2   The Aum Shinri-kyo was established by Asahara Shoko in 1984. A New
    Age cult based on the teachings of Buddhism, the Aum attracted many
    young people in the 1980s through the use of subcultural icons and
    techniques, including animated movies and manga. Members were
    asked to renounce the world and donate all their material possessions
    to the organization. In 1989, a lawyer who acted against the Aum,
    along with his family, disappeared (it is now understood that they were
    kidnapped and murdered by the cult members). After this incident,
    the Aum became a social phenomenon and the fact that most of its
    believers were young and supposedly intelligent people from relatively
    rich families stimulated voyeuristic media attention. In 1990, as if to
    prove their legitimacy, 25 members of the cult ran for Congress,
    though no one was actually elected. During their campaign they used
    many 1980s' theatrical techniques. After that, they grew dangerously
    radical and began to arm themselves. This culminated in the Sarin Gas
    Attack on the Tokyo subway in 1995. Although most of its members,
    including Asahara, are on trial, the organization still exists. In 1999,
    the remaining and new Aum members became active again, while the
    trial continued. The Aum has its own homepage on the Internet
    (mostly in Japanese) and you can see how they utilize the visual and
    multimedia language of cyberspace (aum-internet.org). [Note added
    on 20 March 2008: this HP is already removed. Most of the Aum trail,
    at the time of writing this note, is in its last stages. Asahara, along with

some other chief members of the cult, has been given a death penalty, while other members organized a new membership during the trial. For more detail, see, for instance, a more or less accurate description of their activity before and after 1995 in Wikepedia at en.wikipedia.org/wiki/Aum_Shinri_Kyo]

3   Hirata Oriza (1963–) is a playwright and director of Seinen-dan Theatre Company (the name connotes a kind of 4-H club in agricultural regions). His major strategy is a literalization of realism, in which all notions of the dramatic are consciously excluded from his plays. As is demonstrated in one of his 1991 plays, *Seoul Shimin* (*Citizens of Seoul*), characters gather and converse in a very nonchalant fashion; his plays are always an observation of the everyday life of select people. *Seoul Shimin* is set in the dining room of a house owned by a rich Japanese merchant just before the forced unification of Korea with Japan in 1910. Though the setting is very political, Hirata discusses neither colonialism nor imperialism. Rather, he depicts the closed-down and self-contained world of the Japanese people living in Seoul at the time, surrounded by a noisy 'outside' where the people of Korea are resisting Japanese colonial aggression. This can be read politically but Hirata has stated on many occasions that he is not trying to send a message to the audience, only trying to make 'objective' observations. Accordingly, actors speak quietly and there is no dramatic scene in the conventional sense of the word—there is no beginning (the play has already started when the audience members enter the theatre), middle or end. [Note added on 20 March 2008: Hirata subsequently went on to write and produce two other *Seoul Shimin* plays, in 2000 and 2006, each of which is set in different historical stages in pre-War Korea. Interestingly enough, his sense of politics seems to have visibly increased in these later plays, though his basic dramaturgy remains the same. For more details of his work, see www.seinendan.org/eng/info/-index.html]

4   For further information regarding the originally radical Sho-gekijo, see Goodman (1988) and the Introduction (note 6) to this volume.

5   Gesaku has tactfully explained this phenomena on various occasions by saying that, although the War has ended, many nuclear warheads remain and can be launched by computers.

INTERLUDE 1
FROM 'BEAUTIFUL' TO 'CUTE':
A NOTE ON BEAUTY IN MODERN
AND POSTMODERN JAPAN

The notion of beauty seems to have but disappeared from discussions in the modern world not because it is entirely 'lost' but, rather, because it appears to have been satisfactorily addressed by previous generations. Indeed, in the postmodern world we now live in, greater amounts of time and energy seem to be spent in its defense and its politicization, a conclusion I have arrived at through my experience of Japan and, more specifically, of the world of performing arts. It is a conclusion that also appears to be confirmed by a further examination of the literature dedicated to its study.

In Japan, it is commonly believed that beauty has been awarded a very particular role in the process of modernization. For those thinkers and artists who believe that modernization equals Westernization rather than hybridization, the realm of beauty and the field of aesthetics have assumed significance at various critical moments after 1868, the year in which Japan officially opened its borders to the outside world. Important figures in this academic arena range from Okakura Tenshin (1862–1912), one of the founders of Tokyo School of Fine Art, to the so-called 'Japanese Romantics' (*Nippon Roman Ha*) such as Yasuda Yojuro (1910–81), an influential revivalist philosopher of the 1930s, and include such post-War, high-art cultural producers as Nobel prize winner and novelist Kawabata Yasunari (1899–1972) who called himself 'I—the subject—in beautiful Japan',[1] and, of course, Mishima Yukio (1925–70, pseudonym of Hiraoka Kimitake), considered by many critics as the most important Japanese novelist of the twentieth century. Examining their attempts at theorizing a notion of beauty, we observe several interesting issues that are also extremely relevant to any attempt to revisit the realm of aesthetics in postmodern contexts. How, for instance, has the Western notion of beauty been appropriated by, even invaded, non-Western national and cultural imaginations, particularly within East Asia? More specifically, how can we relate this notion of beauty to the emergence of some notable performance practices usually defined in terms of aesthetics (as in the work of Butoh in the late 1960s), and the notion of cuteness to some high-tech performance practices witnessed in the middle of the 1990s?

BEAUTY IN JAPAN'S HISTORICAL CONTEXT

In Japanese, the noun for beauty, *bi*, which appears to have been adapted from ancient China, is a letter which combines 'fat (big)' and 'sheep'. Therefore, it is logical to infer that the notion of beauty was compared to a sheep fattened in preparation for sacrifice. Thus, visual art was translated as *bijutsu*, the technology of and for beauty, and aesthetics was translated as *bigaku*, the study of beauty, after the Meiji Restoration in 1868.

The Japanese language, since the Middle Ages has developed three major adjectives relating to the noun *bi*, namely, *utsukushi(i)*, *kirei* and *kawaii*. To this day, we use these words in different ways on different occasions, though the field of art practices has been pre-occupied with the notion of *kawaii* (cute) in recent years, paralleling the process of blurring any division between popular culture and other styles. However, it is interesting to note that, while moving away from China's influence in the Heian Period (794–1192), the Japanese aristocratic regime is thought to have established the first indigenous culture subsequent to which *utsukushi* related more to the notion of *kawaii*, as is apparent in the famous diary of Seisho-nagon's *Makura no Soshi* (The Pillow Book).[2] In Seisho-nagon's era, *okashi*—'interesting' or 'funny' in modern usage—was synonymous with the notion of beauty, with what was perceived as emotionally and intuitively moving or impressive, thus relating to the essence of the interiority of the object rather than its exteriority. Heian visual culture, on the other hand, can be characterized as the exact opposite of what is usually referred to as the *wabi sabi* (taste for the simple and quiet, and elegant simplicity) aesthetic, which played an important role in Japan's cultural sphere in later years as a reaction to the aristocratic nature of representative Heian visual culture. It comprises aristocratic art forms, where colour, splendour, grandeur, meticulousness and minuteness were the norm. Visual pleasure was all when the *okashi* principle, later identified as the essence of Japanese tradition by Motoori Norinaga (1730–1801) as *mono no aware* (meticulous sensitiveness to nature and beauty)—*aware* being in very close relationship to the notion of *okashi* in the Heian period—entered more into the sphere of the invisible, the transcendental and the spiritual.

BEAUTY IN MODERNIZING JAPAN

Since the Heian period, the two opposing genres—*utsukushii-kirei-kawaii* line and *okashi-wabi sabi-aware*—have, to some extent, constituted the two basic categories of aesthetics or aesthetic sensibilities in Japan and we can observe, for example, a kind of dialectical working of these two principles in extreme differences in Noh and Kabuki theatre. This dialectical relationship between formality ('appearance') and spirituality ('content'), through history and at a particular historical conjuncture, is certainly nothing new but this (seemingly traditional) deep commitment to aesthetics was crucial for intellectuals and artists living in a rapidly modernizing Japan. These artists were conscious of the prevailing aesthetic 'tradition' as a reaction to the 'invading' Western influence of the nineteenth century, at a time when the discipline of aesthetics was entering the Japanese academic world that was in turn striving to replicate the Western educational system, thus heralding the invention of tradition as *bijutsu*, 'a technology of beauty'.

A curious phenomenon was to follow in pre-World War II Japan. Realized as the anaesthetization of everyday life, this phenomenon is best exemplified in the discourse of the Japanese Romantics, and by extension, in the immediate post-War period, the Nobel prize-winning Kawabata Yasunari declared, 'I could survive the post-War devastation, owing to the sense of beauty that I could feel living in Japan' (see Note 1). Japan thus became a country belonging to an aestheticized category, i.e. 'Japan is beautiful,' as Kawabata designates it. Indeed, beauty has become an absolute utopia—an ideologically and conceptually constructed 'spiritual' sphere in which even history cannot intervene. With the presence of this sphere, most of the art practices in post-World War II Japan became a matter of personal taste, exemplifying the symptoms of postmodern relativism, long before people started to use this term. It may relate to the construction of personal identity, but never to the collective or to the national, at least in theory. For the Japanese Romantics, this was a political gesture, as Harootunian explains in his article 'America's Japan/Japan's Japan' (1993). For the post-War art practitioners, it was deemed a historical truism that the practice of art had come to signify either a personal exploration of the sense of beauty or some kind of research into the existence of utopia (usually arriving at the idea that utopia is possible in everyday life), achieved without indicating any interest in the ongoing historical situation.

The post-World War II visual art world was engaged in this battle of competing notions of beauty, especially between the beautiful and the sublime, and the ugly and the uncanny. There have been several attempts to disrupt the secular 'sacredness' inherent in some art practices, for, when an aesthetic space is thought to be autonomous, it can easily be packaged, sold and consumed without having to be labelled as high art.

One example was, of course, the various kinds of performance practices during the 1960s that later came to be categorized as Butoh. Before escaping into the privileged position of a historically sanctioned notion of beauty in 1970, when Mishima Yukio committed ritual suicide, Hijikata Tatsumi was exploring from a variety of perspectives the as-yet-unexplored terrain of the body as a vehicle of expression. His *Hijikata Tatsumi to Nihonjin: nikutai no hanran* (*Tatsumi Hijikata and the Japanese: Revolt of the Flesh*, 1968) was a most remarkable work (in particular, his apparent reference to Antonin Artaud was inescapably modernist). At the same time, Hijikata problematized a notion of the beauty of 'Japaneseness' through his anarchic bodily gestures and movements—often violently physical movements, simultaneously grotesque, beautiful, masculine, always nullifying and denying easy categorization and perceptive containment. One can, of course, debate how and why this became possible. What is important is that

Butoh attempted to resist a fixed notion of beauty in everyday life and opened up the field of performance to the realms of the unknown and the unknowable. At this moment Butoh became impregnated with the work of Hijikata, and, as is often noted, many attempts at mystification followed. Hijikata himself was not exempt from the ensuing changes wrought by this phenomenon, and his performance style drastically changed after 1970, apparently returning to, or reinventing, a mystified notion of 'Japaneseness' in his later works. In those later years, the idiosyncratic notion of beauty of Butoh was to become defined, codified and fixed into that which we recognize in Butoh-related dance works even today.

FROM BEAUTY TO CUTENESS IN 1990S' JAPAN

A decisive breakthrough for the history of the notion of beauty in Japan came in the 1990s. For many, the 1990s was when the Western version of postmodernism came to develop a very complicated relationship with *otaku* (animation freaks and/or computer geeks) culture which had its heyday in the preceding decade, when anime, manga, video games and related fields, including underground urban club culture, came to exert a peculiar influence on other cultural practices, particularly within the space occupied by high art. *Otaku* culture appeared to be enthralled by the notion of 'cuteness' as a form of resistance to the highly defined and well-circulated notions of 'beauty' in both popular (media) culture and high art. The field of visual art practices was opened up, as it were, to this particular version of popular culture—*otaku* culture is not necessarily popular culture but denotes a specific relationship to its source which is, in this case, a heavily media-bound popular culture with its inherent populist and commercial sensibilities. In a way, works of artists emerging in the 1990s were a reflective and individualized response to an ever-renewing sense of beauty in popular culture.

Dumb Type (founded in 1988) emerged from club culture in the 1980s. Moving through performance work to installations, its work evolved into a type of historical document, detailing the development of the renewed sense of high art in the 1990s. Through works such as

S/N (1993–98), an adventurous attempt at reconciliation between the political and the beautiful; *OR* (1997–2002), a more metaphysical enquiry into the notion of death; *Memorandum* (1999), a thoughtful yet somewhat reactionary return to the personal and the beautiful; and *Voyage* (2002), a failed attempt at an aesthetic response to '9/11', it has been wandering into a potentially explosive minefield, at least in the Japanese context (see Figures 2–4). Falling between high art and *otaku* culture, media and performance cultures, it is continually grappling with the postmodern possibility of beauty and questioning whether high art can function in a globalized situation.

Murakami Takashi (1962–), in this sense, is a problematic yet interesting artist. Trained in traditional Japanese painting and educated in the heyday of *otaku* culture, his work shows an ironic affirmation of contemporary cultural sensibilities from the perspective of a Japanese man living in the Japan of the here and now. We should pay attention to his super-flat theory; seldom using the word beauty, he prefers to use 'reality' as a dominant sensory category in visual arts. Sharing the same methodology as other contemporary artists, Murakami uses everyday objects, in his case two-dimensional images from anime, manga and video games, to which he adds his very singular signature (supported by well-trained technique with traditional Japanese visual art) and transforms them into high-art objects. What is important for Murakami is to bring the overwhelming sense of two-dimensionality (super-flatness) that is present in popular culture into a strong and distilled relief in his work. This attempt to connect his aesthetics to the traditional art forms may not necessarily be meaningful, or even logical—it appears to be both ironic and desperate. The works he curated in *Super-flat Exhibition* (2000) shed some light on the problem with beauty in a contemporary setting.

Where are the traditional aesthetic principles that I briefly discussed in the first part of this Interlude? Predictably enough, they are subsumed by popular media, especially film. Animation film director Miyazaki Hayao (1941–) typifies this movement in one of his latest works, *Sen to Chihiro no Kamikakushi* (*Spirited Away*, 2001). The film contains everything that resonates within Japan's popular imagination—a mythical and fantastic narrative following the storyline of an adolescent

FIGURE 2: *OR* (1997–2002) BY DUMB TYPE. PHOTOGRAPH BY EMMANUEL VALETTE.

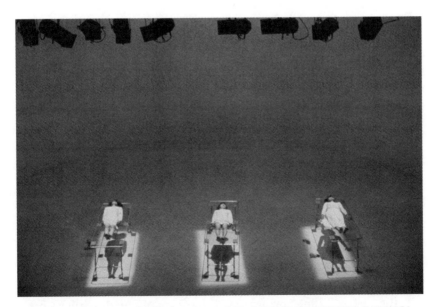

FIGURE 3: *MEMORANDUM* (1999–) BY DUMB TYPE. PHOTOGRAPH BY KAZUO FUKUNAGA.

FIGURE 4: VOYAGE (2001–) BY
DUMB TYPE. PHOTOGRAPH BY
KAZUO FUKUNAGA.

shojo (a young teenage asexual girl, an unlikely existence in post-World
War II Japan) and the reconciliation between certain antithetical categories. Visually speaking, however, the degree of fetishization in the
minutiae in this film is so excessive and outrageous that it is hard to
imagine how such a film became a great success in Japan. It is deeply
disturbing in its emptiness and hollowness if you consider some scenes
in the film where every detail of the background is meticulously
designed and drawn, though viewers may never pay much attention to
it. Unlike Hollywood films, where any available technique and unlim-
ited amounts of money are available to enhance the sense of reality
and speed (thereby enhancing the work's market value in the global
arena), Miyazaki puts great effort into creating a meticulously
detailed, two-dimensional visual closure in this film, as if in response
to Murakami's super-flat theory. We also find a peculiar reconciliation
of the two guiding principles I have mentioned earlier—both
utsukushii-kirei-kawaii and *okashi-wabi sabi-aware* elements are presented.

The apparent celebration of Pan-Asianism reverts our attention to the consideration of the development of aesthetics in late-nineteenth and early-twentieth-century Asia, when Okakura Tenshin was desperately trying to establish the field itself, travelling through Asia and meeting various personalities, including Rabindranath Tagore (1861–1941) in India, and writing manifestos in English. At the same time, the work raises the question of how the avid acceptance of the film relates to seemingly emerging desires to construct a 'New Asia'—Asia as a multi-cultural entity, sharing 'common' values in several intercultural per-forming art projects and connected discourses, searching for Pan-Asian cultural values as an antidote to the all-consuming global media culture (American) which always achieves the most prominent positions.

BEAUTY IN CONTEMPORARY PERFORMING ARTS

In the world of performance and theatre arts, scholars have traced a very different role for the notion of beauty which was revived, or at least reinvented, in the last 20 years. One might even say that beauty was never wholly rejected by theatre practices.

In the context of the performing arts in Japan, beauty as *bi* or *utsukushii* is kept uniquely intact in the traditional forms even as con-temporary theatre or dance artist would not refer to the notion at any time, though s/he may sporadically use the word *omoshiroi*, 'interest-ing'. Dumb Type is an exception as most of its members are from a visual art background. The sole artist who was prepared to discuss the notion of beauty with me was Hayashi Makiko, former director of the Romantica Theatre Company (again, from a visual art background). Hayashi claims to be devoted to the creation of beauty, at any place, at any time, and that this is why she has stopped making theatre; she came to realize that theatre was so impure that it could not provide a suitable site for beauty. Unusually for Hayashi, ideal beauty is to be found in Barbie dolls. How is it possible to recreate the beauty inher-ent in those dolls?—that is the question she is asking as an artist, and, to that effect, shows her work in underground clubs or designs for fashion shows. We may need terminologies of psychoanalysis to under-stand what she means but, living in Japan, watching the super-flat bodies of the younger generation of dancers and taking Murakami's super-flat theory into consideration, it may not be too difficult to understand what she is suggesting here. Beauty is always a commodity, however banal, and it is the role of the artist to transform the site of beauty from the reproducible object into the performer's body and onto the performance space—to materialize, temporarily, the 'original' and singularity that is beauty.

Notes

1   The phrase is from Kawabata Yasunari's famous speech when he received the Nobel Prize for Literature in 1968.

2   In three volumes, written between the end of the tenth century and the beginning of the eleventh.

CHAPTER 3

DECONSTRUCTING 'JAPANESENESS': TOWARDS ARTICULATING LOCALITY AND HYBRIDITY IN CONTEMPORARY JAPANESE PERFORMANCE

In order to frame the main issues, I will first invoke a perhaps unexpected name—the late Heiner Müller (1929–95), playwright and director from former East Germany. In the process of my development as a theatre researcher and critic, and in order to locate my subject position outside the established discursive space which both circumvents and permeates the theatre and performance practices that I witness daily, I, along with some other critics, scholars and theatre practitioners, participated in the formulation of a loosely organized collective called the Heiner Müller Project in 1990. Since then, project members have been trying to open up by employing and theorizing an idea of hybridity in relation to performance practice. This project came about because performance was, and still is, strictly contained within the systematically demarcated confines of academia, journalism and theatre practice.

One of the most impressive aspects of Müller's textual and theatrical practice is the way he confronts the past: not only his personal past but a kind of collectively accumulated textual past, loosely defined as the European literary intertextual tradition of which his *Die Hamletmaschine* ('The Hamletmachine', 1977) is, I believe, the best example. Putting aside its more or less direct reference to the political situation of the declining Communist regime, what is amazing about this implosive text is its intertextuality—it resounds with confessional (though consciously desubjectivized), violent and powerful voice(s). *Hamletmaschine* is a text with traces of the struggles and confrontations of Müller's own history, both imaginary and actual, and there is an obvious attempt to explode a linear political and/or theatre history.

In the face of this challenging text, especially for those working within Japan's cultural milieu where the political and the historical are consensually displaced and are not supposed to be a necessary part of its frame of reference, theatre practitioners, scholars and critics alike, are thrown into a void of impossibilities: the impossibility of staging, theorizing and even speaking about Müller's play. In the same manner as the theory of deconstruction, Müller's text urges us to start examining our assumptions about theatre, history and modes of discourse, the very nature of the ways in which we try to understand and represent ourselves.

All of this may sound naive for those who are familiar with experimental and/or radical performance practices in recent years, or with the more highly acclaimed intercultural (not necessarily intertextual) theatre practices which have gained visibility and theoretical importance through names such as Peter Brook and Eugenio Barba. Intertextual practice is surely an undeniable part of the Euro-American literary tradition, and the discourse of intertextuality sometimes ends up affirming the canonization of 'privileged' texts although it does keep rewriting and revising itself. But in the context of the Euro-American literary tradition, Müller's intertextual modernist approach is perhaps the last of its kind in the great modernist avant-garde tradition.

The concept of intertextuality seems to promise the possibility of articulating and historicizing Japan's contemporary theatre culture apart from a discourse of the 'absolute difference' of Japaneseness. At this particular historical conjuncture,[1] it seems hardly appropriate for those involved in Japan's theatre practice to speak in terms of ideologically and historically loaded concepts of the self and the other— 'our' culture and 'their' culture, or the East ('us') and the West ('them'). Müller's intertextual text, therefore, is useful in deconstructing such a bipolarization in the articulation of theatre cultures in Japan. It also makes us formulate and circulate discourses that are the result of the dynamics of collaborative effort between individuals working within their local contexts.

THEATRE AND ITS TROUBLE IN THE 1980S

I began writing theatre criticism in various forms around the end of the 1980s. What struck me most at the time was the unease I felt towards current theatre practices and the usual narratives of historical and sociopolitical contextualization for these practices. The end of the economic boom in Japan resulted in a new conservatism that informed the critical reassessment of Japan's radical theatre culture usually referred to as the 'Sho-gekijo boom'.

The critical discourse of Japan's theatre culture in the 1980s could be explained by paraphrasing and revising Schechner in his essay 'Decline and Fall of the American Avantgarde' (1982). For this self-styled avant-garde, the prevailing critical gesture was a flat denial and rejection of the ongoing dominant theatre culture and a commodification and reification of allegedly autonomous, therefore more humane and/or transgressive, artistic practice. (A possibility that experimental theatre practitioners of previous decades had secured for the next generation of artists.) This flat dismissal appeared in a peculiarly perverse discursive space, as many of the theoreticians and critics, who had been active and visible in previous decades, chose to silence themselves, presumably to demonstrate their disapproval of the new generation of Japan's theatre culture. This vacuum of critical commentary led to a dramatic decline in the number of critical writings on theatrical practice.

There was yet another segment of critical discourse, if one can call it critical, that unanimously affirmed the contemporary theatre culture and its exponents, sometimes evoking positive images of 'popular' culture practice in the Edo period (1600–1867)[2] and celebrating the unprecedented popularity which the Little Theatre practitioners had sought and eventually secured for themselves, during this decade. (See 'An "Ill-fated" History of Japan's Theatre Culture (3): Opening Up' in the Introduction in this volume.) Most of these writings did not attempt to critique the ongoing theatre culture but, rather, as if intimidated by the sheer numbers of viewers attracted to Little Theatre productions, became journalistic witnesses who chose to faithfully 'describe' the phenomenon from a theoretically conservative perspective within the context of what can be called Japan's version of (pseudo-)postmodernism.[3]

The general unease I felt was thus caused by a juxtaposition of seemingly irreconcilable critical and political positions, whether conservative or progressive, and their modes of enunciation, each basing their discussions on their own local logic(s) but never clearly stating their assumptions about the theatre culture at hand. These radically different assessments of the theatre culture of the 1980s (the reportage mode and the mode of silence) are a complicit resonance which could only be articulated by taking more of the sociocultural process into consideration. Urged by Müller's intertextual historicity (besides contributing from theoretical and dramaturgical perspectives, to a series of actual stagings of his works by the members of the Heiner Müller Project), I increasingly felt the necessity for a more sensitive and persuasive way of writing, speaking and theorizing the theatre culture I was watching.

ALDOUS HUXLEY'S *BRAVE NEW WORLD* REVISITED

To give a more theoretical edge and schematic picture to the personal history I have been unfolding so far, I will evoke another seemingly irrelevant name and work: Aldous Huxley and his *Brave New World* (1984). What is interesting and illuminating about this dystopian novel is that although it was conceived and written in the pre-World War II period, when people felt a growing fear of fascism and totalitarianism in Europe, it shows a very different kind of totalitarian society from the one George Orwell would later invent in *Nineteen Eighty-Four* (1949).

Huxley's New World seems a perfect utopia, constructed after the devastating experiences of global warfare, and after a period of trial and error on the part of rulers in reconstructing the world order. The society Huxley depicts with humour and desperation is the one in which all needs are met, to the extent that there no longer are any needs. Everything is planned and institutionalized. The society's motto is 'Community, Identity, Stability'. Change and transformation are not operative ideas. Total control and manipulation begins from before birth—in the 'test tubes' at the human factory, the 'Hatchery and Conditioning Center'. Here, gene manipulation takes place in order to create humans whose desires (conscious, unconscious, sexual and material) will be predetermined and safely contained. After they are born, people are subjected to an educational conditioning in the internalization of the status quo. There is no room for dissatisfaction, even uneasiness; individual feeling is standardized, mass-produced and internalized. Death and sexuality are strategically built into the stable social structure so that they are neither socially nor culturally marked as taboos: children are encouraged to indulge themselves in 'sex play' at a younger age and are raised to regard death not as fearful and inevitable but as natural, fun and sweet; they are given candies whenever someone dies. Huxley's New World, therefore, is a peaceful world where any factor that might threaten 'Community, Identity, Stability' is systematically excluded. This dystopia is not a place where physical and/or social violence is used to enforce its inhabitants' subordination and conformity to the dominant system.

Huxley's vision extends from the logic of state capitalism using pre-War United States as a model. The word Ford is a symbol of the brand of capitalism and people cry out 'O Ford!' instead of 'O Lord!' In this dystopia, Huxley presents the end of class struggle, the end of history and the end of ideology. What is astonishing about this novel is the fact that Huxley presents us with a surprisingly apt image for Japan's sociocultural space in the 1980s. This manufactured society is Japan's version of (pseudo-)postmodernism of which, among other subcultural genres, theatrical representations were often hailed as the most symbolic.

The fundamental conflict of the novel is expressed by the Savage who signifies the classical antithesis of 'wilderness' and 'civilization', a traveller who returns to his 'origin' (his high-caste mother's tribe) in the New World from the primitive 'old world' (the ghetto land of 'Indian reservation' in New Mexico) in which he happens to have been born and raised. The subsequent plot unfolds his quest for integration between the new and the old but, finally, as he fails to reconcile these value systems, he commits suicide. For the Savage, Shakespeare's *Collected Works* were the only source of intellectual development in the reservation. To express his inner emotions or thoughts, the Savage quotes passages from Shakespeare. Because of this great literary tradition, we are led to wonder whether the Savage really comes from the future; he may only be an image of an European intellectual between two world wars, faced, like Huxley himself, with the commodification, hence the nullification, of everything traditional that he represents. If so, it is understandable why, faced with the socio-economic and cultural hegemony of control by American capitalism, Huxley has the Savage choose suicide.

THEODOR W. ADORNO'S CRITIQUE OF *BRAVE NEW WORLD*

Besides the archaic moralistic overtones and colonial inclinations with which Huxley, consciously or unconsciously, has imbued the narrative of *Brave New World*, there are certain other aspects to be careful about while reading this novel. In his article 'Aldous Huxley and Utopia' (1981), Theodor W. Adorno gives some credit to Huxley's vision of the future in the novel's narrative logic, but a careful examination of its structure and its philosophical and political bases for a critique of the future leads Adorno to become critical of the book which, finally, he condemns as reactionary. He concludes (though the conclusion appears at the beginning of his essay) that the novel is written by an 'intellectual émigré' (ibid.: 97), as a rationalizing of the panic felt on arriving at the 'new' continent (ibid.: 98). I cannot discuss all of Adorno's exacting critique here, but I will quote one passage which seems particularly useful in the context of this chapter. Regarding Huxley's denial of a 'way out' from the totalitarian utopia, Adorno writes:

> Through total social mediation, from the outside, as it were, a new immediacy, a new humanity, would arise; American civilization shows no lack of tendencies in this direction. But Huxley construes humanity and reification as rigid opposites, in accordance with the tradition of the novel, which has as its object the conflict of human beings with rigidified conditions. Huxley cannot understand the humane promise of civilization because he forgets that humanity includes reification as well as its opposite, not merely as the condition from which liberation is possible but also, positively, as the form in which, however

brittle and inadequate it may be, subjective impulses are realized, but only by being objectified. All categories examined by
the novel, family, parents, the individual and his property, are
already products of reification. Huxley curses the future with
it, without realizing that the past whose blessing he invokes is
of the same nature (ibid.: 102).

What Adorno finds problematic in Huxley's novel is not what is said
within the narrative but, rather, the way in which Huxley constructs
the narrative. Adorno tries to deconstruct the rigid binaries of
'humanity' versus 'reification' and 'wilderness' versus 'civilization' as
irreconcilable opposites, from which *Brave New World* acquires its narrative drive and its stable structure as a novel. A similar kind of critical practice seems necessary and useful in dealing with Japan's theatre
culture in the 1980s, in terms of the dominant and bipolarized discourses of denial or celebration. Inside this critical space, the target
theatre culture is made visible as culture. By deconstructing the rigid
binarism by which Japanese culture is narrativized, as Adorno does in
critiquing *Brave New World*, it becomes possible to explain the larger
ideological devices that have made such a critical discrepancy exist
within theatre culture.

THEATRE CULTURE OF THE ANGURA PARADIGM IN THE 1980S

In strictly theatro-historical terms, the Underground Theatre
Movement, or Angura, from the late 1960s to the early 1970s, is now
almost unanimously considered to be an impressive period of both
theatrical innovation and cultural intervention. The formulation of
what critic Nishido Kojin terms 'the Angura paradigm' (1987) became
established so that expectations in terms of what audiences bring to
the conventional and unconventional theatre space were drastically
challenged, if not entirely transformed. This was a time of rare pro-
ductivity and creativity in Japan's theatre history, especially if we com-
pare it with the preceding 20 years of repetitious reflection among
Shingeki theatre practitioners, or the pre-War failure to establish a
'modern' theatre tradition in Japan. This Angura period was productive not only in terms of experiments in theatre language and physical expressiveness, but also because it supported a wide discursive

space, surrounding and permeating those performative practices. Performances were created which in turn gave rise to a variety of critical assessments, from journalistic reports to more theoretical writings.[4]

During the late 1970s and all through the 1980s, when the so-called second and third generation of Underground Theatre artists emerged, everything surrounding theatre culture seemed to shrink and wither away, at least for those critics taking a critical stance similar to Huxley in *Brave New World*. As this whole gamut of newer theatre activities came to be identified as the 'Little Theatre boom', younger generations of theatre practitioners, to escape from the political rhetoric of the previous generation, established themselves in the mainstream commodity culture that was taking shape during this period. The activities of the Little Theatre had no doubt been marginalized within the sphere of hegemonic, media-induced, mass cultures, although they had enjoyed relatively popular (but not necessarily commercial) success, a success that preceding generations of artists had been denied. As a result, some exponents of the Little Theatre boom, such as Noda Hideki, Kokami Shoji and Kawamura Takeshi, were able to become popular cultural heroes of the 1980s.[5]

A discrepancy between two distinctive critical judgements emerged in the theatre culture of the 1980s. This discrepancy does not exactly correspond to the rigidified juxtaposition of 'humanity' versus 'reification' that Adorno criticizes in Huxley, but those who denied Little Theatre practices were close to Huxley in their rejection of the relative popularity that theatre practitioners sought, and the pop fantasy and pseudo-sci-fi quality of their representative works (much like 'Japanimation') with its references to subcultural icons.[6] This theatre was considered infantile, escapist and non-art—commodification of artworks. For these critics, this theatre work looked very much like 'feelies'—the virtual filmic media that the people in Huxley's 'Brave New World' enjoy.

It is important to note here that the two representative writings about theatre culture in the 1980s have a similar methodology in articulating the target culture. Although their critical positions are quite different, they correspond to the above-mentioned two segments of critical discourse. One is Nishido Kojin's *Engeki Shiso no Boken* (*The Adventures of Theatrical Thought*, 1987) and the other is Senda Akihiko's *Nihon no Gendai Engeki* (*Japan's Contemporary Theatre*, 1995). While both of them try to explain how the theatre culture of the 1980s took its distinctive thematics, styles and forms in terms of an ambiguously defined *zeitgeist*, Nishido is critical and Senda is affirmative of this theatre culture. What Nishido calls the 'Age of Informational Capitalism' and Senda the 'Age of Excessive Consumption' is what I am calling Japan's version of (pseudo-)postmodernism. In Senda's case, it is surprising that the book was written, given that the characteristics of the 1980s had passed and the context of the 'bubble economy' had faded. Senda fails to historicize the theatre culture of the last decade, naively repeating what he was writing during the 1980s, mostly in the form of theatre reviews. Nishido's work, from my perspective, is healthier, not only because he dares to speak out, unlike the older generations of critics, but also because he tries to theorize and critique the ongoing theatre culture. As with Senda, however, Nishido falls into the trap of 'the theatre as mirror to Nature' attitude. Here is another wilfully rigid juxtaposition of theatre and reality and an attempt to explain theatre as a faithful reflection of reality, though what they both see reflected is already merely a representation of that reality.

Nishido is very much like Huxley in theorizing and narrativizing the theatre culture of the 1980s, and to that extent we should give him credit. Furthermore, it is crucial that he does not 'create' a character such as 'the Savage' to evoke a nostalgic past and to give his narrative persuasive drive and closure—that would suggest the impossibility of change amidst the total reification of the theatre culture in the period. Nishido writes a sincere description of the emergence of the 'Angura paradigm' and its transformation in the following decades without any critical or theoretical perspectives. We need an Adorno figure to write a more persuasively critical analysis of theatre culture in the 1980s. In order to understand some of the more radical theatre practices that followed in the 1990s, we can turn to Harootunian's persuasive theoretical reassessment of Japan's post-War period in which his concept of 'national poetics' is very useful.

NATIONAL POETICS AND ITS DOOMING POWER

In his essay, 'America's Japan/Japan's Japan' (1993), Harootunian persuasively maps the formulation of Japan's self-narrative and the role
the cultural sphere has been forced to play in that process. According
to him, the 'narrativizing of Japan by the American Occupation' in the
post-War period 'became the central plot of the social sciences in the
1950s and 1960s and what then came to be known as the "modernization theory" ':

> This Occupation narrative and its subsequent articulation in
> countless studies devoted to demonstrating the moderniza-
> tion of Japan combined to establish the terms for constituting
> America's Japan and to mark the place of a new stage of impe-
> rialism and colonialism without territorialization. . . . By the
> same measure, this modernization narrative provided the
> means for not imagining a Japan's America, as if both speak-
> ers were equal, but rather a Japan's Japan. . . . Modernization
> theory, as it was increasingly 'applied' to explain the case of
> Japan, prompted [the] Japanese to incorporate American
> expectations to fulfill a narrative about themselves, produced
> by others, elsewhere, that had already demanded the appeal
> to fixed cultural values—consensuality—uninterrupted conti-
> nuity, and an endless present derived from an exceptionalist
> experience (ibid.: 200).

According to Harootunian, the process in which 'America's Japan'
transformed itself into 'Japan's Japan' was completed in the 1970s
when the 'goals of modernization had been reached, income doubling
secured and high economic growth realized' (ibid.: 215).

> What had originally been conceived as a means to explain
> how societies, in this instance Japan, could become modern-
> ized without relying on the agency of conflict and struggle,
> became an ideological device employed by the state to justify
> the status quo and to eliminate the realm of criticism that
> once belonged to the space of culture. . . . What this entailed
> was a turn to culture to explain the status of contemporary
> mass society, to affirm it rather than to offer the space of cri-

tique, and the subsequent appeal to a pre-modern endowment as an irreducible essence to sanction, not to resist, the
modernizing changes Japan has realized (ibid.: 215–16).

Harootunian is not speaking specifically about the emergence of the
Underground Theatre Movement in the late 1960s nor its transformation in subsequent decades. But his discussion of the transformation of 'America's Japan' into 'Japan's Japan' manifested itself in a
rather symptomatic and drastic way in theatre culture. An 'appeal to a
pre-modern endowment' was easily achieved in the theatrical sphere,
as so-called traditional theatrical forms such as Kabuki and Noh were
inescapably present as guarantees of Japan's 'uninterrupted continuity and an endless present' and, thus, the end of history, though it is
arguable that these forms should be understood in terms of an 'invention of tradition' in the modernizing of Japan.

Even Angura practitioners such as Kara Juro and Suzuki Tadashi
adopted the strategy of appealing and referring to Kabuki or, rather,
to a kind of imaginary Kabuki, as their source of performative imagination.[7] Although their apparent reference to Japan's 'tradition' was a
conscious strategy against the then-dominant Shingeki mode of theatre practice, their theatre practice, along with Shingeki's relative
decline in the 1970s, was also a part of the narrative that explains the
success of modernized Japan.

This kind of reduction of diverse theatre practices into essentialisms may be more acutely observed in the genre of Butoh, a performative practice closely involved, historically and methodologically,
with Angura (Marotti 1997). In Butoh, diverse performative practices
underwent the same kind of reduction into essentialist discourse.
Although at the time of its emergence it was a radically different and
local performative practice, it was nevertheless to be contained within
the discourse of a rigidly self-evident, self-contained art form that was
subsumed within the 'national poetics' supporting 'an ideology of
racio-cultural identity' and an 'endless present' (ibid.).

The repetitious display of cultural ideologies signifying
uniqueness in daily life calls attention to the ceaseless efforts
at persuading the Japanese that they had not become any-

thing other than what they had been since the beginning of
time, in a world where everything else was changing and,
despite the spell of history, constantly strives to hold them in
its grip (Harootunian 1993: 221).

This durable cultural ideology was ultimately deployed in the
post-War nation-state, displacing criticism of artistic and cultural pro-
ductivity with Harootunian's 'national poetics', of which the Angura
Theatre Movement had been an essential part. Both Butoh's and
Angura's performative space was thus ultimately made to function as
an affirmation of the status quo which found its ideological base in the
supposedly never-changing and everlasting Japanese cultural 'tradition', an ahistorically constructed image of 'Japaneseness'.

The strength and persuasiveness of this 'national poetics' ultimately came to nullify, not transform in any positive way, the 'Angura
paradigm' towards the end of the 1980s. It is not at all adequate, however, to describe theatre culture in the 1980s from the perspective of a
normative 'Angura paradigm', because such a perspective was exactly
the one that shaped these bipolarized segments of critical discourse at
that time. Nor does that bipolarity mean that we simply have to consider other important socio-economic factors, as Senda does, such as
the booming economy of the decade that fostered in Japan's entre-
preneurs and public officials a kind of avid eagerness to build theatre
buildings everywhere. Rather, we should confront theatre culture in
the 1980s as a cultural product of the 'national poetics', manufactured
after the completion of transition from 'America's Japan' to 'Japan's
Japan'.

THEATRE AND ITS TROUBLE IN THE 1980S REVISITED

I would like to point out two characteristics of Japan's theatre culture
in the 1980s which have come into being in part by the completion of
the transition from 'America's Japan' to 'Japan's Japan'. The first is a
very persistent sense of anti-intellectualism and the second, an
(almost) total domestication, in commercial and artistic terms, of
theatre practices. In addition, theoretical discourses came to be considered as only a manifestation of pedantic reductionism and univer-

salism on the part of intellectuals. Consequently, the frame of reference in both thematic and formal theatre practice quickly shrank to a kind of naive confession or the intellectuals' love–hate relationships with dominant mass-cultural forms, especially with ever-growing numbers of alluring representations and seductive narratives from the TV and movie industries disgorged at us 24 hours a day.

While more and more foreign theatre works were introduced to our then 'opening' theatre market,[8] 'native' theatre practitioners, as if to protect themselves from external pressure, hastily and with a certain sense of determination, enclosed themselves and their work in a realm in which only the personal and the immediate—what they 'felt', not thought, in everyday life experiences—counted. Theatre culture in Japan became either escapist or conformist/assimilationist. While American performative practice was becoming more politicized, and European contemporary theatre more intercultural, Japan's theatre culture was trying to get rid of any visible signs of influence from the 'outside'. Japanese theatre was supposed to be finding 'itself'—finding a correlative theatrical representation with the ideology of 'Japan's Japan'; finding what were by now internalized self-images of Japan where ancient tradition and advanced technology miraculously met. Thus, there was no politicizing of the arts and very few attempts at experiments in the vein of (at least allegedly) the fashionable interculturalism of the time. Deprived of the possibility of social criticism and of a chance to confront the 'excess of history', theatre practitioners in the 1980s created a peculiar version of the 'art for art's sake' principle in what can be termed subcultural aestheticism. It then became difficult to dissect their eager participation in the formation of 'national poetics' through which they generated a 'privileged' aesthetic space, free from the banalities and unpredictability of daily life. Consensually and carefully constructed by those on stage and by those sitting in the theatre—from Noda Hideki's irrationally fantastic amalgamation of junk culture and irrelevant mythology, a kind of subcultural Disneyland, to Kokami Shoji's easy distortion of Beckett's metaphysical 'Nothing to be done' principle into 'Everything is OK as it is'—they presented the audience with a self-celebratory fantasy world in which if a certain political issue was raised, or a certain social contradiction was revealed, it was effaced almost at the same time by the loud voices of performers engaged in song-and-dance numbers in a pseudo-Broadway style.

THEATRE CULTURE IN THE 1990S

About the time that the Berlin Wall fell, 'category breakdown' was becoming not an idealistic concept of postmodernism but our irreversible political reality. This symptomatic event was followed, in Japan's sociocultural milieu, by the devastating earthquake in Kobe and the Aum Shinri-kyo's attempted attack on the general public in the Tokyo underground. A fictional device, like theatrical representation, seemed to be acutely necessary to articulate the chaotic sociopolitical situation we suddenly found ourselves in. Moreover, some other narrative structures became a necessity in order to rehearse our possible attitudes and behaviour towards these visibly changing sociopolitical structures. Theatre practitioners in Japan, however, from playwrights to highly acclaimed directors, were not at all capable of responding to this need. Subsequently, there arose a strong though marginalized need among those seriously committed to theatre as cultural intervention (instead of as a dream machine reflecting our unconscious fears and escapist desires) to come up with some kind of a performative way to deal with our political reality.

One way of responding to this destabilization of the world order was to restore a 'national poetics' as an effective ideological device to displace our sociopolitical reality from the theatrical one. Around 1994, Hirata Oriza, playwright and director, after 10 years of struggle to gain public recognition, was suddenly hailed as one of the representative theatre practitioners of the 1990s. By claiming to establish what he called a 'contemporary colloquial theatre' that had never existed in Japan, he insisted on getting rid of all excessive theatricality and returning to an 'objective' mode of observation, thereby making it possible to put a faithful reproduction of 'reality' on stage (Hirata 1995: 25–8). Thus, his plays lost their linear narrative drive and become an accumulation of seemingly irrelevant dialogues between various characters who happened to occupy the place of action.

In *Tokyo Note* (1994), for example, a play set in a future Tokyo, characters are gathered in the foyer of an art museum where, because of a devastating war in Europe, famous artworks are stored. Hirata's dramaturgical methodology almost always stays the same: whether the play is set in a gallery, in a scientific laboratory in a university (*Monkeys at the Northern Boundary* 1995–96) or in a dining room of a rich Japanese merchant in Seoul just before the official occupation of Korea in 1910 (*Citizens of Seoul*, 1991). His characters gather and converse nonchalantly as if nothing exists 'outside' this 'privileged' and/or aestheticized space of daily life.

Hirata claims that this is an objective reproduction of our daily life, thereby betraying his naive belief and unconscious participation in the 'national poetics' described previously by Harootunian. It is important to note that Hirata, as well as his audience, feels the necessity to 'persuade the Japanese that they have not yet become anything other than what they have been since the beginning of time'. In other words, this 'national poetics' which, during the 1980s, was not a visible ideological device behind the representative performative practices, has bobbed up to the surface again, apparently as a means to deal with the spell of history that is 'felt' outside of theatre buildings. Faced with the making of history, Hirata chooses not to participate in the process and escapes instead into a localized and personalized space of 'national poetics'.

Another way to deal with our sociopolitical reality is to tackle it head on and to culturally intervene in the making of history. Gekidan Kaitai-sha (Theatre of Deconstruction) and Dumb Type are collectives that attempt this, although their approaches are radically different: Kaitai-sha has chosen to stay within the context of (addressing) the conventions of theatrical practice, while Dumb Type investigates the possibility of a collaborative mode for generating performative work.

Kaitai-sha's director Shimizu Shinjin argues that their critically acclaimed *Tokyo Ghetto: Hard Core* (1996) struggles against the ongoing processes of cultural seclusion ('Japan's Japan') and nationalism (the restoration of 'national poetics' evident in Hirata's plays) in Japan's theatrical landscape. Hence, Kaitai-sha's use of impressively physical images, both violent and provocative (with degrees of affinity with Pina Bausch's Tanzteater pieces)—the space in Shimizu's theatre is filled with abject 'political bodies' whose theoretical background we can locate in Michel Foucault's notion of archaeology, or in feminism's theorization of the 'male gaze'.

More importantly, apart from its technical borrowings and its theoretical foundations, Kaitai-sha tries to locate the female and male bodies of its performers within Japan's sociocultural context, such as the repetitious reference to images of contemporary Tokyo as a dysfunctional landscape, to quote the 'no war' clause in Article Nine of Japan's US-authored post-War Constitution.[9] In the opening scene, a projected image of these words, written on paper and read aloud in English, is burnt.

In another scene, a male performer strikes a female performer's bare shoulders and thighs, as if to suggest that this violent act is the only way left for us to communicate between each gendered existence. However, in due course, he starts to hit himself as hard as he can until he falls to the floor, crumpled and exhausted. The female performer then picks him up, as if he were a baby, and induces him to repeat the same violent acts, thereby revealing the complicit nature of Japan's social structure. Here, Kaitai-sha presents images designed to draw attention to an aspect of Japanese society referred to as a 'patriarchy with seeming dependence on women'. Thus, in Kaitai-sha's performance, bodies are treated not as the site of an essential and autonomous subject but as the result of political and personal histories that include gender, race and class.

The second example of 1990s' theatre intervention is Dumb Type, a collective of visual artists, dancers and musicians, founded in 1984. Dumb Type first toured internationally in 1988 when it performed a variety of performance art and art installations, most notably *pH*. Dumb Type is based in Kyoto (as opposed to Tokyo, centre of Little Theatre activity) and its company members are familiar with gay subcultures in New York. Thus, Dumb Type emerged from a subcultural milieu and an artistic and geographical background radically different from that of the exponents of the Little Theatre boom.

FIGURE 5: S/N (1993–98) BY DUMB TYPE. PHOTOGRAPH COURTESY OF KAZUO FUKUNAGA.

Since its foundation, the collective has been creating mixed-media performance works which, as Daryl Chin has observed, '(utilize) the pop debris and mechanized environment of the contemporary urban centre', thereby presenting us with 'the American-influenced iconography of commercial popular culture' in their scenography (1991: 92–3). Though this description more aptly applies to its earlier works, S/N (1993–98; see Figure 5), the last piece Furuhashi Teiji was involved in, before he died of AIDS in 1995, took a very different turn as Dumb Type underwent crucial political changes to include issues of AIDS, sexuality and prejudice as themes. Soon after the play begins, Furuhashi declares that this is not a theatre piece, as people usually come to the theatre in order to forget the reality of life, but something to help the audience confront its reality and to urge it, in his own words, to 'invent new ways of communication'. By deploying a hi-tech mastery over a series of computer-controlled slides, video clips, music and lighting effects, subculture performative modes of transvestism—the lip-synching songs by 'divas', for example, and a dance of speed, whirling and falling—S/N presents us with a vivid image of late capitalist society where human bodies, surrounded by an excess of information, are pierced by the discursive practices of stereotyping and are entrapped in the futile battle of identity politics. *S/N* is at once political, theoretical, pedagogical, transgressive, resistant, funny and pleasurable.

In some other cultural contexts, this performative practice in the vein of media activism may not be exceptional and may even look naive in its directness. However, Dumb Type is an exception in Japan's theatre culture—informed by various kinds of performative practices, from both 'high art' and subcultural genres—and it has been successful in bringing the possibility of cultural production as a site of resistance into Japan's theatre culture, basing its inception on local subject positions and hybridizing them into a temporal and flexible site of performative space.

Japan's theatre culture is still in the shadow of a 'national poetics' which effectively works to deprive cultural production of its critical power. However, at least the two collectives I have discussed here are trying to establish performative space as a site for critiquing ongoing sociocultural processes in which both performers and audience are invariably involved. Their endeavours to restore the critical perspectives to performative practices may be read not only as an attempt to deconstruct the constructed image of holistic 'Japaneseness' but, in their hybridizing performative practice, it is possible to hear pluralistic, critical and local voices which may remind us of the dissenting voice(s) in Heiner Müller's intertextual practice.

Notes

1   Recent Japanese experience pertaining to this historical conjuncture would include the impact of the decline in economic growth, late-twentieth-century capitalism, inability to bring about political change, corruption in business and government ministries, the rise of the right wing, a turn to cults (most sensationally evident in the Aum gas attacks), etc.

2   During the Edo or Tokugawa era, Japan was united under a centralized feudal-style political rule. As a result of a policy of almost total isolation, Japanese culture tended to develop independent of other

international trends and technological advances. New urban centres were the site of the emergence of the popular theatre culture of Kabuki and Bunraku.

3   The most symbolic event, now considered to be demonstrative of the Little Theatre Movement's coming of age, was Noda Hideki's production of *Stonehenge* (1986), performed in a huge gymnasium in Tokyo and attracting an audience of 26,400 in one day.

4   Arguably the most important sources of critical writing on 1960s' theatre were the journals *Dojidai Engeki* (*Contemporary Theatre*) published by the theatre group Centre 68/70, and *Concerned Theatre Japan*, an English-language companion journal, edited by David Goodman.

5   Noda, Kokami and Kawamura are directors and playwrights of leading theatre groups that gained prominence and popularity during the 1980s. Some observers have pointed to the postmodern characteristics exhibited in 1980s' theatre culture that generally deferred cultural critique in favour of a performance style that exhibits the sensibilities of speed, playfulness and science fiction-like dramaturgy. The above artists are the representative figures of this movement. For a helpful discussion, see Rolf (1992). See also Introduction and Chapter 2 of this volume.

6   Japanimation or anime refers to the often feature-length science-fiction and cyber-punk animation films popular in Japan.

7   Kara and Suzuki, along with Sato Makoto and Terayama Shuji, were the predominant source of theatrical innovation in the early phase of Sho-gekijo. Goodman argues that an abiding interest in traditional theatres and the pre-modern imagination of Japan that is evident in 1960s' small theatre was a strategic resistance to Shingeki and a mode of radical cultural discourse (1988: 15–19). Kara is known to have evoked the image of *kawara kogiki* (beggars of the river bank), alleged originators of Kabuki in his writings (see Kara 1997). Suzuki worked with Noh actors and is known to have developed the Suzuki Method of actors' training, basing his techniques on traditional performance forms (cf. Suzuki 1986).

8   During this time, Japan started to participate in the world theatre market and contemporary Japanese theatre in particular become popular in many centres around the world.

9   Japan's post-War Constitution was (some argue, hastily) written in English by the American-led Allied Occupational Forces following Japan's defeat in 1945. It was later translated into Japanese and pre-

sented to the Japanese authorities without possibility of comment. This has led some to argue that the Constitution is ambiguous and unsuited to Japanese political culture. Article Nine declares that Japan foregoes the right to declare war and can only act militarily in self-defense.

CHAPTER 4
PLAYING BETWIXT AND BETWEEN:
INTERCULTURAL PERFORMANCE IN THE
AGE OF GLOBALIZATION

Cross-cultural exchange in theatre has a long and interesting history in Japan. Since the end of the nineteenth century, we have seen many examples of such cultural exchanges, most of which can be articulated in terms of influences and borrowings and/or in the context of the search for alternative modes of theatre by both Euro-American high modernists and theatre modernizers in Japan. In other words, those traditionally definable cross-cultural exchanges in theatre were possible, in most cases, through an unevenly distributed balance of attention and interest in which innovative Euro-American theatre practitioners were always looking at Japan's traditional theatre while their counterparts in Japan were always looking at the most advanced forms of theatre on the other side. In this kind of cross-cultural traffic, what mattered was the sense of otherness, especially in the sphere of aesthetics, and what could be demarcated as techniques; that which were appreciable yet new, unknowable yet knowable. Therefore, in most cases, contexts and specificities, especially historical and political ones, were not taken into consideration; practitioners on both sides were only looking at what they *wanted* to in the cross-cultural process which thus fell more aptly into the category of cultural translation. It was, in short, a process of appropriation, acculturation or assimilation. And, in either case, there has seldom been a dialogic, immediate and/or physical relationship between those influencing and those influenced. This tendency is still present in today's intercultural theatre practices where a modernist myth of originality and universality continues to be believed as valid and shareable.

The rise of postmodernism complicates the matter, as Patrice Pavis aptly remarks in his influential essay 'Toward a Theory of Interculturalism in Theatre' (1996):

> Faced with this difficulty in articulating the theory and the functioning of the work, it is tempting to postulate a confluence of intercultural theatre and postmodernism. It is certainly arguable that the two phenomena coincide with each other in time, and in the practice of Wilson, Suzuki and Bejart. But these represent only one type of cultural exchange amongst many and one, moreover, which levels cultures and decrees the passing of those radical avant-gardes of which Brook, Artaud and Mnouchkine are the last dinosaurs (ibid.: 19).

At the moment, I would tentatively argue that even postmodernism is passing and what is emerging, especially in the Asian region, is neither the debris left by 'the last dinosaurs' nor works created by epigones of cultural relativists such as 'Wilson, Suzuki and Bejart' but something quite different. In order to understand this something, I feel it is more productive to 'postulate a confluence'—not of 'intercultural theatre and postmodernism' but of intercultural theatre and the process of economic and cultural globalization. For, what differentiates recent attempts at giving rise to or performatively creating an intercultural space, especially after the collapse of the Berlin Wall in 1989, have been two rather obvious traits: the drastic increase in the number of collaborative projects between Asian theatre practitioners, and the varied senses and degrees of self-reflexivity, sometimes strongly manifested, at other times only feebly felt, in those intercultural theatre practices.

The first has to do, apparently, with the ongoing process of visible globalization, by which I mean the simple historical fact that international travel has become easier for some of us. In Japan, as its theatre culture is largely dominated and controlled by the market as elsewhere in Asia, many of the performances we see are still either mainstream ones from Euro-American countries or traditional ones from other Asian countries. Yet, in recent years, an ample amount of public funding has become available, itself a new phenomenon in Japan, from the Japanese government. For instance, the Japan Foundation, a government-sponsored public funding organization, affiliated with the Ministry of Foreign Affairs, is responsible for many inter-Asian collaborative projects that have been staged during the latter half of the 1990s.

The second has to do with the working environment of these projects—how are they envisioned, planned and executed; who is participating; who is responsible and how are they participating or responsible; where is it taking place and for whom? In most cases, the created performance space does not fall into the category of traditionally defined intercultural theatre practice, which almost always carries signatures of the individual. The most typical case being that an individual goes to the target culture, either physically or imaginarily, and 'takes' whatever can be taken from the master—Peter Brook going to India or Eugenio Barba inviting masters from 'the East' or influential Japanese theatre director Ninagawa Yukio (1935–) is invited to the National Theatre of Britain to direct British actors.

In the two cases I am about to introduce, the collaboration falls into the former category as both projects have taken place between two performance collectives. I would argue that we cannot articulate such practices in the discourse of influence nor in terms of power relations between each culture or each nation (that geopolitically defines its boundaries) and that these exemplify recent trends in what I have called an interculturalization of Asian theatre practices in the age of globalization.

A GRASS LABYRINTH IN TOKYO

The first collaborative project I am about to discuss became possible with the initiative of the Japan Foundation, Asia Centre, which, in 1996, set up a programme for the cross-cultural exchange of inter-Asian (between Japan and other Asian countries or regions) collaborative work in addition to the individual funding it had been offering so far. What characterizes this programme is that the Japan Foundation's major concern was to set up an intercultural creative space for contemporary theatre artists. Zuni Icosahedron, a Hong Kong-based experimental performance group, and Tokyo's Pappa Tarahumara were chosen for the programme. After two workshop sessions conducted in Hong Kong and Tokyo, they decided to work on the themes and images presented in the Japanese Gothic fantasy novel *Kusa meikyu* (*A Grass Labyrinth*, 1908) by Izumi Kyoka.

The work is divided into three parts with a prologue and an epilogue. Each part corresponds to themes found in the original text: water, moon, mirror. The epilogue is co-directed by the artistic directors of each company, Koike Hiroshi (1956–) of Pappa Tarahumara and Danny Yung (1943–) of Zuni Icosahedron. Koike directs the first and the third parts, and Yung the prologue and the second. Yung, in a TV interview, explains the project:

> In many ways, we are opening the doors. And then, when we open the doors, we step into people's territory and we learn from each other about our experience. I think in many ways we are also trying to find a common ground, a common vocabulary to start to develop a dialogue. In the work we have been developing, what I hope to achieve is to open as many doors as possible. And, I hope that, like all forms of art, art itself is like a mirror. In the mirror, we see ourselves and we see our environment. We also see how we relate to our environment (1997; author's transcription).

What is interesting about the performance is that it has become the site, at least for the audience, to observe the sameness in presentational style ('common vocabulary') and the difference in attitudes towards what art is and should be. The first has to do with more or less standardized aesthetics and techniques of contemporary performance—its use of bodies, multimedia, means of expression and so forth. Though each director's signature is inevitably inscribed in performance details, it is not so difficult to grasp the meaning of performance within the continuum of an undisturbed perception. The drastic and non-negotiable difference is rather in the content of the work. While Yung underlines the sections for which he is responsible with a very obvious reference to China's unification of Hong Kong (the frequent use of the colour red, for instance) which was a pressing issue in 1996, Koike, on the other hand, does not show any political concern in his sections (is that, in fact, a political gesture?); his is rather a naive, even blatant display of cultural essentialism (the use of Noh masks, for instance). For Yung, art starts with a political concern in his 'environment' but for Koike that is not necessarily the case. The performance space for *A Grass Labyrinth*, therefore, is presented as a mirror, as Yung explains, not necessarily for seeing 'ourselves' but for seeing, at the very least, the basic assumptions and aesthetics of the participating parties, the sameness and the difference, without a forced effort either to erase that difference or to affirm that sameness.

JOURNEY TO CON-FUSION IN TOKYO AND MELBOURNE

The second case is a more and, perhaps for some, even extremely localized intercultural project. Titled *Journey to Con-fusion*, it is a collaboration between the Melbourne-based Australian performance group Not Yet It's Difficult (NYID) and Tokyo's Gekidan Kaitai-sha. This project is envisioned as more long-standing than the Zuni–Tarahumara collaboration as, from its inception, it was meant to last for at least three years; participants were aware that, because both groups were known for their unique physical quality in performance and their political interventionism in each localized context, this particular project would be a great challenge.

The question, therefore, is: how is it possible that two such collectives working in localized politico-cultural contexts could 'open doors' and 'learn from each other'?

In the first case I have presented, the final date of presentation was set from the beginning, mainly because the whole project was publicly funded. For *Journey to Con-fusion*, nothing was settled at first, as they asked for separate funding for each session. Gekidan Kaitai-sha was to visit Melbourne to do the workshop with NYID in the winter of 1999 and NYID was to visit Tokyo in the summer of 2000. Both occasions were thought of and planned as a chance to see and work in each other's localized contexts. If something did come up after these two occasions, they would be able to present something in Melbourne and/or Tokyo in either 2001 or 2002.[1]

The first two sessions that took place were more in the nature of workshops; both companies explained and demonstrated how, why and what they had been doing, and the workshop results were shown to the public. There seems to have been no way to 'collaborate', as the two directors (David Pledger of NYID and Shimizu Shinjin of Gekidan

Kaitai-sha) differed in so many ways, especially about the notion and the concept of the performing body and, more radically, about what a contemporary performance can and should do. It was a difference brought about not only by their respective politico-cultural contexts but also by their individual thinking and beliefs towards the world at large. But they found out that issues and concerns can be shareable, as Peter Eckersall explains about the second workshop session:

> For *Journey to Con-fusion* the same basic model applied [as the first] . . . The theme of media as a cultural and political agency was loosely adopted although neither group adhered to this religiously nor was there adequate time to investigate this theme in any serious manner. Instead, the directors tended to continue in the vein of working within their respective company forms and structures although with an intensity and an eye to detail that was appropriate to a second meeting. The public performance also had more structure.
>
> For example, as the audience entered the studio for the public showing in Tokyo, NYID actors introduced themselves in simple Japanese. This was an often-awkward theatrical device designed to destabilize people's expectations of a seamless and integrated performance. Many of the activities were videoed and projected onto two large screens, extending the notion of a work in progress that was being documented. At the same time, this created an epic visual scale and atmosphere of expectation. There were no seats in the auditorium and audience members were forced to move as the action changed in the space.
>
> There were clearly two halves to the workshop-presentation. Pledger's sports-theatre aesthetics, jogging, interviewing 'players', group chants, etc. dominated the first part. In the second part, Shimizu's theatre of body politics was played out in several sequences (2005: n.p.).

Although I cannot give you any final words about this collaboration, as it is still a work in progress, it is obvious from Eckersall's documentation that the aim was not a seamless performance, as was the case with the Zuni–Tarahumara collaboration. Nor was it integration but, as the title of the project suggests, 'con-fusion'—playing between and betwixt the notions of fusion and con-fusion, between and betwixt the sameness and the difference. As the Zuni–Tarahumara collaboration work was created around the abstract themes derived from a literary work—water, moon, mirror—it was possible for the audience to observe the difference between the two collaborators within a graspable aesthetic frame of a seamless 'finished work'. In the NYID–Kaitai-sha collaboration, the audience was also included in the process of collaboration, as it were: the journey to con-fusion was not only for the collaborators but also for the audience. In short, although the latter was more disruptive, it was provocative and intellectually stimulating. The exploration of common issues—in NYID–Kaitai-sha's case, 'media as a cultural and political agency'—seems to provide a valid ground to generate this kind of collaborative intercultural performative space.

THE SPIRITS PLAY IN SINGAPORE: PART 1

The third case I wish to discuss is also an issue-oriented collaborative project. This too is ongoing, even though the first public performance took place in August 2000. It is worthwhile discussing this project at length, especially in the context of this chapter and in the context of the emerging revisionist movement in Japan, as the project was about World War II and memories of it.

For this project, Ong Keng Sen (1963–), artistic director of TheatreWorks in Singapore, has been working with a text called *The Spirits Play*, written by Kuo Pao Kun (1939–2002) another Singaporean artist. (For scenes from the play, see Figures 6–9.)

Let me start with a few words about who they are and what they have been doing up to their involvement in this project. Kuo Pao Kun is one of the most influential playwrights in Singapore. Although it is not inappropriate to say that he is a nationally recognized figure, it does not necessarily follow that he is a conservative artist nor that he is considered to 'speak for the nation'. In terms of class, because he is of Chinese descent, he inevitably belongs to the mainstream. Nevertheless, the fact that he has been awarded a medal should not be understood to mean that he is an officially and nationally recognized artist. Known for being

FIGURE 6 (TOP LEFT), FIGURE 7 (TOP RIGHT), FIGURE 8 (BELOW, LEFT) AND FIGURE 9 (BELOW, RIGHT):
THE SPIRITS PLAY—6 MOVEMENTS IN A STRANGE HOUSE
A THEATREWORKS PRODUCTION INSPIRED BY KUO PAO KUN'S *THE SPIRITS PLAY*
CONCEIVED & DIRECTED BY ONG KENG SEN
17–19 AUGUST 2000, THE BATTLE BOX, FORT CANNING CENTRE, SINGAPORE
25–26 AUGUST 2000, VICTORIA THEATRE, SINGAPORE
PHOTOGRAPHS COURTESY OF THEATREWORKS

resistant to many national policies and the mainstream ideology, he was even imprisoned for four years not long ago because of his sub-versive artistic activities in theatre. The medal, on the part of the government officials, was an attempt to institutionalize him as a poet laureate, an identity Kuo Pao Kun strategically accepted so that what he envisioned as 'artist-and-activist' could achieve fruition smoothly. Kuo Pao Kun, therefore, is regarded as the 'father' of Singaporean modern theatre—situated between commercial and institutionalized 'national' theatre—and he has been educating and provoking both audiences and artists for a long time.

Ong Keng Sen, alumnus of New York University's Department of Performance Studies, comes from a completely different generation. In his mid-thirties, he can be described as the enfant terrible of the Singaporean theatre scene. He established TheatreWorks in 1985 and has been very active throughout the world. Heavily funded by the national government and cultural institutions in Singapore, TheatreWorks has been a representative contemporary theatre com-pany since its inception and, at least for the current organization, is a kind of producing company with only four regular members. For each project (rather than production), it usually starts by gathering artists and stagehands.

In 1994, Ong Keng Sen conceptualized the Flying Circus Project, which, according to the programme note for *The Spirits Play*, is a 'creative strategy laboratory which is a robust encounter between con-temporary art and traditional performance' (2000: n.p.). His recent interest is amply demonstrated in this passage about the project that was held every two years and out of which grew such intercultural pro-ductions as *Lear* (1997) and *Desdemona* (2000–01).

Ong Keng Sen's work, from the very beginning of his career, has been geared more towards the international theatre market than towards developing Singaporean theatre. But recently, rather than making himself known in the Euro-American avant-garde theatre market, his interest has shifted to networking with Asian artists. As a result, he established a project-based funding network called Arts Network Asia in 1999.

The Spirits Play was first written in Mandarin Chinese and first performed in Singapore in 1997. Prior to Ong Keng Sen's version, there were two productions, both in Mandarin Chinese: the first was directed by Stan Lai from Taiwan for the Singapore Arts Festival and the 1998 production by Kuo Pao Kun himself, in Singapore and Hong Kong. It was subsequently translated into English and the text I refer to is this English version (see Pao Kun 1998).

The play was, according to Kuo Pao Kun, conceived when he visited a graveyard in Singapore for the Japanese soldiers killed during the War (personal correspondence with Pao Kun, 2000). The play deals with the Japanese occupation of Singapore but, surprisingly enough, all the characters in the play are Japanese—spirits of the Japanese who died in Singapore during the War and who are still wandering the earth and gathering, once a year, at the graveyard. All but one are the victims of war. The characters are named The Mother, The Man, The Girl, The Poet and The General. The Mother marries a soldier just before he is sent off to war. She becomes pregnant and gives birth to a son; in the meanwhile, the father of her child was sent off to Singapore where he ultimately died. Hearing of her husband's death, The Mother goes to Singapore to find his body where she discovers, instead, the ruins of war filled with male dead bodies. Every body that she comes across, she cremates as if it were her husband's. Regarding this as proof of her madness, she is shot to death by Japanese soldiers.

The Man is a soldier fighting in Singapore. When the Japanese military decide to abandon Singapore, in the process of withdrawing to the Malay Peninsula, they destroy the bridge connecting Singapore to the mainland, leaving behind thousands of fellow soldiers. These soldiers eventually die from starvation or epidemic diseases. The Soldier's is the story of witnessing the bodies of his comrades pile up amid the ruins of war.

The Girl is sent to Singapore as a nurse where she is raped by soldiers. Persuaded by the commander that it is a very sacred task for women to perform for the sake of 'a sacred war', she not only drops the charges but also becomes a prostitute in order to further serve the nation.

The Poet is an aspiring poet who is sent to Singapore as a reporter. He is forced to write war propaganda and must give up the hope of telling the truth through his poetry.

The General is commander-in-chief for the occupation of Singapore. A true believer in the holiness of the entire War, for him, sacrifice is everything. Everyone condemns The General but he is neither persuaded nor converted.

The Spirits Play is written in a poetic language through which Kuo Pao Kun tries to imbue the play with a mythic quality. Nothing is resolved at the end: a barren and desolate feeling of the spirits wandering about on foreign soil hovers in the air. It is a modern high-'quality' play set within the humanist tradition. What is interesting about it is the political implications of the Japanese War experience being described by a playwright of Chinese descent working in Singapore.

THE SPIRITS PLAY IN SINGAPORE: PART 2

The immediate effect of this production was that Kuo Pao Kun was criticized by the Chinese media in Singapore for being too 'soft' on issues of war (personal correspondence with Pao Kun, 2000). It is a well-known fact that the Chinese government in Beijing assumed a hard stand against the Japanese government concerning issues of war for various political reasons which, in response, triggered off a revisionist movement in Japan during the mid-1990s. Here, Kuo Pao Kun clearly stands on the side of the 'suffering' Japanese or the 'Japanese victims' during the War. Four characters in the play each condemn The General for allowing them to be trapped in the narrative of the sacred war, the official narrative of the militarist government during the War.

Although nothing is resolved, it is clear that, for those familiar with how Japan has constructed its national narrative about the War in the space of post-War democracy, the story of *The Spirits Play* should be very familiar. It is interesting to mention here, however, that the Japanese military's actions in Singapore are not well known to people in Japan. They are aware that Japan colonized Korea and conducted a massacre in Nanjing but not so many know about the the their massacre of Singapore's residents.

'We've heard enough,' a revisionist may say, reading Kuo Pao Kun's play. Yet, on the Japanese side, there was an interesting incident regarding an attempt to produce this play in Japan's New National Theatre. The Ministry of Culture in Japan has been sponsoring The Asian Art Festival for some time and, in 2000, it asked the Black Tent Theatre Company to plan and produce the festival. Sato Makoto, playwright and director of Black Tent Theatre, decided to dedicate the festival to Kuo Pao Kun's achievements. Sato, a professed anti-emperor-system artist, decided that different directors from different parts of Asia would direct *The Spirits Play*, a very natural way of thinking about the project. There seems to have been, however, a very subtle, unclear and ambiguous pressure from the Ministry of Culture to the effect that *The Spirits Play* was not suitable for the festival, especially not for being played at the New National Theatre since Japan's emperor has the right and authority to visit and watch performances at this theatre.

I will not address the censorship issue in this context but simply make it clear that such a play about the victims of war, despite its familiar nature, is considered mildly dangerous and subversive by government officials. When the revisionists are editing a new textbook for junior high schools and the government is trying very hard to enforce its national flag to be recognized as such, this kind of mild critique of the War is felt to be dangerous.

Ong Keng Sen, in deciding to direct *The Spirits Play* in Singapore in August 2000, took a very different approach towards the text and the production itself. One of the major devices for this production was that he added materials from a book about the Lee Geok Boi Oral Archives, published to commemorate the War experience in Singapore. He chose some passages (testimonies of residents who survived the Occupation period) from this book to balance the original text which is exclusively devoted to the Japanese side of the story, so to speak. This was a drastic revision of Kuo Pao Kun's original, significantly challenging his intention of describing only the Japanese experience of the War in Singapore. Secondly, Ong Keng Sen did not follow the sequence and the structure of the play at all—throughout the workshop and rehearsal processes, he distributed passages among the performers and each participating artist chose which lines they wanted to deliver during the performance. As a result, in the final script that was used for the performance, 80 per cent was from the original text and 20 per cent was from the archival material.

As I have mentioned earlier, Ong Keng Sen's recent interest lies in making an intercultural collaborative performance within Asia. After his stay in Japan for six months in 1999, he was acquainted with many from the younger generation of visual, theatre and performance artists, and he chose seven of them to develop *The Spirits Play* in Singapore: four from a group called The Grinderman; Nishijima Atsushi, a sound installation artist; Bubu, a member of Dumb Type and a sex worker-cum-activist; and Shimada Yoshiko, a visual artist known for her work dealing with issues of War memories and comfort-women. After two sessions of workshops with other performers, mainly from Singapore, each lasting approximately two weeks, Ong Keng Sen developed two versions: one, to be performed at Battle Box, the bunkers-turned-into-war-museum, and the other at Victoria Theatre, a more conventional theatre space.

For the first version, the performance was divided into three parts. The first part was in a space called Studio One, the second part was in the bunkers and the third in a space called the Black Box. The audience was first invited into Studio One to watch the performance of The Grinderman who identify themselves, according to the programme note, as a 'Techno-Art-Group whose main concept is to "grind-oneself" through performances that incorporate music, video, sculpture, mixed media, fine art and performance art'. Wearing metal helmets with their faces hidden, their part of the show is subtly evocative of war machinery and the mechanism of turning human bodies into killing machines. The performance is clearly meant to 'awe' the audience with 'strictly-timed synchronized movements and homogenous outfit capped with a black box on the head', as Marcus Tan writes in his review of the performance (2000).

In the next scene, we are invited inside the bunkers where different actions take place in different places:

> The mood radically shifts as the performance is moved into the Malayan Command Headquarters (better known as the Battle Box). Here, the space of performance is redefined as the boundaries of actor and audience dissipate into the eerie atmosphere of the poorly lit bunker. Seven veteran local actors 'float' around the corridors and rooms assuming different roles of lost spirits, each relating a painful story of war and loss. . . . (ibid.).

Then we are led into the Black Box, where:

> The haunting memories of guilt and pain then link the second and third plays together. A play of dramatic 'inaction', we are brought into the psyche of seven post-war characters, each dealing with their own demons. Employing the familiar motif of water, the repetitive ritual of bathing and washing that takes place in a space encircled by barbed-wire fencing becomes the central 'action' as the characters question the sense (and sense-lessness) of war (ibid.).

In the second version, because it was to be performed in a more conventional theatre space, Ong Keng Sen made the setting much clearer—a sex club where each client fantasizes about the War. The first part juxtaposes a drag show and each performer quotes mainly from Kuo Pao Kun's text. The second part was the same performance that The Grinderman presented in the first part of the first version. To conclude the formal presentation, however, Ong Keng Sen showed Shimada Yoshiko's video work about the War or, rather, about recent attempts at erasing the memory of the War in revisionist discourse. At the conclusion of the video clip, the entire set was removed and the audience was invited on stage to join the drag party.

The two female artists, Bubu and Shimada, were actively involved in the shaping of the whole performance on both occasions. They were known to be collaborating with activists for comfort-women issues in Korea and elsewhere and have made many works relating to these issues. Thus, they both provide a sharp contrast to the younger generation of artists (like The Grinderman); for the women, war issues are familiar terrain within the contexts of the ongoing systematic erasure of war memories.

Shimada contributes to this work with a short video clip in which she explicitly critiques the revisionist ways of rewriting history. It is shown at the end of the second version (at the theatre space) and at the bar in the bunkers where she acts as a bartender, 'disguised' as a male American GI.

Bubu, on the other hand, makes her stand very clearly, especially at the beginning of the second version, when she declares:

> I'm a female, Japanese, heterosexual person. I'm a prostitute. I want to tell you who were and are prostitutes. There is nothing wrong with you. Because what is needed to live can only be decided by yourself.
>
> Don't label us with any adjectives. Poor, great, brave, strong, miserable, weak, ignorant, innocent, wise, cunning, sensitive, victimized, stupid. If you have benefited from using us as a subject, you must pay us back. I have never felt miserable or cried at work. I have experienced worse in my life before (2000: n.p.).

For The Grinderman, on the other hand, war issues are remote and unreal. They have nothing to do with their daily lives—at least that was the case until they went to Singapore to work with Ong Keng Sen. For them, this intercultural work was a rare occasion to learn how to collaborate with artists with different ideological and/or aesthetic backgrounds and to learn, more than anything else, about the War. It is not that they did not want to learn, it is only that they did not know. They are also the victims of history for they have been brought up within a cultural sphere where the memories of the War have been systematically and repeatedly deleted. Ong Keng Sen writes about the work in his 'Notes to Japanese Friends':

> The only way we as post-War babies have been able to make sense of WW II has been by thinking of it as a madness in a moment in time which we can slip into again so easily. On the surface, we subvert the war experience by setting it in a Jean

Genet world but at the same time, I feel this has the contemporary relevance which I am seeking. In Singapore today, if you ask a young person 'Do you think there will be war in Singapore in the next decade?' you may get a laugh in your face. War is unreal in Singapore now, it only happened to our predecessors who were probably 'uncool and too traditional, old fashioned' (2000: n.p.).

Ong Keng Sen's two versions of *The Spirits Play* thus become a truly intercultural site, in which each of the participating artists had to take his/her own stance on war issues, bringing different talents, experiences, expectations, ideas, ideologies, histories and aesthetics into play. Then s/he had to start negotiating with the others and within him/herself about the very process of creating a performance dealing with War memories and about making a performance about those memories in 2000 in Singapore for the Singaporean audience. In the process, Ong Keng Sen did not act as an overpowering director/dictator but consciously functioned as a careful and cautious moderator: he only provided a setting, an environment in which every participating artist could start an intercultural negotiation process.

Can it be a model for other intercultural performances to follow? I am not sure. But for me at least, this is the foremost and the most interesting example of what I have been referring to as the interculturalization of Asian theatre practices until now.[2]

Notes

1 For the entire collaboration, including the last stage, please refer to Eckersall (2005).

2 *The Spirits Play* Project was brought to Japan in 2001 and renamed *Dreamtime* at Morishita Studio. The Grinderman continues to participate but the others did not because of various personal and political reasons, considering the sensitive nature of its subject matter. Instead, Toru Yamanaka, a musician, Nishiyama Minako, a visual artist, and Yubiwa Hotel, a theatre company, joined the collaboration.

FICTIONAL BODY VERSUS JUNK BODY: THINKING THROUGH THE PERFORMING BODY IN CONTEMPORARY JAPAN, OR WHY IS ANCIENT GREEK DRAMA STILL PRODUCED?

THE ORIGIN

Performing ancient Greek drama in Japan seems to have become a tradition, at least from an outsider's perspective, as two of Japan's most visible contemporary theatre directors—Suzuki Tadashi and Ninagawa Yukio—have been constantly producing Greek tragedies. In truth, however, Japan does not have a long history of producing ancient Greek drama. According to Ozasa Yoshio's *Nihon Gendai Engeki-shi* (*The History of Japanese Contemporary Theatre*) in eight volumes (1985–2001), the first production of a Greek tragedy was in 1916—*Oedipus Rex* by Geijutsu-za Theatre Company—though an adaptation of the same play is recorded to have been performed in 1894 (its details are lost). In the meantime *A Historical Bibliography on Western Classical Studies in Japan from Late 16th Century to 1945* (2001–02), recently assembled in Japan, records that some translations of ancient Greek drama started to appear towards the end of the nineteenth century and, during the 1920s, translations of representative plays were published (see Watanabe 2001–02).

In the post-World War II period, according to the theatre database of Waseda University, Tokyo (www.enpaku.waseda.ac.jp/db/enpakujo-ho), the first production of a Greek tragedy was in 1958 by an amateur university group (The University of Tokyo Greek Tragedy Research Group). One of the members of this group, responsible for tabulating a chronology of Greek tragedy productions for their performance, says, 'We thought we were the first to produce any Greek Tragedy in Japan, but we unexpectedly found the precedents' (Ozasa 1985: 155). Thus, it is clear that, until the post-War years, producing Greek tragedy was not common practice in Japan.

The university group chose for their first production *Oedipus Rex*, followed by *Antigone* (1959) and *Prometheus Bound* (1960) and continued producing Greek dramas until 1968. The first complete collection of Greek tragedies in Japanese translation was published in 1960 in four volumes by Jinbun Shoin Publishing Company. The first professional production was *Antigone* in 1959 by Engeki-za Theatre Company, a relatively small Shingeki company. The second quiet surge of productions of Greek tragedy was in the early 1970s when the late Noh actor, Kanze Hisao, established Mei no Kai Theatre Company and produced *Oedipus Rex* (1971), *Agamemnon* (1972) and *Medea* (1975), working with emerging 'angry, young' artists from both traditional performing arts genres and Shingeki.

It may be, therefore, reasonable to conclude that ancient Greek drama as text was not at all visible in Japan's wider sociocultural contexts, at least until the 1970s. One of the most important books of Shingeki history in Japan—*Shingeki Sho-shi* (*A Short History of Shingeki*, 1973) by Ibaragi Ken—mentions Suzuki Tadashi's *The Trojan Women* (1974) as the very first production of Greek tragedy in Japan. The reason for this is rather obvious: Shingeki's long tradition of introducing Western modern theatre into Japan during the late nineteenth century continued even into the post-War days. [This is amply demonstrated by the fact that Shingeki's first post-War production was *The Cherry Orchard* (1945) in which many Shingeki artists, who had been imprisoned and/or displaced because of their leftist ideologies during the War, participated to inaugurate their interrupted project.] Their acting master was Stanislavsky and their dramatic masters, Chekhov and Shakespeare, each of whom were well-respected figures in pre-War Shingeki circles.

Searching for an alternative, younger generations of theatre artists in Japan during the 1960s turned to ancient Greek drama as text, while the older generation stuck to safer terrain—modernizing Japan's theatre culture, according to (what they thought were) Western European standards.

Let me briefly draw a post-War political map, especially in terms of the project of establishing a national identity after Japan regained its independence in 1951 with the San Francisco Peace Pact that was signed by 48 nations (excluding the Soviet bloc countries). American occupation in political, economic and perhaps cultural terms—both domestic and international—continued and was a given reality in the 1950s. Especially important was the American military presence before, during and after the Korean War (1950–53), despite which Japan succeeded in concentrating on its economic gain during this period. Under GHQ supervision, many pre-War politicians and economic figures were 'revived', and Japan turned radically conservative. Naturally, the old Left was against this political reactionism, especially in 1960 when the Security Treaty between Japan and the US was to be renewed as the Treaty of Mutual Cooperation and Security. Shingeki kept a close but ambiguous tie with the old Left but, during the 1960s, as it did in Euro-America, the new Left movement started to emerge, culminating in the social turmoil of 1968. While the old Left's ideology was sustained by a strong nationalism, the new Left was more flexible, less organized and less factional.

THE ANGURA YEARS

The emergence of the Underground Theatre Movement in Japan in the late 1960s, in which both Suzuki and Ninagawa played a crucial role, was thus closely linked to the emergence of the new Left with both movements gaining enormous momentum after 1968. These were also anti-Shingeki movements in their own way that viewed Shingeki as too Western, too intellectualizing, too bourgeois, too safe. Japan, we must remember, had accomplished an amazing degree of economic growth during the 1960s. With a peculiar modernist urge, Underground Theatre practitioners turned to 'the popular', to what was apparently lost—the 'origin' and the 'original'. Terayama Shuji turned to the lost imagination of 'the people' as well as to European avant-garde's 'shock values'. Kara Juro tried to revive the image of 'beggars of the bank', the originators of Kabuki in the Middle Ages. Suzuki, perhaps the most intellectual and 'Westernized' of them all, explored the actor's body in an effort to regain its power and aesthetic efficacy. The search was on for some kind of 'origin', for an alternative, for something new that could speak to their contemporaries. Many of the practitioners were delving into the unconscious, into physical memory, into the discarded and/or forgotten cultural and national past.

It was perhaps a natural step for Suzuki to turn to ancient Greek drama in 1974 as a negotiation site for what he thought he had at hand in terms of theatrical apparatus—the actor's body. We must remember that Suzuki did not regard the traditional forms as a source of inspiration; for him they were dead art rather than living and/or lived art that speaks to the audience. In search of the efficacious and affective actor's body during his formative years, he experimented constantly with other non-professional, untrained performers of his generation, using different kinds of dramatic language, from Beckett to Kabuki to plays by Betsuyaku Minoru (1937–) (a prominent absurdist playwright), from lyrics of popular songs to super-nationalist writings from the late nineteenth century. This search was realized both physically and theoretically in the body of Shiraishi Kayoko, a female actor who was to become Suzuki's lead actor during his Waseda Shogekijo years (1966–82). In 1974, Suzuki directed *The Trojan Women* with Shiraishi, Kanze Hisao and Shingeki female actor Ichihara Etsuko. Furthermore, the text was drastically edited and shaped to fit the form of a play-within-a-play format. It was set in post-War Japan, where an old man evokes the dead to enact several scenes of *The Trojan Women*. Suzuki was interested, as he explains on many occasions, in theatrically demonstrating the ontological status of Japanese subjectivities in which the traditional, the modernizing process (Westernization) and the contemporary coexisted in theatrical terms. To that extent, he was both nationalistic and postcolonial.

In the context of this interlude, it is important to note that Suzuki came to discover the efficacy of the 'fictional body' as theorized by his contemporary Watanabe Moriaki (1933–), French theatre researcher, director and Kabuki connoisseur. In the production of *The Trojan Women*, Suzuki and his audience were reassured of the aesthetic efficacy of Shiraishi's body collectively acquired quite unconsciously through the fervent years of experimenting with his fellow members in Waseda Sho-gekijo, by juxtaposing it with the Noh actor's traditionally trained body and the Shingeki female actor's less affective Stanislavskyian body of realist theatre. Eugenio Barba called the fictional body 'extra-daily' after his own line of enquiry; but perhaps 'fictional body', as realized by the traditional genres of Kabuki, Noh and Kyogen is more useful here. Suzuki was, therefore, not saying that there is an essential body of the Japanese to be discovered, nor that traditional acting techniques could be applied to contemporary acting; his intention was more towards universalizing the actor's body as 'fictional'—a physical attribute that is to be collectively acquired through vigorous training and cooperative work in order to be affective in any given theatrical environment.

But why Greek tragedy, we wonder. As we have seen, ancient Greek drama was not and still is not a part of Japan's cultural imagination and knowledge, even if we limit its extent to the intellectual and the artistic. Did Suzuki choose those plays because they were 'Western', as Ian Carruthers (2004) seems to suggest in his most recent book on Suzuki? This idea is quite misleading, at least to me, for he makes it seem as if Suzuki chose Greek texts only in order to be able to perform abroad (specifically in Europe, according to Carruthers). In my opinion, Suzuki was responding to the politico-cultural unconscious of the 1960s. For his contemporaries, Chikamatsu and Euripides were equally remote and, if you will, foreign, whereas Shakespeare was 'our contemporary' because of the Shingeki tradition. And the 1960s, as we have seen, was a decade characterized by its urge to, in more contemporary terminology, invent 'the origin'. And in this case, the imagined 'origin'. The search itself was accompanied by a sense of loss for there is no origin we can return to. Thus, Suzuki's choice of *The Trojan Women* was doubly interesting—text and its language were supposed to have some sense of 'the original' and was, at the same time, a way of drawing our attention to the defeat of World War II as the performed origin.

NINAGAWA YUKIO AT THE 'POPULAR' FRONT

Another exponent of the Underground Theatre Movement in the 1960s, Ninagawa Yukiko, turned to ancient Greek drama a few years later in 1976, with a production of *Oedipus Rex*. But with a reason quite different from Suzuki's. Ninagawa was invited to direct a big commercial theatre production in 1974, with *Romeo and Juliet* followed by *Oedipus Rex* to be played in Nissei Gekijo (Theatre), with 1,330 seats. The text was by Hugo von Hofmannsthal, translated from the

German. Ninagawa was not recognized for his direction of ancient Greek drama until, a few years later, he directed *Medea* in 1978 in the same theatre, which went on to become the most performed Ninagawa production for many years to come. *Medea* featured Hira Mikijiro, a Shingeki actor, also known for film and TV roles, in the lead. What characterized this production were its decorative elements and its theatricality as rich spectacle. Ninagawa is a director known not to tamper with the text although for *Medea*, no mention of any translator can be found in the record and we cannot be sure which version of the text he used. It is without doubt, however, that Ninagawa contributed to popularizing ancient Greek drama in Japan, proving that a Greek tragedy could be a commercially successful production.

The 1970s is also known for the commercialization of the image of Japan within the nation. A famous motto of the time was Japan National Railroad's campaign headline—'Discover Japan'. The decade was a transitional phase from the modern to the postmodern, when, after achieving the unexpectedly high economic growth of the 1960s, Japan seemed to find itself again, especially culturally, in a more popularized and commercialized sphere in the emerging late-capitalist society. It was a new kind of cultural nationalism, a continuation of post-War nationalistic sensibilities with the central question being: how can we adapt ourselves to newly discovered postmodernizing late-capitalist's social, cultural and political environments and formations? Ninagawa's work and its popularity can be looked at as a response to the formation of such a new nationalism, accompanied by a renewed sense of populism with regard to then firmly established middle-class population, especially in the more centralized urban environment of the postmodern metropolis, Tokyo.

In the context of this interlude, it is more interesting to discuss Hira's body, a body not necessarily an 'extra-daily' or a 'fictional' body, as he was not trained in traditional genres, but was (and still is) an idiosyncratic stage and film actor, with a good voice and a charismatic presence. Through the use of this body, and Tsujimura Jusaburo's famous decorative and exaggerated costume design, Ninagawa was able to project the image of the traditional that happened to be *Medea*. Of course, we can argue that Ninagawa's theatrical spectacle has attributes more common with Takarazuka—an all-female revue and musical theatre that is a modern fusion of Kabuki and American musical theatre—than with 'authentic' traditional genres such as Kabuki and others. If we look at the visual image of *Medea*, we will also be surprised by its camp characteristics (although the notion of camp has a very different ideological take in Japan's gay culture). Ninagawa was, therefore, trying to update Kabuki with contemporary contexts through this production of *Medea* with its use of an all-male cast and the Western classic text. However, unlike Suzuki, he lacked the theoretical thinking to develop it further and nor had he a theatre collective to work with. From this time on, Ninagawa operates quite opportunistically, by incorporating emerging young and decisively unprofessional actors (teen idols, in most cases), male and female, into his productions, focusing on ticket sales and performing in huge commercial venues. He has directed not only Western texts from Shakespeare, Brecht and Tennessee Williams but also some modern and contemporary plays by Japanese playwrights. A sense of the theatrical and spectacular extravaganza—some call it 'theatrical decoration as sweet as sugar candy, but without any content'—became his trademark, and he worked very 'professionally'. Whatever he chooses as text, he never touches its content but tries rather to bring 'it' on stage as 'it' is written, with younger and fresher actors.

Ninagawa came back to ancient Greek drama in 1986, with Sophocles' *Oedipus Rex*, with Hira Mikijiro playing Oedipus, for an outdoor spectacle performed in the precinct of a Buddhist temple in Tokyo. It was only a mild success and was never performed again, either locally or abroad. He returned to *Oedipus Rex* after 16 years, in 2002, a decision prompted by his meeting with Nomura Mansai, a Kyogen actor who, like the younger generation of traditional artists in the 1960s and 1970s, was trying to cross the boundaries imposed by traditional ways of thinking. Nomura played Oedipus in Tokyo (2002, 2004) and Greece (2004), though he was known at the time as one of those emerging teen idols of the late 1990s owing to his frequent appearances in TV dramas and commercial films. The production was a commercial success, with its translation language updated for contemporary Japanese audiences.

We must remember that this was in 2002; the intervening 16 years have seen a drastic change in Japan's political, social and cultural environments and formations, and we must contextualize this particular way of displaying the 'fictional body' in *Oedipus Rex*, especially within the matrix of so-called petit-nationalism of 1990s' Japan.

PETIT-NATIONALISTIC JAPAN IN THE 1990S

The Japan of the 1990s is characterized both by the long-lasting economic recession and by the emerging dominance of neo-liberal sovereignty, and their far-reaching effects, politically, socially and culturally. The breakdown of the Berlin Wall did not open up a borderless utopian intercultural space but, rather, created coexisting cultural 'holes' within the nation.

It is well known that Michel Foucault formulated the ontological status of the body in modernity as created through the state machinery of discipline (military, education and others) and surveillance; this is what he called the 'docile' body. Neo-liberal sovereignty, on the other hand, according to sociologist Shibuya Nozomi, creates the subject of self-censorship (2003). The body becomes not the object of domestication through disciplinary processes but the object of self-censorship without any imposed process from outside. According to Shibuya, when the machinery of self-censorship malfunctions, this kind of body tends to run away, run amok. Ootori Hidenaga, a cultural theorist, called this kind of body, which we can today observe everywhere around the globe, 'the body of dementia' (2003). And I would argue that cultural manifestations of the body in 1990s' Japan need to be understood from such a theoretical perspective.

In more theatrical terms, the 'fictional body', both in Underground Theatre practices and in traditional genres, came to lose its validity in a wider sociocultural context and, therefore, was considered to lack the actuality that could resonate with the body-state of the audience. As I have argued elsewhere, Japan's performance culture in the 1990s is characterized by the dominance of what I call a 'junk body', the exact opposite of the 'fictional body'; untrained, undisciplined, a loose kind of body-in-performance. Sakurai Keisuke, a dance critic, named this 'child's body', in his attempt to privilege it as an unconscious resistance against the state of globality (see Chapter 6).

In the context of this interlude, however, this transition from the 'fictional' to the 'junk' has a tremendous influence on Japan's performance culture. Suzuki Tadashi, for instance, kept directing ancient Greek drama; his productions have grown more refined and he has risen up the political ladder even though his work is largely ignored by the younger audiences. His name is now equated with the notion of high art which does not have any historical ground within Japan's performance culture. Ninagawa, on the other hand, is ever present, as he is always aware of his market value and continues working in that peculiar domain of popular, commercial and high art. For a younger generation of performance practitioners, the 1990s were a difficult time. Miyagi Satoshi, a theatre director heavily influenced by Suzuki's work, is a typical case in point. He was exceptionally interested in directing ancient Greek drama and he came up with an interesting solution, given the sociopolitical context I have outlined. In the postmodern age that we live in, according to Miyagi, it is not possible to collectively acquire the 'fictional body', which was possible in the 1960s and the 1970s within the matrix of constructing an alternative national identity. So he appropriated the Bunraku puppet theatre's methodology of splitting up the puppet and the voice. In his production, the movement and the voice are separated, again, as the 'extradaily-ness' of characters in Greek tragedies can only be performed this way.

In the context of this interlude, I would argue that the disruption between the language and the body (though in Miyagi's case, the disruption itself is not necessarily foregrounded but, rather, intellectually resolved) points to the contemporary ontological status of the body in everyday life which, in my terminology, can only be described as 'junk body-ness'. The 'peculiar aesthetic quality' acquired by experiencing this divide is more likely to have something to do with our 'junk body-ness' than with traditional genres of Bunraku puppetry, as the expected synchronicity between language and body movements, though achieved beautifully in Miyagi's productions, is visibly betrayed and the possible gap and/or rupture inevitably emerges.

In concluding this section, I would like to mention a performance by the very young theatre company, Chelfitch. As we will be looking at their work more closely in the following chapters, I will note here their 'faithfulness' in trying to represent the rupture between the language they speak and the body movements the language is supposed to induce. The actors speak a super-colloquial language used by young people in Tokyo now, but the body movements do not match the content of their words. Rather, they betray each other; as they speak of everyday trifles, their bodies react very strangely, in some cases lapsing into a Butoh-like dance.

One may say that all they need is discipline, but isn't discipline the very thing that neo-liberal sovereignty has decided to deprive its subjects of? Coming from one of the most advanced neo-liberal states and the city of Tokyo, where you can observe and sense this particular kind of 'junk body-ness' on every corner of every street, I wonder what kind of body movements can be induced if we gave any of those bodies the lines from ancient Greek drama, written centuries ago, to speak.

CHAPTER 5
POP, POSTMODERNISM AND JUNK:
MURAKAMI TAKASHI AND 'J' THEATRE

Some of the key words in understanding contemporary Japan are *kire-ru*, to snap, *hikikomo-ru*, to lay up or to retreat (into a house or into a room, never to come outside) and *iya-su*, to heal. People are 'snapping' everywhere and committing absurd forms of violence, and young people are retreating into their houses, often confining themselves to their rooms, refusing to go out to school, to work, to therapy, sometimes even slashing their wrists in an act of terrorism against their own bodies. In response to these urgent expressions of individual anomie and social dysfunction, cultural products in different media—from high art to mass cultural genres—that claim to 'heal' are flourishing. People visit Bali to be healed, people visit the theatre to be healed and people retreat into their rooms to be healed. At the same time, there has also been an enormous increase in the numbers of violent (and bizarre) crimes for which no rational motives can be easily located. A typical example would be as follows: an 'ordinary' citizen, without any apparent reason, snaps one day and kills others or him/herself. The mass media declares that 'society is sick' and tries to locate the problem within the realm of modern rational thinking—society is sick because of the long-lasting recession, because of the loss of traditional values or because of the loss of national pride.

Does psychoanalytic knowledge help us to understand and to survive? Saito Tamaki, a psychiatrist, seems to say so in *Ikinobiru tameno Lacan* (*Lacan for Survival*, 2006), first published as a series of articles on the Internet, while Kayama Rika, another psychiatrist, reaches almost the same conclusion based upon observations made in the course of her own clinical practice: 'There were many maddening incidents in the world this year [2001]. We must not, however, forget there were many maddening incidents in this country [Japan] too' (2001: 114). After mentioning some bizarre criminal cases as well as the publishing of a photographic book of Japan's Prime Minister Koizumi (2001–06) and the 'much-ado-about-nothing' nature of the media spectacle around his son's debut as a TV star, she declares: 'The world has gone mad. There is no mistake about it, because I, as a psychiatrist, say so. Or put it somewhat differently, the world has gone mad, to the extent that the pre-existing notions of madness cannot explain what is happening' (ibid.). Her diagnosis, somewhat forced, is that the entire population of Japan is suffering symptoms of depersonalization disorder. [I say 'somewhat forced' because Kayama claims to not really understand what is happening; all the traditional explanations of typical clinical psychological dysfunctioning are not enough.] The psychological dysfunctioning identifiable as depersonalization disorder is so widespread in Japanese society that it is difficult for Kayama to decide who should be clinically treated, especially since a decisive 'gap' between the traditional medical notions of the normal and the abnormal no longer seems to exist. People in Japan seem to be living in the gap—in a jumble of sane and insane relations with the world—until they snap; their snapping makes their condition visible through bizzare criminal acts. According to Kayama, everyone in Japan is experiencing the same psychological dilemma.

It must be noted that Kayama's thoughts on Japanese life are being aired not in a popular medical forum but in an art magazine in the context of Murakami Takashi's work. Kayama is interested in why Murakami's work, usually categorized as contemporary visual art, has gained such enormous popularity in Japan.

It was in 2000 that Murakami proudly declared in his 'The Super Flat Manifesto' that 'The world of the future might be like Japan is today—super flat':

> Society, customs, art, culture: all are extremely two-dimensional. It is particularly apparent in the arts that this sensibility has been flowing steadily beneath the surface of Japanese history. Today, the sensibility is most present in Japanese games and anime, which have become powerful parts of world

culture. One way to imagine super flatness is to think of the moment when, in creating a desktop graphic for your computer, you merge a number of distinct layers into one. Though it is not a terribly clear example, the feeling I get is a sense of reality that is a very physical sensation. The reason that I have lined up both the high and the low of Japanese art in this book is to convey this feeling. I would like you, the reader, to experience the moment when the layers of Japanese culture, such as pop, erotic pop, otaku, and H.I.S.ism fuse into one (ibid.: 5).

Although Murakami's super-flat theory is both simplistic and ethnocentric, his notion of the 'super flat' is relevant to Kayama's analysis of people snapping, isolating themselves and wanting to be healed.

Kayama diagnoses Murakami's work as an indication that he is not a victim of depersonalization disorder precisely because he strategically jumps over the gap by managing the traditional categories of high and low art—creating his super-flat work. Furthermore, Kayama explains that this is exactly the reason why Murakami's work is so popular in Japan. Murakami's sense of reality, which he identifies as 'a very physical feeling', seems to be shared and appreciated by his audience who are experiencing symptoms of depersonalization disorder while 'society, customs, art, culture' are all becoming 'two-dimensional', as Murakami puts it. Two-dimensionality, or a flat surface, does not allow us to acquire depth or 'gap'; it does not allow us any psychological defense mechanisms in dealing with the world.

What about the body, we may naturally come to wonder. For Johannes Birringer, the body has 'special qualities and a personal history' but is also that which 'is written about and written into social representations of gender, race, and class' (1986: 86)—the body with depths and dimensions in various levels and directions. When we say the body becomes two-dimensional, super flat, what does it mean, especially in Japan, where, as Kayama says, 'the world has gone mad'? What does it mean, especially for those involved with contemporary performance, in which the body still seems to be the dominant vehicle of their performing practice?

PERFORMING BODY IN THEORY

Ishimitsu Yasuo, a cultural theorist, in his 'Hisyteric na Shintai no Yume—Shintairon no Yukue' ('The Dream of the Hysteric Body: Whereabouts of Body in Theory'), traces theories of the body in modern Euro-American discourse:

> What is certain is that what we mean by the word 'body', when we say 'body in theory', is no other than a body image and therefore, is only a 'cast-off skin' of the lived body. The body that is lived, here and now, by us, without any meaning attached to it, stays outside of our knowledge and, when we can experience the body via our knowledge, it is always, already represented by figures that can be felt and grasped by and through the five senses. If the body ever presents itself as a unified volume, it is, without exception, constituted through images and the power of images. As for the unified volume, it can sometimes be totally replaced and dissolved by 'textual body' (body as text), and at other times it can only be that, though there is a certain logic working there, the logic itself can only be articulated through metaphors ('grotesque body', 'tremulous body', etc.). In the former, the body is annihilated ('the morbid negation of the body'), and in the latter, our intellectual endeavour to theorize the body becomes very difficult, even impossible (2000: 22–3).

Following this passage, Ishimitsu says that, as far as modernity desires to 'negate the hysteric body' in aesthetic representations, metaphoric bodies flourish. At the same time, it is equally natural that 'body in theory through speculative language can only be very poor' (ibid.: 31).

To sum up Ishimitsu: firstly, the body can only be felt and grasped by the five senses as representation. Secondly, the body that seems to present itself as a 'unified volume' before our eyes can only be either text or metaphor, never a lived body itself. What is the body image that is 'totally replaced and dissolved by textual bodies, body as text', and what is the metaphorical body that Ishimitsu says is flourishing in aesthetic representations in contemporary performance practices?

PERFORMING BODY IN HISTORY

In contemporary Japanese theatre culture, the dominant body at the moment is that which can be 'totally replaced and dissolved by textual bodies'. This can typically be observed in Hirata Oriza's Quiet Theatre works. The actor's body belongs wholly to the character as a linguistic construct and serves the Bakhtinian notion of 'commentary to language and action'. In other words, the 'morbid negation of the body' has given rise to a mode of theatrical representation called modern realist theatre, what we are witnessing in theatre in Japan today is exactly that: the body of (revived? revised?) modern realist theatre.

Among those who confronted 'the problem of how to visualize the body, excluded from the discourse but visibly remaining in the periphery' (ibid.: 14–15), were the so-called Angura Theatre practitioners in the late 1960s. In Japan's theatre, historically speaking, and according to the official narrative of its history, in the bodies of Angura practitioners such as Suzuki Tadashi and Kara Juro, 'the internal body that had lost any figuration or form' and lacking any textuality (verbal articulation) displaced itself onto the external visible body that was in a way filled up with that subversive energy usually called 'passion' (ibid.). With Angura Theatre practices, the Bakhtinian 'grotesque body' as an aesthetic metaphor was able to be constituted through the complicity between the practitioners and the audience. It was a time of political revolt and cultural upheaval when the physical and/or the visceral was the centre of attention on both the political and the cultural fronts.

In the following years, dominant theatre practitioners desperately tried to prevent this type of passion, the most obvious example being the body in Hirata's Quiet Theatre. Except for a few noteworthy cases, bodies in Japan's contemporary theatre practices are dominated by 'the morbid negation of the body', by bodies that are given the concrete role of commenting, at various levels, on the characters, linguistically constructed entities in written texts. Nevertheless, there are moments during the performance when commentary fails. In Hirata Oriza's earlier works, his actor's bodies were amateurish, convulsive and spasmodic. Or there are cases when the process of displacing the internal to the textual is interrupted and/or ruptured. According to modern realist theatre aesthetics, the failure/interruption of valuing the body as an interpreter of text lowers the aesthetic value of the given performance. The notion of good or bad acting thus relates to this very issue of erasure/negation of the body in the modern realist theatre tradition that is still dominant in Japan's contemporary theatre culture.

From a broader perspective, it is possible to say that the two kinds of body images made possible by modernity's desire for the 'morbid negation of the body' have always co-existed. In Shingeki, for example, even though the body was theoretically constructed to serve as a transparent representation of the 'Westerner's' body (after Stanislavsky), the here and the now in the performance space was represented by the 'Japanese body' and which was aspiring to the transparent representation of the 'Westerner's' body and was thus necessarily an unsaid manifestation of the notion of 'the morbid negation of the body'. We can assume that the 'Japanese body'—something to be denied and annihilated, according to historical Shingeki conventions and aesthetic principles—was nevertheless undeniably visible in the performance space. Angura Theatre practitioners, therefore, were those (in the post-War cultural space where such doubled 'textual bodies' were to dominate the representational sphere) who interpellated and represented the Japanese body in the periphery as a Bakhtinian 'grotesque body' and it was understood as such by the audience, i.e. as an aesthetic metaphor.

'JUNK BODY' IN CONTEXT

In contemporary Japanese theatre culture, the body is only allowed to function as a commentary to dramatic text. Due to the pressures created by what may be regarded as a dialectical necessity, the desire to make something else of the body seems natural; it is no wonder that we have seen theatrical representations in which 'lived bodies' are displaced onto aesthetic metaphors. At the peripheral of dominant theatre culture, this has something to do with the emerging of what can only be called the 'grotesque body' or the 'junk body', wherein the notion of the character as a linguistically constructed whole does not function at all. Nevertheless, what we are witnessing in some male-dominated theatre collectives such as Gokiburi Kombinat (Cockroach

Kombinat—Kombinat means an industrial complex in Russian) and Potsu-doru [untranslatable], where bodies can only be described as 'run-away bodies', is not the same as the aestheticized bodies of Angura or 'grotesque body' as an aesthetic metaphor. What we see are simply naked bodies, 'literal bodies', not metaphorical at all and far removed from those of high art. Or, in the case of some female-the-atre collectives such as Yubiwa Hotel (Ring Hotel) or Kegawa Zoku (Tribe of Fur), what is being presented is a very particular kind of 'grotesque body' that has nothing to do with the notion of 'the morbid negation of the body'. The displacing movement from 'internal body'/'lived body in real time' to 'external body'/'body as representation' seems to be totally lacking. These bodies are not there to comment on the character as a linguistic construct; uttered words and bodies are far removed from each other. The body is presented de facto and only by being involved in a performance structure is it allowed to inscribe its existence, quite temporarily, into a space.

In these typical 'J'/'junk' theatre practices, what is presented is not what Ishimitsu describes as 'the morbid negation of the body'; that is, the negation of the hysteric body, the body, which has a possibility of suffering the symptoms of hysteria, the body as a stage, where repression and realization of highly charged desire translates and expresses itself in the body phenomenon' (ibid.: 30). If, as Ishimitsu says, 'the drama of repression and realization of desire can only be performed through the struggle with language', we must presume, in those bodies, that language—supposed to repress desire—is already and always lost.

'THIN BODIES' IN DANCE

As for dance-oriented performances in Japan, Kumakura Takaaki, art critic and scholar, sees in them what he calls 'thin' bodies. When he saw one of the performances by Mezurashii Kinoko Buyodan (Strange Mushroom Dance Company) in 2001, he said, 'I felt that the twenti-eth century, or rather, the modern has finally come to an end':

> 'Thin subjects'—bodies—must be kept alluring. I must keep excessively covering my own super flat with incessant series of simulacra. From *bihaku* ('beautiful white skin') to mobile

phone e-mailing. From 'dispatched' jobs to chatting at a fashionable cafe . . . it is nevertheless 'thin'. If I am not techno-
logically well-equipped, I might fail in jumping or I might
break through thin ice. Then, the black hole—that black hole
I have been desperately evading—is waiting with its huge
mouth open. 'The animal', 'violence', and 'the unconscious',
supposedly exorcised by super-visible simulacra, are whirling
down there, waiting to swallow 'the I', the subject. Once swal-
lowed, my 'thin' subject—the body—is easily destroyed. Watch
out! I must grasp the nearest simulacra, must somehow rise to
the surface, and keep skidding along the super-visible super-
flat surface (2002: 124).

The 'thin' subject—the body—can put on series of simulacra and keep
skidding over the super-flat surface with its own movement, the dance.
The 'drama of repression and realization of desire' that 'can only be
performed through the struggle with language' simply does not
happen; therefore, 'the lived body' can never become visible as an
aesthetic metaphor. In the same vein, the junk body is only 'the
grotesque body' as simulacra and not an aesthetic metaphor; it is
physically present, burdened with nothing. Female bodies in Yubiwa
Hotel or Kegawa Zoku are literally there, as if there is no repressed
desire, sometimes communicating, anti-aesthetically, and aesthetic
and political vulnerability.

But, as Kumakura observes, this body technology does not get rid
of 'the lived body'. 'Desire', 'the animal' and 'the unconscious' are all
forgotten but not entirely repressed. The hysteric body is not morbidly
negated but vacantly forgotten in order to continue skidding over the
super-visible super-flat surface:

I didn't learn how to deal with 'the darkness', 'the animal'. At
home, at school, I only learnt to cage 'the animal'. They did-
n't even teach me how to build a cage properly. That's why
sometimes 'the animal' suddenly breaks the vulnerable cage,
and tries to eat up 'thin' me (kireru—to snap). Or it tries to
drag me into the cage (hikikomoru—laying up) (ibid.).

Not having learnt of ways to repress our desires, releasing them may cause our body to run forward (snap) or go into isolation (lay up). To prevent this, the Strange Mushroom Dance Company must dance, Gokiburi Kombinat must exhibit their naked bodies and Yubiwa Hotel must stand on stage. As for Potsu-doru, as is typical in what they call their semi-documentary works such as *Naito Club* (Knight/Night Club, 2001)—they are trying to tell people: let's learn how to tame 'the darkness', 'the animal', so that our bodies do not run away.

It is certain, as Kumakura says, that we are at the moment when 'the twentieth century, or rather, the modern has finally come to an end.' But we must be cautious not to succumb to the idea that the universal theory of psychoanalysis can convincingly explain what is happening to our bodies. It is not, and should not be understood as, only a psychological and thus a 'personal' problem, as both Kayama and Kumakura seem to think. We need to ask whether what we are confronting is a new historical phase and whether our bodies are passing through a particular historical conjuncture.

EMERGING BODIES OF 'THE MULTITUDE'?

To what degree are contemporary bodies always-already fictional? What is the historical process of globalization inscribing onto our bodies?

In their much-acclaimed *Empire*, Michael Hardt and Antonio Negri tell us of the emerging bodies of 'the multitude': 'Bodies themselves transform and mutate to create new posthuman bodies' in the process of 'the anthropological exodus' (2000: 215). Should we just wait for Benjaminian 'barbarism' to take hold of us and/or for Donna Haraway's 'cyborg fable' (ibid.: 218) to become our reality? Should we welcome the transformation of our bodies into posthuman bodies? Should we regard Kayama's description of the omnipresence of depersonalization disorder in Japan as the beginning of an 'anthropological exodus'?

From a sociological perspective, Sakai Takashi gives us a more concrete image of what is happening:

> While the division is becoming deeper and wider in the form
> of class stratification and economical polarization within the
> nation-state [Japan], the in-between space, the room for
> dropouts to keep on living or to resist against the current
> trend is increasingly filled up. Notwithstanding the ignoring
> of social rights, if we look at the Personal Information
> Protection Act [that has passed the National Diet quite
> recently], even freedom of speech is on the verge of being
> extinguished. Only languages of self-responsibility [the lan-
> guage of self-accountability] and morals [the language of
> good or bad, a simple dichotomy, according to bourgeois
> morality] are overwhelmingly advanced as acceptable and
> normative, and people are deprived of languages to express
> themselves in order not to be forced into desperate manifes-
> tations of antagonism (murder, terrorism, suicide, etc.) . . .
> neo-liberal sovereignty attacks language first. I am very sur-
> prised at this paranoiac urge within those in power to domi-
> nate and prevent any kind of antagonism even before it takes
> any visible, tangible form (2001: 68).

Although this observation is theoretically and empirically accurate, it
is not shared by the majority living in Japan. As we have seen, the
dominant discourse explaining contemporary 'desperate manifestations of antagonism' is preoccupied with universal psychological
explanations. But it is not too unreasonable to imagine, as Sakai
acutely observes, that a neo-liberal sovereignty in Japan has so far succeeded in depriving its subjects of a 'language to express' any forms of
non-desperate antagonism—that bodies in the real world are alto-
gether 'running away', i.e. showing symptoms of depersonalization
disorder. On the other hand, the younger generation of theatre and
dance artists desperately try to put their 'thin' and 'flat' bodies (which
may 'run away', if left alone) into an aesthetic frame, in order to contain and tame them. Perhaps we should ask them to let the animal out
of the cage, to let the 'anthropological exodus' take place, at least within the framed space of contemporary performance. Then, that may
become a site of resistance against 'the paranoiac urge within those in
power to dominate'.

CHAPTER 6

GLOBALITY'S CHILDREN: THE 'CHILD'S' BODY AS A STRATEGY OF FLATNESS IN PERFORMANCE

This chapter, like the previous one, constitutes a part of my ongoing project to theorize and historicize the body-in-performance in contemporary Japanese performance. I call this project 'Super Flat Japan: Thinking about "Flat" Bodies in Contemporary "J" Performance'. The last chapter, the first version of which was read at a performance studies conference at Dokkyo University in Japan in 2002, was subsequently published in *Dokkyo International Review* (see Uchino 2003). I examined the theoretical status of the body-in-performance through some 'edgy' performance practices in contemporary Japan. Referring to Ishimitsu Yasuo's (2000) theoretical and historical analysis of 'the body as text' and 'the body as metaphor' in the context of modernity's 'morbid negation of the body', I gave a historically informed overview of the ontological status of the body in Japan's theatre culture. But something else, in my observation, is happening in contemporary Japan. My essay attempted to address some of the most pressing issues regarding 'flat' bodies and 'run-away' bodies because a sense of 'flatness' and/or violent 'running-away-ness', rather than 'depth' and/or formal containment of the body, mark the performance practices of some of the younger generation of artists. By way of conclusion, I argued that one needed to understand the sociopolitical actualities of a Japanese society dominated by neo-liberalism in order to grasp what was happening with these younger artists. Or, to put it another way, much of today's Japanese performing arts need to be analysed in terms of the social, economic and political actualities of globalization. This chapter is a continuation of that line of research and I will be looking at three performances that comprise part of my theoretical mapping of the ontological status of the body-in-performance in contemporary Japan.

THE THEORY OF THE CHILD'S BODY

Since the publication of my 2003 essay, a certain critical discourse has become available to explain 'flat bodies' on stage, most notably Sakurai Keisuke's theory of *kodomo shintai*, children's bodies—the immature and/or asexual body. Sakurai discusses the reason why some of us find kinesthetic pleasure in watching those bodies, or more precisely, watching those bodies-in-performance (2004). Drawing upon Homi K. Bhabha's notion of 'mimicry' (1994), Sakurai discusses Japanese dancing bodies (which he associates with children's bodies as opposed to Western dancers' adult bodies) perfectly mastering Western dance techniques in their training. As *kodomo shintai*/children's bodies, they are intentionally 'misusing' these techniques, deconstructing them and thereby subverting the intended impression. Sakurai is referring to dance companies such as Mezurashii Kinoko Buyodan and Nibroll Dance Company, groups that many in the Japanese contemporary dance world consider 'edgy', 'avant-garde', 'more advanced' and 'more contemporary'. Sakurai tries to locate Mezurashii Kinoko Buyodan's and Nibroll's 'unique' displays of movement within a (pseudo-)postcolonial discourse in which an imagined geopolitically isolated Japanese performance culture developed its own aesthetics, conceptions of dance and critical standards. In doing so, Sakurai tries to isolate Japan's contemporary dance culture and vocabulary within a globalized standard of dance and discourse. His goal is to protect Japan's dance culture from the continuing pressure of romantic ballet, modern dance and diverse contemporary dance practices. Though Sakurai's specific observations are relatively accurate in terms of describing the particular contemporary dance performances that he discusses, his discourse itself is formulated within a parochial contemporary dance community, constituted of dance and movement 'freaks' (somewhat fanatical fans), a band of artists and critics with a renewed sense of aestheticism which resonates with the ideology of 'Japanese cool' that inevitably betrays their ideological naivety.[1]

Despite such shortcomings, however, Sakurai's theory—or more precisely, his labelling—helps to reformulate a local way of articulating Japan's contemporary dancing bodies-in-performance and to explain why Sakurai and his peers are so enthralled with Japanese dance.

My interest in the notion of *kodomo shintai* as an aesthetic category is not in its pronouncements of 'Japanese cool' but in its failure as another form of post-World War II Japanese junk[2]—this time, the junk body—which betrays and exhibits the postmodern rupture between language and the body by using super-flat surfaces on which diverse simulacra are projected. Instead of 'Japanese cool', the super-flat choreographic architecture of the body becomes a two-dimensional masquerade.

It is useful to consider *kodomo shintai* in relation to the more popular image of *shojo*—teenage girls—though Sakurai very cautiously uses the gender-free word *kodomo*. The image of *shojo* is very difficult to either historicize or theorize, as it has been part of Japan's cultural sphere for such a long time and, accordingly, has come to possess a certain degree of normative power in its subject construction. It is obvious that the image of the *shojo* itself is a product of a phallocentric, if not a phallogocentric, imagination, at least by origin. But, over the years, the image has been circulated, romanticized, commodified, duplicated and so on to such a degree that it actually operates as a part of a wide range of fiction concerning modern Japanese female subjectivity.

The subject of this chapter is an investigation into how the flat-body *shojo* image has entered the field of contemporary dance and visual arts (in Murakami Takashi's work, among others) in recent years.

Two images by Murakami Takashi state my case visually. The first, from his older work (Figure 10, 1997) is a typically Murakamiesque gigantic 'figure' work in which the male fantasy of the *shojo* in the phallocentric *otaku* imagination acquires not only sexually charged exaggerations but, more importantly, a simultaneous three-dimensionality and a super-flat glossy quality.[3] Another, more recent, example is from an exhibition held in Tokyo between May and June 2004.[4] Sato Eriko, dubbed Satoeri, who became a famous young celebrity in recent years through her constant appearances on TV shows, poses for

FIGURE 10: HIROPON, 1997. OIL PAINT, ACRYLIC, FIBREGLASS AND IRON. 223.5 x 104 x 122 CM. COURTESY OF GALERIE EMMANUEL PERROTIN. © 1997 TAKASHI MURAKAMI/KAIKAI KIKI CO., LTD. ALL RIGHTS RESERVED.

Murakami's *shojo* figures. The poses in the series of five gigantically enlarged photographs (2004), in which Satoeri masquerades in various costumes, are taken from Murakami's previous figurative works. As far as Satoeri's body is concerned, therefore, no artificial or technical modification is made. In the exhibition, being held at a small downtown factory-turned-gallery space, there are two small figures by Mr BOME, Murakami's design collaborator, which are modestly exhibited in separate glass cases,[5] surrounded by the five large photographs of Satoeri. Murakami is theoretically interested in the reciprocal process of imagined figure-body without origin—reciprocal in that the two small figures are not from real life but from manga, another representational medium with indistinct origins. All we see are two tiny figures and five gigantic photographs. Our gaze is forced to wander between one and the other. Which is the original? Where is the original? Through this experience, Murakami presents the relationship between the original and the copy, illustrating the much-famed loss of originality and the unstoppable proliferation of simulacra in postmodernity. But more obviously, they can be read as a desire to contain the real-life body, the body per se, in two-dimensionality, to render its palpable fullness–roundness into/as flatness, in the name of visual art. The two figures in the centre of the room signify the origin of the photos; yet, compared to the photographed bodies, they are disproportionately small and timid. Satoeri's body actually exists as it is, breathing and moving 'out there', constituting an implied metaphoric relationship to the photographs. Surrounded by photographed bodies, the two figures seem to shrink, making them a twice-removed reminder of Satoeri's 'lived body', the body which we know, at least intellectually, is being lived by her.

It is ironic that the exaggerated *shojo* figure in the *otaku* imagination was finally 'found' or 'realized' in Satoeri's 'lived body' and that the body, caught as a photo-image, is at once threatening and comforting to the *otaku* imagination. This is because the 'lived body' appears forcibly flattened on the super-flat surface, on which the imaginary violence accompanying the transferring process is concealed or sealed. Nevertheless, the detectable violence of the aesthetic rendering that makes the exhibition itself possible can be read as marking a crucial moment when the *otaku* imagination finally has to confront the otherness of the other. As the *shojo* image is virtual, not real, in the *otaku* imagination, it represents the *otaku's* escapist desire to avoid the real—escapist, for what it actually wants is the real body. Remember that the *shojo* image was basically a simulacra. But in the photographed images of Satoeri, a series of *shojo* images is embodied by Satoeri, then captured and enlarged in the photographic prints. Through this process, the image of the *shojo*, the other without otherness, the disembodied vehicle of the otherness of the other, i.e. the otherness as lack, arguably undergoes a historically important transition, which makes us rethink Sakurai's *kodomo shintai* from a completely different perspective. Continuing in this theoretical vein, the bodies in the Yubiwa Hotel Theatre Company, for instance, have become more interesting for me than Sakurai's exemplary 'fashionable' and 'cool' dancing bodies-in-performance. Sakurai's theory is certainly useful in thinking about the simulacra of *shojo* images floating in the subcultural space of manga and the visual art space of Murakami's older work. Murakami's efforts at containing the 'lived body' in flat space resonates with the emerging tendencies of exploring the 'lived body' in Japan's performing culture. How then does Hitsujiya Shirotama, artistic director of Yubiwa Hotel, deal with the 'lived body' in her performance?

In the following section, I will explore this issue in relation to *Passion*, one of the more recent productions by Yubiwa Hotel, performed in March 2003 at the rooftop open-air tennis court in the heart of downtown Tokyo (Figures 11–13). The narrative very loosely follows a dramatic text (*Doru* [Doll], 1983) by the late Kisaragi Koharu (1956–2000). The performance was dedicated to the playwright who died quite unexpectedly in 2000. The text itself is the product of a 1980s' imagination and is considered a kind of manifesto for the 'fighting *shojo*'—an attempt to give voice to silenced female subjectivity, quite affirmatively vocalizing what Kisaragi, masquerading as *shojo*, feels and thinks through a narrative of mythic collective *shojo* suicides. In Hitsujiya's version, the production consisted of several unrelated scenes in which female performers, sometimes in male high-school students' uniforms and sometimes in female tennis wear, quoted—

FIGURES 11 (TOP LEFT), 12 (TOP RIGHT), 13 (BELOW, RIGHT).
PASSION BY YUBIWA HOTEL, INSPIRED BY KISARAGI
KOHARU'S TEXT, CONCEIVED AND DIRECTED BY HITSUJIYA
SHIROTAMA, PERFORMED AT THE ROOFTOP TENNIS COURT OF
ROSA BUILDING AT IKEBUKURO, TOKYO, MARCH 2003. IN
FIGURES 11 & 13, WE CAN SEE REAL HIGH SCHOOL FEMALE
STUDENTS IN THEIR UNIFORMS PARTICIPATING IN THE PER-
FORMANCE. © 2003 YUBIWA HOTEL. ALL RIGHTS RESERVED.
PHOTOGRAPHS COURTESY OF SAKIKO NOMURA.

rather than enacted—some of the lines from the original text. The scenes are a loosely structured series of Hitsujiya's impressionistic, both literal and visual, interpretations of the original text.

POSTHUMANIST VERSION OF THE BODY?

In her well-known theorization of performance, Peggy Phelan reminded us of 'the hysteric body' as theorized by Ishimitsu Yasuo:

> Performance uses the performer's body to pose a question about the inability to secure the relation between subjectivity and the body *per se*; performance uses the body to frame the lack of Being promised by and through the body, that which cannot appear without a supplement (1993: 150–1).

In Yubiwa Hotel's performance, 'the inability to secure the relation between subjectivity and the body *per se*' was a given sociocultural condition rather than a psychoanalytic determination. The sense of 'lack of Being' became one of the issues that the performers, consciously or unconsciously, dealt with. Here, both the notion of *kodomo shintai* and the image of the *shojo* came into play as their performing bodies, aspiring to become the image of *shojo* itself, always failed. In *Passion*, what clarified Hitsujiya's rather ill-articulated—some see it as too ambiguous, if not downright dubious—political project was the introduction of 'real' female high-school students in school uniforms into the performance. The diverse kinds of 'junk-bodyness'—so removed from the Satoeri-like, romanticized, mediatized super-flat body—of the students' bodies were unexpectedly highlighted as none of them was asked to act in a traditional *shojo*-like manner, something in direct contrast to the performers' use of diverse costumes and continuous masquerading. The lack of modern subjectivity 'promised by and through' the students' 'real' junk bodies intervened in the process of the performers' endless and unachievable project of becoming the image of the *shojo*. By and through the masquerading, the audience was made aware of the discrepancy between the *shojo* image that the performers tried in vain to embody and a different kind of junk-body-ness—aesthetically undesirable physicality—that they nevertheless inscribed onto the performance space. Modernity's project of transforming the 'lived body' into an aesthetic metaphor is not only made visible in its failure in Yubiwa Hotel's performers' bodies, but another project of modernity—'how to visualize the body, excluded from the discourse, but visibly remaining in the periphery' (Ishimitsu 2000: 14–15)—seems to be, somewhat surprisingly, reactivated in a post-modern context. Hitsujiya is more interested in the failure of the metaphorical process than in its success. The performers, as a result, can only be said to be performing 'themselves' in their failure to embody the *shojo* image. In the end, we never really know who they are apart from their failed embodiment.

Especially noteworthy in this regard is the fact that in the performance, even though she uses a dramatic text, Hitsujiya does not seem to have found a way to stage the text by enacting its written characters. In Hitsujiya's production, the lines of the play are merely spoken by some of the performers and none of them sufficiently enacts any character in the text, thereby making it impossible to make the body exclusively serve the language. Through this distancing device—the performers sometimes make unconscious comments using their physical appearance to distance themselves from the original narrative—the relationship between the body and the language is reversed: as the *Passion* performers enact only 'themselves', not the characters of the play and the language they speak is quoted, not 'lived' as in orthodox theatre.

The way in which Yubiwa Hotel's production of *Passion* inscribes the *shojo* image poses an important question: why are they performing 'themselves' in vain? The socio-psychological explanation I have given earlier—that Japan's social reality is dominated by a neo-liberal philosophy—may answer this question[6] for some of us. But I am more inclined to look at the effects of the performing group's sense of failure, flatness, discrepancy, inadequacy and a certain degree of vulnerability. In short, 'junkness'. The performing bodies are neither 'the body as text' nor 'the body as metaphor', to use Ishimitsu's categorization. Through diverse technologies of performance, Hitsujiya seems to intuitively make a positive gesture towards the cyborgian nature of postmodern female subjectivity's 'lived body'—the body as it is lived by its owner, which can only be perceived as coexistence of body parts. Is this only another version of 'the metaphorical body', 'the body as representation'? Or is this a much celebrated, at least theoretically, posthumanist version of the body, the body as surface, for instance? Ishimitsu's statement that 'the drama of repression and realization of desire can only be performed through a struggle with language' (ibid.: 30) does not describe what is happening here. Rather, Yubiwa Hotel members perform the failure of their search for language, or languages, and to perform 'themselves'. For this company, 'the drama of repression and realization of desire' no longer takes place. Whatever the conclusion we may arrive at, given the constraints of space, we must now leave behind the discussion of the ontological status of the collectively constructed image of *shojo* in order to look at a performance in which the relationship between everyday language and body-in-performance is a reflexive experiment.

CHELFITSCH AND ITS *FIVE DAYS IN MARCH*

In terms of theatre history, the experiments of Okada Toshiki of Chelfitsch Theatre Company in recent years can be defined as an attempt to synthesize Hirata Oriza's Quiet Theatre[7] and contemporary dance genres with *kodomo shintai*.

The story of Okada's (2005) *Sangatsu no Itsukakan* (*Five Days in March*, 2004; Figures 14–16) is very simple: in March 2003, just when the US is starting its war in Iraq, a young couple is having sex for four consecutive nights at a love hotel (a Japanese institution made expressively for sexual trysts) in Shibuya. The story unfolds through a very complex narrative structure and all the characters/performers speak in the most contemporary colloquial Japanese, though there is no improvisation either of language or of movement. The prescribed text and movements were found during rehearsals and then set. Here is the beginning of the text:

No set.

Male Actor 1 and Male Actor 2 enter . They are standing together.

MALE ACTOR 1 (*to audience*). OK, I think we should start *Five Days in March* the first day, first of all this is set in March last year, I think that is what we think we are going to do, waking up in the morning this is the story of the man Minobe, it was a

FIGURES 14 (LEFT), 15 (TOP), 16 (BELOW): *FIVE DAYS IN MARCH* BY CHELFITSCH, WRITTEN AND DIRECTED BY OKADA TOSHIKI, PERFORMED IN SPHERE MEX THEATRE AT TENNOZU, TOKYO, MARCH 2004. PHOTOGRAPHS COURTESY OF KATAOKA YOTA.

hotel when waking up why am I in the hotel he thought, and who is this girl sleeping next to me, I don't know, I don't know why but she is sleeping—that kind of story—but he soon remembers, 'Oh, I remember last night, I remember last night I kinda got drunk, this is a Loveho [love hotel] in Shibuya' he soon started to remember.

MALE ACTOR 1: And I am going to tell you the story of what the real first day was like, 'Oh, I was in Roppongi last night,' ughh, in Roppongi, last March, and Roppongi Hills was not there yet, and the story is before it was built, that's where I am starting the story, right, now the Roppongi Station, we walk up to the ground after getting off the subway, and when we walk up, we go down the slope heading for Azabu, where Roppongi Hills now stands there is something, not quite a crossover, we have to go up and down to get towards the Nishi Azabu crossing now, but about a year ago we could walk straight, and the story I am going to tell is, at that time, there was something like a live house [the name of a Japanese institution for live music, mainly for young kids]. I am going to start the story when he went to see the live performance, and, it was a very good one, that is what I am going to tell, and yes, and, he met a girl at the place and they had sex instantly and without a condom, this kind of story I am going to tell from now, but before all that, ughh, when he went to the live house on the first day of five days in March, two went there together, a male and a male (*vaguely pointing to himself and to Actor 2*), to see the live performance, ughh, let's go to Roppongi, there were two males thinking so and I start the story by telling about those two males (I think) (ibid.: 27–8).

Through this stream-of-consciousness speech, or a literal transcription of how 'we'—that is, Okada's contemporaries—speak, Actor 1 declares several times during this first speech that 'I have a story to tell'. In the subsequent 10 scenes, the story of the loser (Minobe), an exemplary male youth in globalized Japan, is told within a very complex structure in which narration and first-person dialogue are intentionally mixed-up. The narrative is almost never enacted by the performers in a 'realistic' way: one of them speaks his lines standing in an awkward pose and jerking his body; another speaks with dance-like movements; yet another, putting his hands on a stool, very slowly collapses to the floor without any psychological motivation.

This rupture between language and body is the physical reality that each performer brings to the performance. The performers try to speak the lines 'naturally', not according to modern realist theatrical convention but according to their own physical realities, i.e. according to their 'lived body' sensibilities they experience in everyday life. This sense of spontaneity set against the sense of a construct is found and then restored during the rehearsals. Thus, inevitably, their movements are 'twice-behaved' behaviours[8] in actual performances, at least at a theoretical level. Nevertheless, it is interesting to note that a displacing process of the 'lived body' onto 'the external body', the body as image, is not only made visible through their performance but also triggered off by the particular kind of language they have agreed to speak—a language given from outside. Theoretically speaking, we can grasp Okada's use of language by expanding Hirata Oriza's colloquialism (see NOTE 8), but Okada does not limit what comes from his performers' bodies into the unified and coherent boundaries of the characters' bodies. He does not define the performer's body as 'commentary to action and language' (Bakhtin, quoted in Ishimitsu 2000: 15). This, perhaps unintended, display of a rupture between language and body in Hirata's work is exactly what Okada is interested in exploring.[9]

What, then, is Okada inscribing into his performance space? Is it, again, modernity's project of 'how to visualize the body, excluded from discourse, but visibly remaining in the periphery'? Yes and no. While in Yubiwa Hotel's performance, 'the drama of repression and realization of desire can only be performed through the struggle with language,' there is no such struggle made visible in Okada's performance (in ibid.: 30); instead, rupture is everything, making Okada's theatrical use of the body not metaphorical but metonymic to the 'lived body'. Not an aesthetic translation but a performative reconfiguration of the 'lived body'. Perhaps, then, the sense of the plurality of the performing body that we witness in his work is symptomatic of a drastic paradigm shift, displaying the performing body that is occurring under the domination of Japan's neo-liberal economic–social–political reality.

Five Days in March is quite intentionally set in March 2003 at the start of the American-led war in Iraq. Considered against the proliferation of anti-US campaigns in the mass media, in street demonstrations and leftist (read neo-nationalist) theatre practices in Japan, where a reductionist notion of 'evil' versus 'good' inevitably prevailed (some argue that we had regressed to the Middle Ages), Okada's sense of politics is simply more nuanced and postmodern.

There is a scene in which two of the characters reluctantly and somewhat accidentally participate in an anti-US demonstration in Shibuya. Though the scene is not an overt re-enactment of the experience, it is obvious that Okada cannot fully validate the idea of the demonstration as a political option. He does not criticize street demonstrators but perceives an unbridgeable gap—not a gap rendered by postmodern political scepticism but, rather, a gap that has grown from sincere desperation. Do we really know what we think we know? How can we know anything at all apart from the matrix of the neo-liberal economic powers? What about the true losers, those of us who are not able to participate in the morality play of the Middle Ages? Okada seems to point out that we must begin looking at what is happening to our private selves, to our bodies and our languages; we should not explore new aesthetics for their commodity value but to find ways to validate politics in the context of a vacantly apolitical performance culture.

Notes

1 In reading any of Murakami Takashi's writings, his ideological naivety should be obvious, especially in the context of so-called 'petit-national sentiment' which came to be problematized in a wider discursive space towards the end of the 1990s. Sakurai's (2004) ideological positioning is manifest, though subtly, in his serial perform-

ance reviews in *Butai Geijutu* (*Performing Arts Magazine*, published three times a year since 2001, by Kyoto University of Arts and Design). His notion of *kodomo* itself is formulated against a strategically simplified version of the West as adult, grown-up.

2 The notion of junk here refers to a complex set of sensibilities, not meanings, that artists try to embody in their work.

3 For a recent history of contemporary visual art practices, see the bilingual catalogue for *Little Boy: The Arts of Japan's Exploding Subculture* (Murakami 2005). According to Murakami, *otaku* is 'literally "your home"; obsessed fans, primarily of anime and manga' (ibid.: xiv). The term refers to the fact that these fans, mostly boys and young male adults, were calling each other *otaku*; in colloquial usage, it is sometimes used as the pronoun 'you'. The notion became popular towards the end of the 1980s and loosely parallels the notion of the 'nerd' in English: 'A person who is single-minded or accomplished in scientific or technical pursuits but is felt to be socially inept' (*The American Heritage Dictionary of the English Language*, 2000). But in the case of the *otaku*, it is not necessarily scientific or technical pursuits that they are after but mainly anime and manga. *Otaku*, in Japan, is usually derogatory in its connotations.

4 The exhibition was titled 'Satoeri Ko2Chan' (Miss Ko2-Satoeri) and was held at Koyama Tomio Gallery, Tokyo, between 24 May and 16 June 2004. I intended to publish one of the photos here but, according to Kobayashi Nozomi, a representative in Murakami's office, Satoeri is such a huge celebrity that obtaining copyright permission is very complicated; I was advised not to pursue it. I refer instead to the website www.tomiokoyamagallery.com/kako_show/040524.html (accessed 10 October 2005).

5 Ko2Chan is the name originally given to the figurative work created by Murakami in collaboration with Mr BOME.

6 In recent theorizations of subject construction in Japan, a malfunctioning of the disciplinary system is emphasized. In other words, critics observe that the notion of disciplinary power, as analysed in Foucault's earlier writings, is on the decline, as Japan's neo-liberal sovereignty has lost interest in disciplining its subjects through family and school systems. Its subjects are expected to discipline themselves, if they want to be a part of the system which, not surprisingly, has resulted in the proliferation of junk bodies—undisciplined bodies—both in everyday life and in performance cultures.

7　Hirata Oriza and his Seinendan (Theatre Company) was founded in 1983. In the 1990s, Hirata turned to what he calls 'contemporary colloquial theatre', in which he gets rid of almost all theatrical and dramatic elements in the production while actors speak 'naturally', as they do in everyday life. His theatre was dubbed 'Quiet Theatre' by critics. See Introduction, Chapter 2, NOTE 3 and Chapter 3 in this volume for further information on Hirata and Quiet Theatre.

8　I refer to Richard Schechner's famous conceptualization.

9　In Hirata's earlier works, actors who were not yet used to his methodology had a difficult time 'not acting' and getting rid of all exaggerated movements and gestures. They were asked to speak and move 'naturally' but became so tense in their attempt 'not to act' that, in conflict with Hirata's intention, they seemed to be trembling. I am referring here to this phenomenon. Okada, on the other hand, lets actors move as they wish, not limiting their gestures and movements to 'non-acting'.

THEATRE AFTER THE ATTACK ON IRAQ: INTELLIGENCE IN ORDER TO AVOID REVENGE

Right after 9/11, one of the most oft-repeated phrases in Japan was 'it's as if we were watching a Hollywood movie.' The phrase suggests the distance that people living in Japan are disciplined to sense towards what is happening on the TV screen. While Slavoj Žižek wrote, somewhat ecstatically, 'Welcome to the Desert of the Real!' right after 9/11 (see Žižek 2002), Japan's mainstream perception of the same incident was the virtual one; the kind that was easily incorporated into an ever-permeating narrative of the national border as something that secures physical and symbolical closure; a closure that Japan as a nation-state had been and is still enjoying, culturally and economically. This particular violent incident, witnessed on their TV screens, had, for many of the people living in Japan, nothing to do with their daily lives. Even though about 30 Japanese nationals had been killed in that same incident, as far as the average citizen was concerned it was no more than one of those unfortunate accidents that tend to happen at any time and at any place. Thus, after a short-lived media hype, a familiar sense of amnesia took over and various forms of cynicism followed, except, perhaps, within more intellectually sensitive discursive quarters.

Therefore, it is no wonder that within what I call a J-theatre continuum, 9/11 was never an issue—except on some occasions where the spectacular image of the collapsing Twin Towers was used as a metaphor for the collapse of the Japanese regime of economic prosperity after 1991, and its supposedly direct outcome in the increase of crime rates and of the numbers of suicide.

The cultural climate, at least in Japan's theatre scene, did begin to change after America's military action in Afghanistan, followed by its incoherent accusations against Iraq. Completely coincidentally, this change in the cultural climate was accompanied by a rising tension between Japan and North Korea (covered extensively in the media) which came to a head with the attack on Iraq by America and its allies (mainly the UK). Interestingly, however, the protest against the US aggression assumed only a very traditional form: street demonstrations and public rallies at some places in Tokyo. Mainstream theatre practitioners gathered in an auditorium and adopted 'An Oath of De-war' (not anti-war, but 'de' as it connotes an absolute denial of any mindset related to war), unconsciously admitting that what was happening was a traditional war, the antithesis of which was peace. In the face of the dichotomoy inherent in liberalist-humanist views, it is difficult to know where mainstream theatre practitioners situate their work, i.e. how they continue to create theatre within such direct political concerns.

As Japan is distantly implicated in the attack on Iraq—although this distance itself is an extension of a huge mass delusion, as I have mentioned earlier—mainstream theatre practitioners acted accordingly and participated in a subdued form of traditional anti-war campaigns in which the notion of peace was heralded as sublime and undebatably good. There was no exploration of the politics of their own work nor did they produce any significant work that resonated with the issues raised in their de-war rallies.

Unakami Hiromi described this attitude as 'theatre-centrism', in which the value of theatre as cultural and political currency in a liberalist-humanist tradition (in Japan, usually referred to as post-War democracy) is thrown seriously into doubt (see Unakami 2002). Accordingly, those theatre-centrists, in a seemingly humble manner, continue to make theatre, with historically and culturally defined methods and content (with a few predictable transgressions and variations) and without ever betraying the expectations of their mainly middle-class audience. Their social and public responsibilities are thus thought to be fulfilled by organizing protest rallies in a theatre space, rather than by confronting critical issues in theatrical terms; as if to say that all theatre can do in a late-capitalist society is entertain its ticket-buying audience.

Theatre, therefore, has become more pronounced in its insistence on being the site for escape from the complexities of the world; a site in which audiences can immerse themselves in their nostalgia for simplicity and communicative instantaneity. Even if they are watching a play that tackles the Iraq issue, the dominant frame of mind in Japan is incredibly obviously informed by the traditional narrative of the war-or-peace dichotomy, fuelled in turn by the universalizing impulse to make the productions safely detached from reality. Those who would like the theatre to be a cultural forum for debate, where progressive and interventionist actions and ideas can be contemplated and/or enacted, experience great difficulty even in staging a simple discussion of current issues in their work. This tendency—a kind of cynical aestheticism—is growing fairly powerful because Japanese cultural nostalgia goes hand in hand with the political nostalgia for Japan as a nation-state of closure in the post-9/11 days. 9/11 reaffirms the imagined closure of Japan to outside influences, an imaginary which, nevertheless, has led to absorbing cynicism. At the same time, there is a sense of crisis within select J-theatre practices and, during the attack on Iraq, we finally began to see some theatrical attempts at confronting and analysing the complexity of the post-9/11 New World order.

That one such attempt was by Noda Hideki, one of the most popular theatre practitioners today, raises some important issues. One of Noda's most recent works, produced during the attack on Iraq, was *Oil*. The word 'oil' in the title has a double meaning: oil in English and *oiru*, to grow old, in Japanese. *Oil* has a typical Noda Hideki setting, where the ancient and the modern, the East and the Middle East (in this work) magically, theatrically and half-jokingly meet. The ancient 'here' is inhabited by people, not of Japanese ancestral ethnicity but of a minority group (mentioned in some classical myths; their image is doubled with people in the deserts of the Middle East). In the play, they do not have a sense of time and thus do not understand the notion of getting old. They will be taught about growing old by Japanese ancestors (usually referred to as the *Yamato* race), during the course of the play, through a process of ethnic cleansing and nation-building. The modern 'here', on the other hand, is towards the end of World War II, when America is about to drop an atomic bomb on Hiroshima.

The audience come to know, towards the end of the play, that the whole theatrical landscape they have been witnessing is in fact a desperate fantasy imagined by a young woman named Fuji who can, in her imagination, live in both the ancient and the modern worlds because of her mystical power as a prophet. She received these powers through the tragic experience of her younger brother, a runaway *kamikaze* (suicide) pilot, who was killed at Hiroshima and thus deprived of the opportunity to live in post-War prosperity. Noda seems to be critiquing not only US racist violence but also the post-War Japanese people who seem to forget (and forgive) the past so easily. The character Fuji asks the audience 'How can you forget the past?' and, at a crucial moment in the play, she demands revenge. Fuji imagines her brother and his friend flying two Zero fighter planes into the Twin Towers in retaliation for the bombing of Hiroshima and Nagasaki. Here, the ancient, the recent past and the contemporary (and very remotely, the East, the Middle East and the US) all come together in the phantasmagoric imagining of Fuji, and the audience members are invited to acknowledge that Noda is asking them to think through the current chain of retributions outside Japan as their own. Noda's is not necessarily a universalizing project but, rather, a pointing towards different and alternative ways, at least for those living in Japan, to respond to the post-9/11 world.

Sato Makoto, one of the exponents of the Underground Theatre Movement during 1968 and in the post-1968 era, with the Black Tent Theatre Company, produced *An Absolute Plane* (2002) in which he directly tackled the issue of 9/11 by making Mohammed Atta one of the main characters in his play. But the work was not an attempt at re-narrativizing Atta's now-well-known pre-story, so to speak, but to present a site for Sato's very personal response to Atta's action as a terrorist. At the beginning of the play, Atta is almost clashing into one of the Twin Towers when his eyes accidentally meet the eyes of a female worker in the tower; she is drinking coffee at the moment of the attack. Time freezes. They exchange words, fragments of unrelated stories are enacted by various characters—as if these episodes and images rushed through Atta's mind at the time of the attack. Some references are naturally made to a few mediatized episodes about Atta in Germany and elsewhere but they are divided and connected by Brechtian songs and have no direct connection with 9/11; rather, they all seem to be concerned with notions of flying, travelling, wandering and moving in both mythical and secular senses. There is a story about a woman and her brother living in a waiting room for third-class passengers at the Central Station, whose mother has committed suicide by swallowing diamonds; there is a scene between a street vendor, a traveller and an old man collecting small stones on the street; another, between ancient and mythic birds—between an owl, a thrush, a humming bird, a swallow and a parrot. What these fragments succeed in doing is to very remotely suggest something of the ancient, the Islamic, the mythic and the European with which Atta may have had subconscious or unconscious ties.

Sato is interested in the consciousness of the terrorist which he explores through a wide variety of irrelevant and fragmented stories and images. The work is neither an accusation nor a rational explanation as to why Atta did what he did but, rather, is a theatrical intervention into Atta's mind via the working of an artist's imagination. At the end of the play, Sato lets the female office-worker speak in a stream-of-consciousness manner to Atta:

> I won't hate you/ You are a solider even if you are an enemy
> soldier I will not hate you as I am not a soldier I will accept
> you I don't want to make a mistake I don't make a mistake/You
> made a mistake/ It is simply so and nothing more (2002: n.p.).

Through these two obvious examples I have tried to show how some of Japan's theatre practitioners are responding to the sense of crisis after 9/11 and the attack on Iraq. At least in these works, theatre practitioners are using their theatre-centrist's resources in providing the audience with alternative ways of looking at the current issues that are mostly excluded from the theatre space.

But what about the title of this interlude? What form of intelligence is necessary to avoid revenge and cut short the chain of retribution? This particular phrase, as I understand it, comes from the words of Noda Hideki. In one of the interviews concerning his work, particularly the most recent *Oil*, Noda says to Ootori Hidenaga that he still trusts the ability of people to think through a situation before embarking on an act of revenge, while admitting, at the same time, that this notion and the hope it generates is a little old fashioned (see Noda 2003). Old fashioned or not, Noda is referring to the very problem with which we are confronted today—the death, or at least the declining power, of the project of enlightenment.

In his film, *Minority Report* (2002), Hollywood director Steven Spielberg asks, rather desperately, and by an intriguing coincidence, the same question. In this dark film about a futuristic society of surveillance, Spielberg saves the modern project of enlightenment at the very last minute in the film by letting the villain make a choice. Instead of killing the hero, as is predicted by the usually accurate precogs, the villain kills himself. However premeditated the fate of all the inhabitants of this society of terror, something happens at the moment of the act of killing: they can still make a choice rather than being emotionally driven to the act of violence. But can we believe this? Isn't Spielberg's very trust of so-called humanity not only 'a little old fashioned' but also reactionary, as his trust in human intelligence is the very idea that the liberalist-humanists want to hear?

These questions open up a wide range of issues, relating the role of theatre to globality. Can we call liberalist humanism's project of enlightenment reactionary and/or neo-colonial? Without sinking into postmodern cynicism, without imprisoning oneself in the safe closure of cultural relativism and without being trapped in theatre-centrists' arrogance? Admitting that the universalist (or its updated version, new cosmopolitanism) positioning is impossible, what is required for us at the moment is what Rustom Bharucha calls 'cross-border imaginary of resistance':

> To juxtapose imaginatively, and with artistic rigour, the violence of terrorism against the continued brutality of the civilized world, we may need more than a new dramaturgy or performativity. We need a new cross-border imaginary of resistance. Out of its inner necessities, perhaps, we may yet be

able to reclaim chaos as a dissident creative principle in embracing—and betraying—the terror of our times. The task today is not to fight terrorism with counter-terrorism, but to counter counter-terrorism with irreverence and critically renewed internationalist vigilance (2003: n.p.).

TRACING THEORIES: IMPERIALISM, CAPITALISM AND GLOBALIZATION

The call for action seems inescapable. The world is, to use Samuel Beckett's phrase, turning 'Worstward, Ho!' This is no time for writing a theory, making theatre or, worse still, talking of theatre which is what we are doing right now. Or are we not? 'Act, no matter what!' some say, though many dismiss the call as no more than an inner cry from a morally hurt bourgeois conscience. Žižek, on the other hand, in *Iraq: The Borrowed Kettle* (2004), tells us not to act. There is no easy way out; there is no ideological alterity for action available. The only thing we can do is to keep thinking.

In fact, the world we are looking at today seems so complex that we are intimidated by its grotesque complexity and are tempted to act in immediate (read heavily mediatized) contexts, often falling prey to an open-mouthed reductionism, the kind that insists that America is the bad guy and we should punish it by, for instance, following the melodramatic dramaturgy and/or becoming—or perceiving ourselves as—actors in a mediaeval morality play. Žižek's warning, of course, is against this kind of reductionism, but where is the theory we can use to start thinking about all of this in the first place? Žižek, unfortunately, does not answer this question, though, as usual, he is critical of everything. Are we to return to abandoned notions of liberalist-humanist-universalistic terms such as 'responsibility', 'justice' or 'freedom'? History says we cannot, as those terms have been hijacked quite severely by neo-liberalists and neo-conservatives for their own self-centred purposes. Accordingly, most humanist terms of value are so heavily appropriated and relativized that some activists even admit that now is the most difficult time. As Arundhati Roy writes in *Power Politics*: 'What is happening to our world is almost too colossal for human comprehension to contain. But it is a terrible, terrible thing.

To contemplate its girth and circumference, to attempt to define it, to try and fight it all at once, is impossible. The only way to fight it is by fighting specific wars in specific ways' (2002: 86). Although I would like to agree with her, I would also like to argue that we should not lose sight of the larger picture, however vague it may be, however politically ambiguous it sounds. This is where theory, or in Žižek's term, 'thinking', comes into play and some leftist intellectuals, such as David Harvey and others, as well as Žižek himself, are starting to give us some appropriate analyses and starting points so that we may think for ourselves before engaging in 'specific wars in specific ways'.

In this vein, Harvey's *The New Imperialism* (2003) is useful, if not illuminating. More descriptive and analytical than philosophical and theoretical, Harvey's writing is clearly targeted at what is happening to the world right now, including the American invasion of Iraq and subsequent events. But the main issue in the book is to articulate imperialism as an ideological and political manifestation of capitalism's desire to accumulate capital, from a larger historical perspective, and its transformation through modernity and postmodernity vis-à-vis various kinds of imperialist projects of power and domination. According to Harvey, there are two distinctive logics at work in the process: the territorial logic of power and the capitalist logic of power, and it is crucial, especially now, for us to see the difference:

> The fundamental point is to see the territorial and the capitalist logics of power as distinct from each other. Yet it is also undeniable that the two logics intertwine in complex and sometimes contradictory ways. The literature on imperialism and empire too often assumes an easy accord between them: that political economic processes are guided by strategies of state and empire and that states and empires always operate out of capitalistic motivations (ibid.: 29).

In this way, Hardt and Negri's much-contested notion of 'Empire' without any articles ('a' or 'the') attached to the word Empire with a capital E, and the notion of 'the multitude', is subtly rewritten and updated by Harvey. Thus, according to Harvey, from 1973 until 2000, the territorial logic of power receded while the capitalist logic of power grew stronger, crossing national borders and resorting to the methodological ideology of what he calls 'accumulation (of capital) by dispossession', thus creating various dispossessed classes of people around the globe, even in so-called 'advanced' or 'developmental' states. National borders are easily violated by capitalism's renewed neo-liberal projects while invisible borders are erected everywhere, intra-nationally and internationally.

This is globalization. The emergence of invisible classes of the dispossessed gives rise to various types of anti-globalization movements. Advocates and practitioners of neo-conservatism in the US, namely the current [at the time of writing] Bush administration, are not necessarily operating under the capitalist logic of power but more in accord with the territorial logic of power, making the US operate like an old type of empire (Harvey compares current America with the turn-of-the-century British Empire).

What we need to question today is how we are to go about resisting these two distinctive logics of power—the territorial and the capitalist—operating simultaneously. It is obviously easier to say 'no' to the older type of empire, comparable to the US today; accordingly, we have been witnessing much resistance from all quarters of the globe, including in the US itself. The coming elections may bring a halt, if not an end, to this doubly reactionary imperialistic regime. But it is tougher and trickier for us to resist the capitalist logic of power that is omnipresent around the globe and, as Hardt and Negri admit, there is no outside to this logic. It is the question of whether we can bring ourselves to say 'no' to capitalism. If so, how? That is why a confessed Marxian like Žižek says we have to think, rather than act, as we have either nationalism or religious fundamentalism as tangible and viable alternatives (and not only in the Arab countries; the US too is driven by Christian fundamentalism). That is exactly why Roy, whom I quoted earlier, says we can only fight 'specific wars in specific ways'.

On the other hand, Harvey calls for a seemingly realistic, and thus temporary, solution:

The only possible, albeit temporary, answer to this problem within the rules of any capitalistic mode of production is some sort of new 'New Deal' that has a global reach. This means liberating the logic of capital circulation and accumulation from its neo-liberal chains, reformulating state power along much more interventionist and redistributive lines, curbing the speculative powers of finance capital, and decentralizing or democratically controlling the overwhelming power of oligopolies and monopolies . . . to dictate everything from terms of international trade to what we see, read and hear in the media. The effect will be a return to a more benevolent 'New Deal' imperialism, preferably arrived at through the sort of coalition of capitalist powers that Kautsky long ago envisioned (2003: 209).

He admits this proposal has its negative sides, but he also argues that the 'construction of a "New Deal" led by the United States and Europe' may just 'assuage the problems of overaccumulation for at least a few years' (ibid.: 210) and that at 'the real battleground where this has to be fought out' is 'within the United States' (ibid.: 211).

Harvey does ask for help, at the end of the book, for such a battle to be fought. I say so because what he proposes here, however, is very unlikely to happen: an overnight revolution, violent or not, subverting what the US stands for or has stood for for the last 30 years. Harvey's realistic solution is, in short, too utopian. Is it not more realistic to think that this battlefield within the US will inevitably be lost and things will get even worse?

If so, how about proposing a new form of cosmopolitanism and a new kind of imagined but not-necessarily territorially defined civil society? This line of thinking may lead to what Ootori Hidenaga describes as 're-imagining the boundary'.[1] Does this, then, also sound too utopian? Žižek would definitely say yes, as the liberalist-humanist tradition, according to modern and postmodern history, has only been operating to prolong the life of capitalism, secretly aligning itself to and/or being co-opted to accommodate both the territorial and the capitalist logics of power. If, however, the capitalist logic of power works both internationally and intra-nationally, is it not obvious that a certain form of international and intra-national form of resistance should be imagined?

When Bharucha calls for a new cultural front of internationalist resistance, he seems to speak to us about that imagined cultural front to resist against two logics of power at hand (see Bharucha 2003). In other words, we should fight our specific wars in our specific ways but the specificity should be defined by thinking and acting both locally and globally. Or, to put it yet another way, the specificity should be defined by going against imperialism's territorial logic of power and its capitalist logic of power. Imagined cultural spheres may be able to become sites in which we can tackle the impossibly intertwined problem of how we can translate this kind of thinking into real and efficacious action.

Note

1 This is the overall title of the theatre festival Ootori curated for Laokoon Festival at Kampnagel in Hamburg, Germany, in 2004. The full title was 'Re-imagining the Boundary: Transnational, Intranational'.

The purpose of this chapter is to draw a cognitive map of what is happening in Japan's theatre culture at present. For the July 2005 issue of the literary magazine *Eureka*, in which 'Little Theatre' was the main feature, I was asked to supervise the structure of the issue and I decided to present a map in which I would select 40 theatre companies (or 'units', as they are often called now), individuals and dance companies. As English-language readers do not necessarily share historical, cultural and/or political contexts with readers of *Eureka*, I would like to use the map a little differently and show the range of Japan's contemporary theatre culture as I see it now. I am not going to refer to all the 40 companies I have included in the map, but I will discuss some representative groups and individuals for the sake of readers who are not at all familiar with any of the 40 entries I chose.

This map assumes that what I am going to say is only in terms of how I see what is happening and that there is no theoretical reason, for instance, for the chosen number of groups. Japan's theatre culture is now so manifold and compartmentalized that nobody can really have a unified image of the field. I was interested in the diversity of performance that we see every day in Tokyo, and 40 was the number required to give the map a certain degree of validity and reflect my understanding of Japan's contemporary theatre culture. In addition, I deliberately chose to highlight the younger generation of practitioners, most of whom were born after the 1970s. I thought that this choice would enable me to cast a certain light on the future of Japan's theatre culture. For the sake of greater clarity, I have decided to add three more entries, all belonging to an older generation of theatremakers who are still active in the contemporary scene.

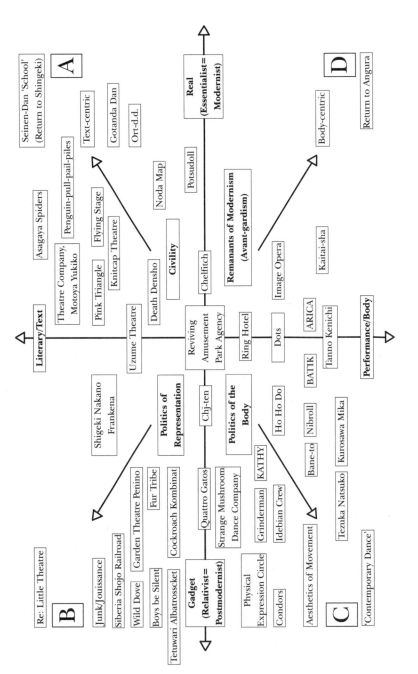

A MAP OF 'J' THEATRE

MAPPING/ZAPPING 'J' THEATRE

The map is divided by vertical and horizontal axes and I have named the four sections divided by those axes as follows: Plane A (top right), Plane B (top left), Plane C (bottom left) and Plane D (bottom right). For the vertical axis, I have put 'Literary/Text' at the top and 'Performance/ Body' below. This means that by going towards the top of the axis, you will see the stronger presence of 'literary' and 'textual' influences in the performances of those designated at a particular place on the map. On the other hand, stronger elements of 'performance' and/or 'body' come into play towards the lower part of the same axis.

For the horizontal axis, I have put 'Real (Essentialist=Modern)' towards the right vector and 'Gadget (Relativist=Postmodern)' towards the left. I chose the word 'real' because, in Japan's contemporary theatre vocabulary, the notion of 'real' as opposed to 'fictional' and/or 'fantastic' is supposed to have a positive value. The notion of 'real' as it is currently constituted in Japan also has some resonances with notions of 'faithful', 'sincere' or 'authentic'. It also relates to an ideology of 'essentialism'—when, for instance, the transparency of representation, of the literary text, or of the performer's body, is firmly believed in in performances as belonging to these planes (Planes A and D). Here, the notion of 'originality' is still key to the practitioners.

Moving towards the left on the horizontal axis, the sense of 'gadget' becomes stronger: 'gadget' refers to the postmodern sensibilities of 'playing', 'borrowing', 'masquerading', 'quoting' and 'self-reflexivity'. According to practitioners belonging to Planes B and C, there is nothing new anymore; all that remains is the question of how to arrange and combine already known performative elements. Both the notions of 'originality' and 'essence' are obsolete for them. Hence, my putting the word 'relativist' in opposition to 'essentialist'.

PLANE A: THE 'SEINEN-DAN SCHOOL', OR THE RETURN TO SHINGEKI

In terms of the number of events and market share, most of Japan's contemporary theatre practices belong to this plane, and this is where a traditional dialogue-oriented theatrical performance style dominates. For groups clustered around Plane A, the origin of performance is a dramatic text in which characters enact their stories; thus, we see characters as a linguistic construction. Actors are expected to represent, as faithfully as possible, already-always-written characters in the play. In most cases, the transparency of representation is assumed and characters are supposed to have a unified psychology, i.e. a rational interiority is assumed in their mode of presentation. This is representational theatre, where the modernist myth of 'humanity' is still operating and—ranging from big commercial theatres to the New National Theatre—most performances in Tokyo belong to this category. The recent developments in theatres along this plane are twofold: a modern-realist theatrical revival—the 'Seinen-dan School'—and 'the return to Shingeki'. Although somewhat updated in the 1990s, this category of theatre dominates the Japanese scene. Seinen-dan's plays, coined 'contemporary colloquial theatre' by writer-director Hirata Oriza and journalistically called Quiet Theatre, are most typical of this genre and have been very influential.

A trend for formerly marginal and innovative works to become mainstream is also evident. Artists associated with the the 'Little Theatre boom' of the 1980s, like Noda Hideki, are now in their 50s and, with a few exceptions (such as Kawamura Takeshi and Miyazawa Akio), their performances can be considered to belong to this plane. Although works by these artists are not in the style of modern realistic theatre (along with Noda, we can include Keralino Sandrovitch and Matsuo Suzuki), they nevertheless exemplify an essentially text-oriented play of characters, albeit with some physicality involved.

Second on Plane A, I chose the word 'civility'. This reflects the fact that most of the younger generation of theatre practitioners now show a sincere concern for society—however strange that may sound. Noda Hideki, for example, was known for his fantastic and playful Little Theatre extravaganzas up to 1990. Since then, however, he has been taking-up so-called 'national themes' in his work such as the war on Iraq, Japan's emperor system and the bombing of Hiroshima and Nagasaki. Even in the field of sexual politics, which is hardly manifested and/or debated in the public domain, there are now at least two sexually identifiable theatre companies: Pink Triangle and Flying

Stage. The former explores the issue of lesbian identity and the latter of male homosexuality.

PLANE B: RE: LITTLE THEATRE

Plane B is where new voices are heard, showing a marked characteristic of what I call 'J' theatre, especially those who have started working in the last five years. The 'J' here stands for 'Japan as Junk' where the notion of 'art' is always-already elusive. From the perspective of 'high art' in the Euro-American context, where certain universal aesthetic values and methodologies are supposed to be shared, these performances look like junk—lacking value as either economic or cultural capital, they appear to be 'artistic garbage'. Whether consciously or not, 'J' theatres defy and ignore history, shared values and 'common sense'. Their frames of reference and of knowledge are deeply subsumed in the sub-cultural genres of manga, anime, computer games, midnight TV programmes, B-grade movies and 'V' cinemas (films especially made for video release). In short, they are self-admittedly subcultural.

Historically speaking, the Angura Theatre Movement from the late 1960s and early 1970s—including practitioners such as Terayama Shuji, Kara Juro and Suzuki Tadashi—and the early works of Noda belong to this quadrant, though their frames of reference were much richer. However, as the sense of newness and outrageousness of their work came to be accepted by a larger population, they can also be said to have turned mainstream.

This is in any case not of any concern to contemporary 'J' theatre practitioners, and one of the most interesting characteristics of their generation is that they do not seem to have a sense of antagonism.[1] Unlike early periods of contemporary theatre, 'J' theatre artists do not seem to explore notions resistant to authority and mainstream power structures. Yet, in a strangely original way, such artists are trying to make performances that suit the taste, sensibilities and aesthetics of a community of urban youth. Their frame of reference is extremely limited if looked at from outside, although—as expressed by the term 'Re: Little Theatre' for Plane B—the frames of reference for 'J' theatre inevitably fall into a rich resource of theatrical vocabulary. This is the very same vocabulary that Little Theatre practices kept exploring after the 1960s. Hence, at this axis, we may encounter so-called neo-Angura companies such as Gokiburi Kombinat and Kegawa Zoku, where images of Angura are appropriated and (mis)used for their own purposes. At the same time, because of their naivety (and embracing this naive approach), 'J' theatres are extremely sensitive to their immediate environments and contexts wherein, as mass media proclaims 'the Japanese society is terribly sick.' In other words, 'J' theatre performances have a certain degree of resonance with the sensibilities and psyche of the youth who sometimes withdraw from society to a pathological degree (*hikikomori*), or who may engage in acts of self-mutilation. This is why I refer to the Lacanian notion of 'jouissance' in connection with these activities; not a simple joy, but more complicated, even pathologically critical, aesthetic sentiments are suggested here.

Yubiwa Hotel is one such company, whose work, as mentioned earlier, always deals with the *shojo*, an image of teenage girlhood. *Shojo* themes are an important phantasmagoric site for Japan's popular culture, including the now-famous *otaku* culture. For groups and artists gathered along Plane B, there is room, therefore, to tackle important issues such as the politics of representation. In fact, most of these companies or units are dealing with such questions, though they often remain unconscious of the political implications of what they are doing. At the other extreme, there are companies like Tetsuwari Albatrosscket [untranslatable], which makes purely junk and meaningless short performances, as if to say there is nothing 'meaningful' that theatre can do in the postmodern world.

PLANE C: CONTEMPORARY DANCE

'Contemporary dance' is a term designating newer kinds of dance in Japan which came to flourish during the 1990s. Influenced by choreographers such as Pina Bausch and William Forsythe, a younger generation of dancers started to create completely different and diverse kinds of dance forms. Their work decisively broke away from the traditions of classical ballet and modern dance and they were not interested in a linear narrative nor in expressing their inner emotions and personalities. Contemporary dance was geared towards exploring an idiosyncratic movement vocabulary and was a peculiar kind of post-modern dance: a 'J' kind of postmodern dance culture. Basing their work on everyday life and incorporating/zapping diverse kinds of movement from ballet, modern dance, jazz and the like, these artists were successful in establishing a new aesthetic category which can only be called 'junk' in a positive sense: a 'junk' aesthetics of movement. The genre of 'contemporary dance' became an interesting site for reading and analysing trends in performance, and a younger genera-tion of critics are now interested in writing about 'contemporary dance' as Japan's cutting-edge performance culture.

Characteristic of the work of Nibroll, for example, the most cele-brated young dance company in Japan today, is an erratic and some-times violent relationship among young people and their everyday existence. Violence is expressed in Nibroll's dancing bodies and their pedestrian movements. Deepening this interest in everyday life, Okada Toshiki of Chelfitsch has begun a provocative experiment in form (perhaps moving towards Planes A and D). Okada is a young playwright who won the prestigious Kishida Playwrights Award in 2004, and a director who is interested in creating a vocabulary of phys-ical gesture which is at once mundane and fictional. His performance *Five Days in March* (2004) is revolutionary in its rejection of traditional ways of unifying word and body (as in modern realist theatre), and Okada has been successful in capturing the relationship between con-temporary spoken language and physical gesture. In *Five Days in March*, contemporary bodies are shown in ceaseless conversation while their movements unfold, as if operating with an alternate, estranged and unknowable corporeal logic. A physical stammering contrasts with the flow of dialogue and the combined effect is everyday yet uncanny.

PLANE D: RETURN TO ANGURA?

This is the plane that is most under-populated at the moment, where physical expression is the main resource for performance. We have sel-dom seen newcomers working in this field over the last 10 years.

However, two notable exceptions in the 'plane of physical theatre' in recent times are Image Opera and ARICA.

Image Opera is a production unit in which a very young Butoh dancer, Wakikawa Kairi, is the main performer, director and choreographer. Although he has only presented three works, Wakikawa has shown a keen interest in working with influences from the Western avant-garde tradition while maintaining his formally disciplined Butoh presence as a cornerstone of the work.

ARICA was founded in 2001 and its members include a poet, actor, director/designer and musician. Their most well-known performer is Ando Tomoko, one of the main actors in Ota Shogo's Tenkei Gekijo (famous for their *Mizu no Eki* [Water Station, 1981]). By updating the legacy of Angura's theatrical vocabulary in their work, ARICA's collaborations have shown new ways of thinking about the notion of physical theatre.

And while somewhat in decline, a physical theatre tension between Plane A and Plane D is indispensable for a 'healthy' theatre culture. From a historical perspective, this tension was associated with the spirit of anti-establishment experimentation of Angura. Yet, at the moment, it is obvious that Plane D companies are losing their audience. Some critics would say that this is because audiences have become more conservative.[2]

ON THE BORDER: THE POSSIBILITY OF CHANGE

While we have only briefly discussed each plane of my 'J' theatre map, what is most interesting are the groups working at the borders of each axis—groups that are not satisfied with inclusion in a particular plane. Among those I have already mentioned are Chelfitsch and Yubiwa Hotel. Also resisting in this way is Miyazawa Akio of Reviving Amusement Park Agency, whom I have placed at the centre of my map.

Novelist, playwright, director and filmmaker, Miyazawa was one of the leading Little Theatre figures of the 1990s. He is currently struggling to update his established method of performance-making. In his later work *Tokyo/Absence/Hamlet* (2004–05) based on his novel,

Miyazawa moved through several layers of experimentation, trying to find some sort of a contemporary physical gesture along with a variety of ways of presenting theatrical images which can speak to an audience, through different channels and registers.

Nor is Miyazawa attracted to the conventional notion of 'good acting' or straightforward ways of representing dramatic text. In a recent production, he asked Yanaihara Mikuni of Nibroll to work with him and interestingly, the performance became a site for showing the difficulty that artists face in updating the notion of 'acting' in a postmodern age. At the same time, Miyazawa's urgent need to update theatrical vocabulary was critically provocative and an important gesture if, as we hope, Japan's theatre culture is to survive as an important cultural capital.

More than 10 years have passed since Aum Shinri-kyo attacked Tokyo's subway in 1995, the same year that Japan also experienced the Hanshin Awaji Great Earthquake. Many cultural theorists are currently looking at 1995 as a historical watershed in Japan's socio-psychological milieu. For some critics, these events have become a *zeitgeist* for the 1990s—they descibe the decade as: 'the age of impossibility' (Osawa Masachi), 'animalizing the postmodern' (Azuma Koki), 'romantic cynicism' (Kitada Akihiro) and Japan the 'psychologizing society' (Saito Tamaki). Although with differing emphases, these theorists share the same understanding of the 1990s. As Azuma suggests, we are now living with a sense of 'pervasive postmodernity'. The 'age of enlightenment' has finally ended and a Lacanian symbolic order has lowered its threshold as well. These factors have brought about the unbalancing of the triptych of the Real, the Imaginary and the Symbolic.

The last 10 years are also characterized by an unprecedented increase in public funding for the performing arts in Japan. This has meant that performance culture, including theatre and dance, for the first time in Japan's history, was finally 'officialized' by the state. The relationship between this officialization of performance culture and the aforementioned postmodern sociocultural–psychological formations is very complex and obviously beyond the scope of this short chapter. But there are many reasons for us to read Japan's contemporary performance culture as symptoms of a 'sick', 'psychologizing' society as its inhabitants are living in the 'Age of Impossibility'. Sociology and psychoanalysis, rather than aesthetics and literary theories, are more appropriate methodologies from which to begin understanding what is happening here. This chapter, I hope, will be the first step towards that kind of sociological and psychoanalytical exploration of Japan's performing arts culture.

Notes

1   Unlike the former generations of artists who were always responding to the work of elder peers with a sense of antagonism and frustration.

2   Although we see quite a few companies that are still very active from an earlier generation of artists in Plane D, including Gekidan Kaitai-sha, OM-2, DA-M and Storehouse Theatre Company.

Yuenchi Saisei Jigyo-dan (Amusement Park Regeneration Agency
Theatre Company), lead by the playwright and director Miyazawa Akio
and its manager Nagai Ariko,[1] emerged in 1990 with its production of
Yuenchi Saisei (Regenerating Amusement Park). Yuenchi Saisei Jigyo-
dan produced idiosyncratic but well-made theatrical works such as
Hinemi (1992; awarded the prestigious Kishida Playwrights Award),
Chikaku no Niwa (The Garden of Perception, 1995), *Juyonsai no Kuni*
(The Country of the Fourteen-Year-Old, 1998) and *Suna ni Shizumu
Tsuki* (The Moon Drowning under the Sand, 1999). After a brief gap,
Miyazawa wrote and directed *Tokyo Body* (2002–03; see Figure 14), the
final performance of which emerged after a long series of workshops
conducted during 2002. 9/11 has had a profound impact on Miyazawa:

> On that day, the World Trade Center collapsed so easily. It
> was as if the collapsed towers symbolized the fragility of my
> notion of the idealized body: what was left was standing
> blankly, without any sense of rootedness. In order to try and
> reclaim a visceral body sustained through 'dramatic lan-
> guage', without going back to old theatrical forms, I went on
> a search for an alternative body, aware that the unrooted,
> blank body did exist in the past. It was therefore not a coin-
> cidence that, during the process of creating a new work, I
> came across various kinds of bodies of 'here and now'. On
> stage the 'now-ness' of the body is inevitably deformed, but
> the more visceral 'now-ness' of the body, with some blood-
> stained scars, should be much closer to us, very close to
> those who are reading this passage right now, and to myself,
> who is writing it right now (Miyazawa 2002: n.p.).

After 9/11, Miyazawa found himself wondering 'Then, what?', a question he tried to answer or at least grapple with through *Tokyo Body*, *Tokyo/Absence/Hamlet* and his two projects in 2006. This same question lead him to performative explorations of past theatrical forms and classical texts and to attempt a *literal* performance/staging of the 'now' of the 'J' locality. In his own words therefore, Miyazawa achieved his realization not only because of his optical and historical experience of the World Trade Center collapsing 'so easily' but also because he had a surprising number of people—approximately 360—show up for his audition to create the work which was to become *Tokyo Body*. Previously, Miyazawa had conceptualized the 'unrooted, blank body' as a 'non-construction', differentiating it from both 'construction' and 'deconstruction'; in his production, the actor's body was conceptually articulated and physically located. But he had to move on to find 'an alternative body', being aware that such an 'unrooted, blank body did exist in the past'. An 'alternative body' was 'a self-injurious body'; the body of the so-called 'wrist-cutters':

> After 1995, our body came to experience a more difficult state than simply being dysfunctional. Being dysfunctional means that there is something wrong with the function, but it is still functioning. It was possible, therefore, for Furuhashi [of Dumb Type], with his own dysfunctional body, to create *S/N*. His death seemed to herald a shift in which the world was not even dysfunctional anymore. Something beyond being dysfunctional has arrived, and at least in Japan, bodies are behaving very strangely in the streets. . . . And I would call these bodies 'bodies of dementia' (Ootori 2003: 106).

How can we deal with such psychoanalytic bodies on stage? Must we deal with them at all? Miyazawa believes that although those living 'bodies of dementia' can only be 'deformed' on stage, he should nevertheless find a way of dealing with them in theatrical terms because those bodies belong to 'those who are reading [this passage], and to myself, who is writing it right now'. And this is exactly what contemporary theatre has to work towards, especially after 9/11.

Miyazawa thus abandoned his dramaturgical and theatrical style while preparing *Tokyo Body* and made full use of his knowledge of theatre history. Two particular elements of Tokyo Body, as a result, stood out: the many quotations used to create both complexity and a sense of the ad hoc, and the use of dancing 'children's bodies' as a means of displaying idiosyncratic body movements.

TOKYO BODY AND HAMLETMASCHINE

Heiner Müller's *Die Hamletmaschine* (1977) was a major reference in *Tokyo Body*. Müller's work is now a canonized intertextual minimalist text in which, some say, there are no original words, only quotations. Following Müller, Miyazawa (though turning Müller's reticence into garrulity) also quotes a classical Kabuki text (*Shinju Ten-no Amishima*), *King Lear*, *Hamletmaschine*, even the definition of capitalism by Karl Marx—at both textual and performance levels. Different stylistic languages are scattered between the colloquial dialogues of the characters and the self-reflexive utterances by a character as he repeats, 'I was a playwright,' referring both to Miyazawa himself and to *Hamletmaschine*. Contemporary works by Gilbert and George and John Jesurun's 'live broadcasting' performance style are 'quoted'[2] at the performance level—in some scenes, a screen shows the audience what is being enacted through a video camera set up at extreme back centre stage—and 'children's bodies' are mobilized between the scenes to perform a series of non-narrative body movements.

Despite the use of what appears to be no more than a series of random 'quotes', there is nevertheless a sense of narrative. 'Teacher'—like King Lear with his three daughters, yet also blind like Oedipus— comes to Tokyo to find Toriko, the youngest of his daughters and happens to meet his former students, one of whom is working in Shinjuku at a sex shop that 'Teacher' happens to enter. We never know whether he finds Toriko, not even at the end of the play, and, hence, he never reaches Colonus; there is no death, revelation nor salvation. The play ends as abruptly as it begins and the narrative is only an excuse for Miyazawa to performatively inscribe his vision of the ontological and physical shapes and figurations of Tokyo's urban space, utilizing the enumerations of fragmented languages, both textual and colloquial, and mobilizing and inserting newly found theatrical languages of the body. In this work, Miyazawa does not reside over the whole performance as a transcendent author but exists only as a 'brain', functioning as a quotation machine. The machine, however, is dysfunctional and so the performance never aspires towards totality; it remains dispersed and fragmented, unable to cause any form of aesthetic closure.

As in *Hamletmaschine* that began with 'I was Hamlet' (Müller 1977: 6), Miyazawa starts his play with 'I was a security guard' and then proceeds to repeat the format of this sentence throughout the play: 'I was a playwright,' 'I was capitalism,' 'I was a woman,' 'I was a man,' 'I was a poet,' 'I was a lesbian,' 'I was a dead body,' 'I was Mecca,' 'I was Domino's Pizza' and even 'Here was Tokyo.' Other than being a reference to *Hamletmaschine*, each of these repetitions serves as an identifier for characters who are otherwise designated only by numbers (Male 1, Male 2, Female 1, Female 2 and so on, except 'Teacher'). The historical burden of Western modernity bestowed by Müller with the simple but shockingly apt line of 'I was Hamlet' is thus easily removed and wilfully degraded by Miyazawa. Even though the quoted material has its feeble but significant resonances with the content of the play, each 'quotation' is given a sense of degradation—a sense of what can only be described as *shoboi* in Japanese—made to look cheap, shabby and low-brow.

In this production, a number of performers (Performer 1, Performer 2 and so on), including Kohama Masahiro (of BOKUDESU) display their dance-like body movement between scenes. Kohama is a regular participant in Sakurai Keisuke's Azuma-bashi Dance Crossing and is considered a typical performer possessing Sakurai's notion of the 'child's body'.[3] While video images taken by a surveillance camera at a video shop are shown on a screen, the performers imitate the actual people in the shop although their movements are inevitably delayed and rendered somewhat awkward on stage.

Thus, in both performative and linguistic spaces and times, we encounter the sense of absolute *shoboi* that, for Miyazawa, permeates the current sociocultural spaces of Japan as junk in which Sakurai's 'child's body' is the physical agency of Tokyo, its symbolic capital. The 'child's body' is *shoboi*, both junk and pink innocence and creating a

cultural dysfunction that severes knowledge from knowing and movement from action. The actor's body cannot aesthetically suture these
dispersed elements on stage, by creating a hierarchy of meaning
among those elements. *Tokyo Body* begins and ends as a performance
of fragmented languages and bodies. There is nothing to 'see' yet
there is so much to 'see' that we do not know what to look at.

TOKYO/ABSENCE/HAMLET

For Miyazawa's next project, *Tokyo/Absence/Hamlet* (2004–05; I will refer
to the work as *Absence* hereafter), he first wrote a novel (*The Absence of
Akihito*, 2004; see Miyazawa 2005a) and then, through workshops and
performances conducted over a year, adapted it into a theatrical production that proceeded from a staged reading of the play (May 2004,
Kagurazaka die pratze Theatre). Following the reading, Miyazawa
asked three film directors to participate in creating an anthology—*Be
Found Dead*—of five short films of which Miyazawa directed two (July
2004).

The third phase—called 'an experimental production' (September, 2004, Yokohama ST Spot Theatre)—was an attempt by Miyazawa
to use different theatrical styles to further explore the extremes of
John Jesurun's live broadcasting presentation style. In this phase, the
'fourth' wall of the stage was almost completely covered by several
panels with a video screen at the centre. Actors entered the stage from
the audience through a 'hole' created by removing one of the panels.
Their performance on the stage, coupled with some pre-recorded
images, was projected live onto a screen. The audience was thus forced
to see the action either through the small 'hole' or as a 'live' projection.

The fourth phase—called 'a preparation production' (October
2004, Azabu die pratze Theatre)—was a straightforward theatrical
presentation without any sets, where the text of the work-in-progress
was questioned. Miyazawa randomly shuffled the order of the scenes,
even going so far as to ask the actors to speak their lines in reverse
order in one scene. In doing this, Miyazawa discarded the naturalness
of performance that had foreclosed the actors' spontaneous physical
(re)actions—the actors had been working with the text for almost six

months and had grown too accustomed to their roles and lines—forcing them to concentrate on what and how they spoke.

As I have noted, Miyazawa has questioned the idea of reclaiming a visceral body and the possibility of a 'dramatic language' that can sustain that body. While in *Tokyo Body* the question was the constituency of the work itself, in *Absence*, an initial response to the question was attempted through 'dramatic language'—by positing a linguistic construction of the novel/play as a starting point and transforming it into a theatrical performance.

What was important for Miyazawa's 'dramatic language' was the deployment of history within the play. Although some original plot and narrative elements—the assassination of Hamlet, the Father, the marriage of Claudius and Gertrude, the appearance of the ghost, the killing of Polonius and the death of Ophelia—are translated into the contemporary story of the Mure family living in Kitakawabe-cho, Kita Saitama-gun, Saitama Prefecture, Miyazawa's intention lies in a thick description of the figurations of the Japanese sociocultural space with its two axes, historical verticality and contemporary synchronicity, which grew out of his encounter with the typical town of Kitakawabe-cho in the north-western periphery of the metropolitan Tokyo area:

> There was a discovery of the area called 'Northern Kanto' at the beginning. It came with a small incident when I got interested in a strange sound of the language in a play that I had a chance to read. I found out, in the process of doing some research, that it was a northern Kanto dialect. I looked at the map. In February 2004, I decided to go to this place where Saitama, Gunma, Tochigi and Ibaragi prefectures meet at one point. The town was called Kitakawabe-cho, Kita Saitama-gun, Saitama Prefecture, which looked all too common . . . To collect material for my new novel, I visited the town many times. During summer, the landscape was filled with a vast space of green rice fields and I saw almost no people. But I noted a few things. Now the technique for embankment work has developed but in the past it was strange that people wanted to live in a place with such poor environmental condi-

FIGURE 14: *TOKYO BODY*. YUENCHI SAISEI JUGYO-DAN #14. 22 JANUARY–2 FEBRUARY 2004, AT THE-
ATRE TRAM, TOKYO. PHOTOGRAPH COURTESY OF NOBUHIKO HIKICHI.

FIGURE 15: *TOKYO/ABSENCE/HAMLET*. YUENCHI SAISEI JUGYO-DAN #15. 19–23 JANUARY 2005, AT
THEATRE TRAM, TOKYO. PHOTOGRAPH COURTESY OF NOBUHIKO HIKICHI.

FIGURE 16: *MOTORCYCLE DON QUIXOTE*. YUENCHI SAISEI JUGYO-DAN PRODUCTION, 23–29 MAY 2006, AT YOKOHAMA RED BRICK WAREHOUSE. PHOTOGRAPH COURTESY OF NOBUHIKO HIKICHI.

tions. If so, I do understand why, as is written in Kawashima Junji's *Kanto Heiya no Kakure Kirishitan* [Clandestine Christians in the Kanto Plain], the first clandestine Christians in Kanto area appeared in Kitakawabe-cho and could only live there secretly. I literally discovered Kitakawabe-cho. There was certainly something special about this all-too-common town but, if I could make it more general, I thought I would be able to write a more universal story (Miyazawa 2005b: n.p.).

Though the Hamlet story underlies the narrative structure of the novel, it is difficult to find a sense of what Miyazawa calls 'universality' which can only be defined by a liberal-humanist tradition where history or historic specificities should erase themselves for the sake of celebrating ahistorical 'human' values. If we consider the original *Hamlet*, in which the notion of revenge is a crucial issue, then we can understand Miyazawa's 'universality'. Especially after 9/11, with the emergence of a global state of war in which the notion of revenge has visibly and universally been made into a key component of terrorism. Focusing his attention on a local community with its specific historicity, Miyazawa, by verbalizing, abstracting and structuring the 'all-too-common town' of Kitakawabe-cho into an authored narrative text, has attempted to summon a 'universally' applicable issue of today.

Miyazawa develops a thick description of the current state of war in the locality called 'J'—where history appears only as a result of a set of uncontrollable contingencies—by presenting Shinjuku as Tokyo at the other extreme of the geographically active location of the text, though its main action takes place in Kitakawabe-cho.[4] His description ends not only with the concealed history of clandestine Christians in that particular area: from the typically oppressive air of the closed community in Kitakawabe-cho and the land-development politics that dominate community affairs—the Mure family is the most powerful land-developer in town—to the typical lifestyles of young people in the semi-urban local community, Miyazawa incorporates elements, atmospheres and particular articulations that relate to the historical transition experienced by Japan in the post-War and the 'post-bubble' years. Especially noteworthy are the young characters in the play—

who gather in front of a local convenience store on weeknights and visit Shinjuku to have fun on weekends—who serve as symbolic embodiments of the 'noisy' and dysfunctional elements of a neo-liberalized society. We also see a housewife who has moved from Tokyo with her husband only to be dissatisfied with the unexciting everyday life in that local community. Accordingly, perhaps even against her will, she derives sexual excitement from crank calls and ends up having an affair with her husband's younger brother.

Here too, the sense of *shoboi* looms over the setting and the narrative details of characters' lives; one of the characters actually says, 'All is very *shoboi*, isn't it?', both at the beginning and at the end of the play[5] (although in the novel it is spoken only once). *Shoboi*, however, is not positively affirmed but posited as an unchangeable underlying premise, a historical given, of the 'J' locality. The absent protagonist of the play is Mure Akihito, a Hamlet figure and an indication of the indexical existence of the emperor system—he shares his name with the current emperor of Japan. Unlike Hamlet in the original, Akihito seems to have already thrown himself into the act of revenge; Ginsekai, a snack bar in Kitakawabe-cho, was blown up when some power-brokers gathered there over drinks for a secret meeting. Akihito surely became a terrorist and Kitakawabe-cho emerged as an appropriated metaphor for the 'J' locality that thereafter entered into a state of war. Akihito, however, continues to be absent until the end of the novel; therefore, the *shoboi* people of Kitakawabe-cho can only witness—and confirm after the fact—the results of Akihito's action, imagining the violent body of a terrorist and the state of war in which such violent bodies may proliferate. The emperor system is implicated in all of this not only as a remote background but as a hotbed of acts of terrorism.

The narrative world constructed in the novel was not necessarily faithfully duplicated in the play version. For instance, in the novel, one of the characters merely walks past a poster advertising Tom Stoppard's *Rosencrantz and Guildenstern are Dead*. In the play, however, the Stoppard element is expanded: Rosencrantz and Guildenstern are introduced as a pair of idiotic clerks at a sex shop in Shinjuku. On the other hand, as if to guarantee the sense of continuity from novel to play, passages like the following are inserted into the play:

VOICE 2. I was not Hamlet.

VOICE 3. I was not necessarily Hamlet.

VOICE 4. I was not even Hamlet.

VOICE 5. I was Hamlet within a remote memory.

POET. I was Hamlet. I stood at the shore of Watarase River
and spoke with the stream BLABLA at my back the ruins
of Kita Kanto.

VOICE 4. *Anmeizousumareya*.

VOICE 5. I was Hamlet.

POET. *Anmeizousumareya*.[6]

VOICE 2. I was not Hamlet. (See Miyazawa 2005c: 6.)

Interventions such as these were devised when Miyazawa was writing the play. And, as if to stitch together the disjointed acting and presentational styles, Miyazawa invited Yanaihara Mikuni, a dancer and choreographer known for her violent dysfunctional physical movements (and usually considered the embodiment of Sakurai's 'child's body') to participate as a choreographer for the final production.

The final production incorporated choreography by Yanaihara as well as the linguistic, gestural and optical elements and techniques. Miyazawa was obviously not interested in working in a conventional way; he was not interested in making 'good theatre' with 'good actors'. Thus, many of the actors who went through the long period of preparation deviated from the dominant and institutionalized value system of 'good acting'.

I came to realize through conducting many workshops that there are those anonymous young actors with full passion for expression, wondering how to forge their inner energy to exterior forms. By borrowing some time from them, can I not discover a different theatrical style? In order to answer this question, I thought I would experiment with many different approaches, spending almost a year. That idea has led to different kinds of preview productions and the accumulation of a long period of training. I am expecting a different kind of expression by simply accumulating time. . . . The accumulated time itself becomes the work (Miyazawa 2004: n.p.).

How can we discover a new theatrical body by working with 'anonymous young actors with full passion for expression, wondering how to forge their inner energy to exterior forms'? The question in *Absence*, therefore, was almost the same as in *Tokyo Body* but in *Absence*, with the narrative world of Kitakawabe-cho as its base, Miyazawa attempted to present a thick performance description of the 'J' locality in the state of war. While *Tokyo Body* was a performance of fragmented languages and bodies, *Absence* was a performance of fragmented bodies set within a well-constructed narrative world.

AFTER *ABSENCE*—UNDOING THEATRE HISTORY

Two of the projects that Miyazawa worked on after *Absence* have similar characteristics in that both pushed him to find a contemporary response to classical texts. One was commissioned by the Setagaya Public Theatre as part of the contemporary Noh performance series and was a project for contemporary playwrights to rewrite a Noh text; for this project, Miyazawa chose Zeami's *Nue*. The other was called the Cardenio Project which I commissioned him. The project was originally proposed by Stephen Greenblatt of Harvard University. For the project, Greenblatt thematized the notion of 'cultural mobility' by asking artists from different cultural backgrounds to work on Shakespeare's 'lost play', in which Cervantes's Cardenio is supposed to have been a protagonist. The materials at hand were several Shakespearean scholars' research material on the 'lost play', a developing play co-authored by Greenblatt and American playwright Charles Mee, Jr, and Cervantes's *Don Quixote*. Using these, Miyazawa came up with a new play called *Motorcycle Don Quixote*, first performed in Yokohama in May 2006 (see Figure 16).

Nue opened as *Contemporary Noh Play III Nue* in November that year, at Setagaya Public Theatre's Theatre Tram. An attempt at explicitly expressing Miyazawa's interest in exploring different styles of performing bodies while using the narrative structure of the original text as a framework, the play is set in the transit room of an international airport where an internationally renowned theatre director and his crew, on their way back to Japan after a successful European tour, meet the ghost of a legendary Angura actor who had worked with the director a long time ago. At the end of the play we come to know that the forgotten Angura actor died that very day in Japan. The reference is obviously to Ninagawa Yukio, the director; accordingly, the script includes some scenes from playwright Shimizu Kunio's work (with whom Ninagawa had worked in his Angura days). The role of the director is played by Uesugi Shozo, an actor who emerged during the 1980s, with Noda Hideki's Yume no Yumin-sha Theatre Company, and the old Angura actor is played by Wakamatsu Takeshi, former member of Terayama Shuji's Tenjo Sajiki Theatre Company. Other cast members include Nakagawa Anna, a Shingeki female actor; Shimousa Gentaro, member of Rinko-gun Theatre Company (known for political plays of Sakate Yoji); and young actors who have worked with Miyazawa in the past. Different bodies from Shingeki, Angura, and 1980s' theatre to contemporary 'J' theatre are all engaged in this play of mourning; the original *Nue* is exactly that, in which a wandering spirit in the form of Nue, an imaginary bird in mediaeval Japan, is pacified by a Buddhist monk. At the end of the play, the dying body of the Angura actor is carried away by the director to the airport where a huge black airplane is waiting to take off.

For the Cardenio project, Miyazawa set the play in a suburban motorbike repair shop in Tsurumi district, Kanagawa Prefecture, where a complicated yet melodramatic love story unfolds. Tadao, the owner of the shop, is a Quixotian figure who yearns to leave, to ride-off into the sunset on his bike. He is a typical post-World War II Japanese figure who grew up blindly admiring the American counter-culture of the 1960s. His wife is dead and his daughter wants to study theatre at university. Tadao is now married to a much younger Machiko, a former actor who once tried to kill herself after being discarded by a fellow-actor in a Shingeki company. The Cardenio plot is a play within a play; the sub-play is one in which Machiko as Lucinda and her former lover as Ferdinand perform Shakespeare's 'lost play'. Tadao, as Don Quixote, sometimes intervenes, in his daydreams.

Sakazaki, an assistant repairman at the shop, is both Sancho Panza and the figure in the Cardenio story who tries to seduce Machiko on Tadao's behalf who doubts whether Machiko really loves him. Other important characters are: a *'freeter'*, a job-hopping part-time worker and a *hikikomori* (introvert) youth living next door who never shows up in the play. Tadao is played by Oda Makoto, former Waseda Sho-gek-ijo (Suzuki Tadashi's company during his Angura years) actor; Machiko by Takahashi Fusae, a Shingeki actor; and Sakazaki by Shimousa Gentaro who appears in *Nue* again.

Miyazawa has skilfully cast different performing bodies: Shingeki, Angura and Little Theatre styles of physicality and acting (almost a catalogue of historical performing bodies since Angura days in Japan) are thus deployed, enacting a contemporary story of family–love–betrayal, the boredom of everyday life and a longing to go away, with references not only to Shakespeare and Cervantes but also to 1960s' American pop culture and Japanese modern and experimental theatre, Shingeki in particular, which has historically admired both the work of Shakespeare and Chekhov. The Shingeki 'body' was expected to merge with the antique language of Shakespeare (in the play-with-in-a-play) and with the more mundane yet poetic language of modern colloquialisms *a la* Chekhov. The Chekhovian references are obvious in Miyazawa's construction of dialogue as well as in the scene when Tadao's daughter practises the lines from *Three Sisters* after she has entered university to study theatre.

Miyazawa is well aware that he cannot return to the collective for-titude of Angura's physical formulations of resistance nor to a 'blank body' for his project of finding a different body which resonates with the 'J' locality in a state of war.

What should be emphasized is that Miyazawa does not escape into history; rather, he introduces history in order to undo it. In 'J' theatre, history is usually summoned as historicity, 'history as image'. Worse, historicity returns as 'universality' and within the matrix of the ideol-ogy of what should be called 'theatre fundamentalism'.[7] That is prob-ably why Miyazawa started the project of explicitly deploying various histories—of dramatic literature and theatre, of local community and so on—within his narrative and performative spaces, thus causing those

histories to be radically undone. Inevitably a losing battle, it is nevertheless the right kind of battle in an age of globalization, especially
after 9/11.

Notes

1 I would like to thank Nagai Ariko, Miyazawa's company manager, for
   making available to me various unpublished documents, including
   acting versions of *Tokyo Body* (2002–03) *Tokyo/Absence/Hamlet*,
   Motorcycle Don Quixote and *Nue*. *Tokyo/Absence/Hamlet* was later published in *Teatro*, (January 2005, Kamomiru-sha, pp. 110–53) and *Nue*
   in *PT*.

2 Some still images of Gilbert and George's famous works are presented
   by live performers in the work. John Jesurun was a visiting professor
   at Kyoto University of Art and Design in 2002 and 2003, during
   which time Miyazawa was a professor at the same university. Jesurun
   directed his *Snow* (2002) and *Bardo* (2003) with the students.
   Miyazawa expresses his indebtedness to Jesurun's work on many
   occasions, including in his blog diary (u-ench.com/index.html).

3 In order to demonstrate his notion of the 'child's body', Sakurai has
   worked as a dance curator for an event called Azuma-bashi Dance
   Crossing in which select dancers are given 20-minute slots to show-
   case their work. Azuma-bashi is the location of the performance
   space where this event takes place in Tokyo (Asahi Square). The first
   took place in July 2004 and since then the event has taken place
   twice a year.

4 In the final production, most scenes which take place in Shinjuku
   (Tokyo) were enacted behind a slit wall and were displayed live on
   the screen hung on the right side of the stage (see Figure 15).

5 'All is very *shoboi*, isn't it?' is spoken by one of the young characters in
   the play, Yukimori. In the acting version, Yukimori speaks it during
   the last scene. In the final production, however, the last scene is also
   played at the beginning of the performance, thus lending it a circu-
   lar structure.

6 I have faithfully Romanized Miyazawa's text. It sounds like 'Annei
   Zeus Mariya' and may be translated as 'Give us peace, Jesus and
   Mary'. Perhaps clandestine Christians' words of prayer?

7 'Theatre fundamentalism' is an underlining anti-intellectual ideology
   that is growing stronger in Japan. It presupposes that there are universal theatrical values that everyone can understand without any education or knowledge. Its idea can be summarized in the tautology of
   'Good theatre is good theatre,' in which its goodness should never be
   defined nor explained as it belongs to the sensory domain. According
   to this ideology, history is summoned in such a way that 'good acting',
   whether in ancient Greek drama, in Elizabethan theatre, modern psychological drama or in Angura Theatre, is all the same; it is simply
   'good' and, therefore, universal and undisputable.

In a recently updated article, originally written in 1992, called 'Five
Avantgardes . . . or None' (2006), Schechner categorizes avant-garde
theatre and performance under five headings; the intercultural avant-
garde comes last, following the historical, the current, the future-look-
ing and the traditional-seeking. Schechner seems to be pointing out
that, in the age of globality, the intercultural avant-garde is the only
possible form of performance culture that can accommodate, either
positively or negatively, the late capitalist, planetary, sociocultural and
geopolitical configurations.

> For whatever reasons—left over colonialism, American impe-
> rialism, the hunger of people everywhere for material goods,
> the planetary spread of modernism, the ubiquity of a 'cos-
> mopolitan style' in everything from airports to clothes—artists
> of the avantgarde are producing works on or across various
> borders: political, geographical, personal, generic, and con-
> ceptual. In a world where each day so-called universal values
> run up against deeply held local values and experiences, the
> result is clash, disturbance, turbulence, unease about the
> future, and hot argument about what the past was (ibid.: 21).

Schechner goes on to discuss three intercultural artists, Peter Brook,
Guillermo Gomez-Peña and Ong Keng Sen, and argues that Gomez-
Peña and Ong Keng Sen are avant-garde while Brook is not because,
in *The Mahabharata*, 'Brook wants to elide difference, he is looking for
what unites, universalizes, makes the same' (ibid.: 22). In Schechner's
definition, intercultural performance is avant-garde 'when the performance does not try to heal over rifts or fractures but further opens
these for exploration' (ibid.). It is the ideological difference between

the two traditions: between a now-almost-extinct liberal-humanist kind of tradition which values those abstract notions of 'humanity', harmony and/or universality, and a still-alive (high) modernist kind of tradition which values, to use Schechner's words, 'clash, disturbance, turbulence, unease about the future, and hot argument about what the past was'.

Somewhat in contradiction to this discussion in the following section called '. . . Or None', Schechner declares 'the avantgarde is yesterday,' as nothing new can be expected to happen anymore because 'the current avantgarde is neither innovative nor in advance of. We note that the avantgarde is a style or a genre—or a clutch of genres, and not a "movement" ' (ibid: 24–5). I agree with Schechner. The questions, therefore, should be, as Schechner notes, 'Who cares? Does it matter?' (Ibid.: 26.) I am, of course, inclined to say, 'No one cares' and 'It doesn't matter,' but I am not entirely sure. This is not because I believe in a bright future for the avant-garde or in their ethical or political efficacy in the present tense. It is rather because I think that Schechner's seemingly cynical rhetorical questions should be taken at face value at the moment; we should and can keep asking 'Who cares?' and 'Does it matter?'

This is especially true while thinking of two powerful contradictory categories that seem to inform the whole gamut of our globalized societies: 'the universal' and 'the particular', which we have now substituted with the 'the global' and 'the local', in accordance with the apparent hegemonic domination of the economic over the cultural. As Schechner notes, 'in a world where so-called universal values each day run up against deeply held local values and experiences, the result is clash, disturbance, turbulence, unease about the future, and hot argument about what the past was' (ibid.: 21).

The three artists discussed by Schechner are all privileged, in one way or the other, to be intercultural. In the case of Peter Brook, there should be no need for further explanation. Guillermo Gomez-Peña, as quoted by Schechner, 'physically live[s] between two cultures and two epochs'. Furthermore, when he is in the US, he has 'access to high technology and specialized information'. When he returns to Mexico, he gets 'immersed in a rich political culture' (ibid.: 21). A border crossing, it seems, is not a problem for Gomez-Peña because he is privileged as an artist and an intellectual. Furthermore, he is not a theatremaker but a performance artist, which makes it much easier for him to be geographically mobile. In the case of Ong Keng Sen: though a decisive sense of 'Asia-ness' is usually made a visible marker in Ong Keng Sen's intercultural theatre work—as his Flying Circus Project and his intercultural *Lear* (1997; growing out of his experience with the Flying Circus Project) testify—there is always the danger of his work being considered a performative duplication of the logic of global capitalism, in which the tensions and the contradiction of 'the global' and 'the local' are referred to from the privileged height of an auteur tradition. To put it more bluntly, his project is reminiscent of Singapore's national policy—a feeble narrative which the Singaporean government is eagerly fabricating in order to survive in a globalized market as a city state. Ong Keng Sen's work, accordingly, tends to become a celebration of the multiculturalism of Singapore which at times conceals the intracultural tensions, contradictions and competition of that city.

If intercultural theatre today only means to symbolize the mobility of the privileged artists between the global and the local, as is the case with these three artists, and/or between different localities within the context of the state of globality, there is nothing much to add to the way in which Schechner abruptly ends the section dealing with the intercultural avant-garde and his somewhat hasty conclusion that 'the avantgarde is yesterday.' I would argue, however, after 9/11 and its ensuing drastic geopolitical re-configurations, we must consider and complicate the categories Schechner has put forward more deeply, in order to deconstruct the binary of global and local. We all know that the global and the local can be so easily reconciled into the notion of 'the glocal' manifest in the motto 'think globally, act locally,' valued as the global capitalists' bittersweet currency for material success. If the dialectical thinking between the global and the local and its *Aufheben* ('the glocal') is always-already hijacked by global capitalism, what can we do? The only resistance to this hegemonic dialectic can be formulated as 'think locally, act globally.' This, I would argue, is what should become an underlining principle for any intercultural theatre work in the present.

What then does it mean to 'think locally'? In the age of globalization, 'deeply held local values and experiences', in Schechner's words, are often essentialized as a given, something that the local should naturalize and 'protect' against the global. From the alleged seamlessly transmitted traditional forms of performing arts to 'here and now' feelings and sensibilities of an immediate everyday reality, theatre artists appropriate many different kinds of resources to generate their work. Those local practices, including the textual and especially the traditional, in the earlier intercultural works of Peter Brook or Ong Keng Sen, necessarily suffered a radical decontextualization within an aesthetic closure authored by a privileged artist, thereby being made a legitimately global, i.e. universal high artwork, that can be displayed (and consumed) in the first worlds of Europe or the US or Japan. Of course, we can claim such sites as an experimental space for 'cultural negotiations', as Ong Keng Sen does (in ibid.: 23). This notion of culture clearly shows that culture is supposed to be a pre-fixed entity with which one can negotiate with other cultures. To 'think locally' means to abandon this cultural essentialism and question the pre-fixed notions of all forms of culture. This will inevitably necessitate a serious and attentive critical enquiry into the existential status of performing arts in modernity, now globalized, in one way or the other, usually defined by an Euro-American project of enlightenment and somewhat influenced by the romantic notion of artist as genius, outcast and/or 'naturally' privileged. In this process of enquiry, we will think about the democratization of theatre—who is the audience and what is reception?—but also how the place of creation is managed. To 'think locally' will then lead us to 'act globally', that is to say, to revisit interculturalism as it is defined by Rustom Bharucha, as a site of 'internationalist vigilance', which should be triggered by what he calls a 'cross-border imaginary of resistance' in the age of terror, especially after 9/11 (2003: n.p.).

INTERCULTURALISM REVISITED AND BEYOND

Let me be more specific about what I have in mind about theorizing the intercultural: at the moment, it has certain practical resonances with the historical development of what the Japan Foundation has been pioneering for the collaborative projects they initiated in the early 1990s.

For the first 10 of the Japan Foundation projects, there were some that were groundbreaking and experimental that brought Asian artists to Japan or sent Japanese artists to Asia, to create intercultural works, including Ong Keng Sen's *Lear* in 1997 (see Chapter 4 for a more detailed discussion on earlier intercultural works by the Japan Foundation). But a real break came with *Memories of a Legend: A Multimedia Theatre Collaboration of Bangladesh, India, Nepal, Pakistan, and Sri Lanka*, which premiered in Tokyo in 2004, and was performed in New Delhi in 2005. It was an adventurous effort in which five young theatre directors from India, Sri Lanka, Pakistan, Bangladesh and Nepal were invited to collaborate. The project began with producer, Hata Yuki visiting each area in 2003 and selecting five directors, after watching many performances and video clips and meeting with as many artists as possible. The first meeting was held in November 2003 in New Delhi. One of the major criteria for selection was the relative youth of the director and his/her emerging within that country's theatre tradition: Abhilash Pillai from India, Azad Abul Kalam from Bangladesh, Anup Baral from Nepal, Ibrahim Quraishi from Pakistan and Ruwanthie de Chickera from Sri Lanka. Quraishi is somewhat exceptional because he does not work in Pakistan but in Paris and New York; this later cast a very interesting and disturbing light on the process of collaboration and on the kind of collaboration in general as he brought the historical, cultural, theoretical and even the personal Euro-American contexts into the collaboration.

At the first meeting, each director introduced his/her work to the other and discussed possible ways to collaborate. The next step was in March 2004 when each brought his/her short work to Tokyo, along with critics and/or scholars who gave lectures about theatre culture in each respective country. At the same time, after a heated discussion, *The Baburnama* was chosen as the text to work on. The third meeting was held in New Delhi between late April and early May, in which each director proposed what s/he wanted to bring to the collaboration, using *The Baburnama*. Each director was also asked to present who s/he would bring to the collaboration by way of actors, musicians and other artists. The fourth meeting was in July in New Delhi, in which other collaborators were invited to do a workshop. And the final stage came in October and November in Tokyo when rehearsals were conducted for three weeks and the work, *Memories of a Legend*, was presented at Tokyo's Japan Foundation Forum.

The performance consisted of a series of episodes, both literal and imaginary, from Babur's life, depicted in various native languages by actors, dancers and musicians, with many video monitors defining the performance area. The episodes were framed by a contemporary image of a displaced traveller returning to his 'native' land in South Asia. Though the story followed the life of Babur, it was fractured in terms of narrative structure and execution because five directors had struggled to find a democratic way of collaboration. The questions varied from the notion of the aesthetic—what is beautiful and what is not, what is good acting and what is not—to defining the efficacy of performance in terms of the theoretical, historical, political, social and/or cultural implications of what they were making. There were sometimes explosions of frustration, dissatisfaction and anger just as, at other times, there were quiet negotiations, expressions of tolerance and patience, with the entire process permeated by a sense of (both positive and negative) confusion. In the final stage of the collaboration, a practical resolution was taken to let each director be responsible for his/her part of the production, though opinions of the other directors were welcome.

I would like to point to two issues raised by this collaboration. First, despite the fact that the entire production cost was provided by the Japan Foundation, only a costume designer and technical staff members were from Japan. Hata Yuki, the producer, took a dangerous yet adventurous risk of being easily condemned from both sides—by Japan and the collaborating countries. On the Japanese side, people may wonder why taxpayers' money should be spent on a collaboration where no Japanese element is emphasized. On the side of the collaborating countries, people may wonder why Japan was interested in eliciting artists for this project backed by 'Japan money'. Wasn't this yet another form of cultural imperialism? The latter may sound too ridiculous to consider seriously, though some cultural essentialists may not agree. The former was expected by Hata from the very beginning and she cautiously prepared contexts for the final production. It was, however, an obvious political gesture for Hata and for me as an advisor. As I have articulated in various instances throughout this volume, theatre culture in Japan has securely enclosed itself, and this collaboration, in terms of its content and its aesthetics, was meant to be completely about 'the other' and 'the otherness'. In that sense, as expected, the collaboration was successful in provoking criticism by strategically presenting 'the otherness' of 'the other'.

Second, that there was no single authority to decide what participants should or should not do. The process was everything, especially for the five directors who were placed into this unique and radically democratized working environment. At every stage of the process, each director had to invent his/her own way to negotiate, persuade and/or insist. It was a long and tiring process but, for me, it was a valuable experiment. Therefore, it did not really matter whether people in Japan 'got it'; their lack of understanding only indicated that the project had not given them what they wanted to see—stereotypical images of the five participating countries. Whether the issues that this project raised, in terms of its content and the political implications of the project itself, further provoked the audience still remains to be seen but at least the five directors were greatly encouraged to keep working in their home countries with a continuing sense of what Bharucha calls 'cross-border imaginary of resistance' (ibid.). Their collaboration may be seen as an attempt to create a site of 'internationalist vigilance' against 'the violence of terrorism' and 'the continued brutality of the civilized world', not only through the content of their work but also through the very process of creating that work.

Back in 1996, after dismissing the then dominant Euro(-American)centric intercultural work as too culturally relativist, Pavis wrote:

Instead, a third term is taking shape and it is that intercultural theatre which still aspires, for the most part, to exist at all, but which nevertheless already possesses its own laws and specific identity. It is in the search for extra-European inspiration—Asian, African, South American—that the genre of intercultural theatre has every chance of prospering, much more so than in the cooperations between European countries, which so often restrict themselves to accumulating capital, multiplying selling points and confirming national stereotypes and the standings of actors. If there is one attitude that we must move beyond, it is that pan-European self-protective huddling which is only interested in Europe in so far as it forms a barrage against the rest of the world: even more reason for placing one's hope in an extra-European interculturalism which may lend a strong hand to the theatre of today (1996: 19).

We must not get too upset about Pavis' obviously Eurocentric neo-colonial discourses but ask ourselves whether our intercultural work is not 'accumulating capital, multiplying selling points and confirming national stereotypes and the standings of actors'. And to paraphrase Pavis further, 'if there is one attitude that we must move beyond', it is not just 'pan-European self-protective huddling' but any kind of 'self-protective huddling against the rest of the world'. *Memories of a Legend* was a small step towards radically revising Eurocentric, neo-colonial interculturalism at a time when such a site of 'internationalist vigilance' was acutely needed. In that sense, the work surely lent 'a strong hand to the theatre of today'.

FROM INTERCULTURALISM TO 'CON-FUSION': *PERFORMING WOMEN*

If *Memories of a Legend* was, for some, a confusion to be affirmed, and for others, a product of detestable artistic compromise, the next project I am going to discuss is what Eckersall calls 'con-fusion'—originally the title of a three-year collaboration project between NYID in Melbourne, Australia, and Gekidan Kaitaisha in Tokyo from 1999 to 2001. Eckersall writes:

The title of the project 'Journey to Con-fusion', at least in English, conveys a productive montage-like notion of praxis, rather than an overreaching concern with the smoothing-out of difference. The performance presentations that concluded each workshop phase of the project were fragmented and disrupted (2005: 209–10).

'Con-fusion', therefore, suggests neither a pure confusion nor a coercive erasure of differences in the name of the aesthetics and its market value.

The next intercultural project funded by the Japan Foundation was *Performing Women: Medea, Jocasta, Clytemnestra*, the first version of which was seen in Delhi in January 2007, and the final version was presented at Tokyo's Theatre Cocoon in October 2007 and then in Seoul, Korea. In Tokyo, the title was changed to *Performing Women: Three Reinterpretations from Greek Tragedy*.

For this project, three directors were selected: Ovlyakuli Khojakuli from Turkmenistan, working in Uzbekistan; Abhilash Pillai from India; and Mohammad Aghebati from Iran. The degree of experimentation was not as great as in *Memories of a Legend*, because the participating directors did not have common historical, cultural or political contexts. The collaboration process was, from the beginning, expectedly very difficult. I, along with Anuradha Kapur from the National School of Drama in India, participated in the process from the beginning, as advisors. This time, however, Hata determined from the beginning that the structure of the production should consist of three parts, each directed by a selected director. It was a practical and professional choice, considering the budget and the time allowed for this project.

The major challenge was deciding on a subject. *The Arabian Nights* was the first suggestion because it is a text with a complex history in the Arab world, in Europe and even in Japan. The text, we thought, may shed an interesting and provocative light on issues concerning contemporary neo-colonialism, stereotyping and cultural essentialisms. But it was flatly rejected by some of the directors who felt the material was too difficult for such a project. Our second suggestion was ancient Greek drama, which led to the theme of 'women' in Greek tragedy. As Anuradha Kapur writes in her programme note:

> Across the world there seem [to] have been more productions
> of Greek tragedy in the last two decades than in most preced-

ing decades. In our disturbed times texts that deal with individuals and their place in society; with people who refuse to conform or surrender or forget; whose sense of revenge dishonor or courage can never be underestimated and who will face questions of mortality unflinchingly—become more like kits of survival than narratives of deliverance (2007: 20).

Each director worked on the selected material after the initial meeting held in Tashkent, the capital city of Uzbekistan, in November 2005, and in Delhi, May 2006. Khojakuli chose Medea, Aghebati, Jocasta, and Pillai first Clytemnestra for the Delhi production, and then Helen for the Tokyo and Seoul productions. Each director was allotted a 45–50-minute portion of the programme.

Khojakuli decided to tell Medea's plight in a mostly linear fashion; he used the original Medea text, along with some additional texts, so that his own interpretation of Medea becomes clearer and more accessible to the contemporary audience:'Medea is not a villain. Her killing her children is an act of sacrifice. It is a tragic attempt on her part to mankind from falling into the abyss of immorality and discord' (2007: 7).

Khojakuli's production was characterized by his intensive use of stylized acting accompanied by chanting and percussions. How much of the performance can be characterized as 'traditional' is a difficult and delicate question to answer, but, compared to a more modern theatrical style of theatre company like Ilkhom Theatre in Tashkent, it is not too mistaken to say that Khojakuli's interest lies in a 'total theatre' kind of collective and stylized performance style he has been developing with a small theatre company called Eski Masjid in the small town of Kharsi. As a result, as Kapur notes:

Ovyakuli's performance of Medea from Uzbekistan hurls us into a world that is not populated by psychologically driven introverted characters that are self-regulating and autonomous. Instead characters who, even as they rage against the social arrangement, are aware that they are part of society and not separate from it occupy the stage. The performance is mindful of a more social and relational view, a more interactional view of the self, where families, groups, and the world are of necessity around you and from which you may never find release (2007).

Aghebati was interested in exploring what he calls 'modern human consciousness' using the Oedipus story as a structural base. Thus he asked Mohammad Charmsir, an Iranian playwright, to write a dramatic text. Charmsir's play is a kind of dramatic poetry, consisting of rather short segments of symbolic dialogues between Jocasta and Oedipus. Loosely following the original storyline of the famous Oedipus story, Aghebati's production emphasizes that both Jocasta and Oedipus are inflicted with the blessing and curse of their self-consciousness, their reflexivity. Thus, as Aghebati writes:

> If in the original, as the latest moment of the play, Oedipus and Jocasta noticed that fate has destroyed them, in our reading, Oedipus and Jocasta knowingly try to murder, and their marriage is in process of being aware of it in order to humiliate the mechanism of Fate and God's will. Their knowing deed has enabled them to revolt against traditional values and to found their definition of conceptions such as 'sin', 'taboo' and 'human's will' (2007: 11).

This assertion of 'human will' over the seemingly transcendental was presented in fragmented and disrupted, yet poetic fashion. Thus our imagination goes easily beyond the immediate (and obvious) contexts Aghebati is referring to: a totalitarian regime that he thinks he now lives in. We are led to witness and be emotionally involved with complex and contradicting aspects of modernity which still cannot be overlooked, even though we wish to believe that we now live in a postmodern time.

Pillai's Helen, written by Sujith Shanker, an Indian playwright, is the most political and most abstract of the three parts of this project. Helen is on her deathbed, recollecting her past, filled with revenge and thoughts of war, love and hate. She is kept alive by an injection of oil rather than that of medicine. She is a symbol of the object of male desire, now reduced from the beautiful to the profitable. Thus, the Trojan War is half-hilariously fought, and, after the killing of

Agamemnon and Clytemnestra, Orestes, as almost Bush, appears as an Americanized neo-liberal computer game player. The performance, without much explanation, oscillates between the past and the present, between the Ancient Greek and the contemporary Iraq. Pillai notes: 'The text is set in a post apocalyptic no-man's-land. Characters confront each other with lengthy monologues often overlapping with each other. We are confronted with a kind of associative prose poem, a blueprint for a performance event set for/in an abstract post apocalyptic world' (2007: 15).

Pillai intentionally mixed the traditional with the contemporary and the authentic with the falsified. He was not afraid of being kitsch in his celebratory but dystopic portrayal of today's world. As Kapur notes: 'Excavation to death, quarrying the body, bleeding dry its remains, this is the topology on which the politics of oil and the clash of civilizations is staged' (2007).

These completely different takes on Greek tragedy were staged on the same set designed by Nakayama Daisuke, a Japanese visual artist, and were sewn together, as it were, with an intermission and an interlude. For some, the performance was understandably a showcasing of different cultures. As Theatre Cocoon is well known for more commercial works, the degree of Eckersallian 'con-fusion' escalated at this venue.

Watching the nationally televised broadcasting of 'Performing Women' in January 2008, I wondered what kind of political and/or ethical impact this production could have on viewers in Japan. I hope that both audience members in the theatre and the viewers watching on television came to realize that, in the phantasmagoric space called Asia, there are still people 'who refuse to conform or surrender or forget; whose sense of revenge, dishonor or courage can never be underestimated and who will face questions of mortality unflinchingly'.

ADORNO, Theodor. 1981 [1967]. 'Aldous Huxley and Utopia', in *Prisms* (Samuel Weber and Shierry Weber, trans.). Cambridge, MA: MIT Press.

AGHEBATI, Mohammad. 2007. 'A New Interpretation of Sophocles' Oedipus the King'. *Performing Women*, Programme Note, p. 11.

BHABHA, Homi K. 1994. *The Location of Culture*. London: Routledge.

BHARUCHA, Rustom. 2003. 'Genet in Manila: Reclaiming the Chaos of Our Times', in manuscript for Japanese translation in *Butai Geijutsu* 4.

BIRRINGER, Johannes. 1986. 'Pina Bausch: Dancing across Borders', *TDR* 30(2) (T110): 85–97.

BUBU. 2000. 'I'm This'. Text distributed for the performance.

BUTLER, Judith. 1988. 'Performative Act and Gender Constitution: An Essay on Phenomenology and Feminist Criticism'. *Theatre Journal* 40(4): 519–31. [Also published as 'Performative Act to Gender Kosei: Gensho-gaku to Feminism Riron' (Yoshikawa Junko trans.). *Theatre Arts* 3 (1995): 58–73.]

CHIN, Daryl. 1991. 'Interculturalism, Postmodernism, Pluralism', in Bonnie Marranca and Gautam Dasgupta (eds), *Interculturalism and Performance*. New York: PAJ Publications.

CARRUTHERS, Ian (with Yasunari Takahashi). 2004. *The Theatre of Suzuki Tadashi*. London: Cambridge University Press.

ECKERSALL, Peter. 2005. 'Theatrical Collaboration in the Age of Globalization: The Gekidan Kaita-isha–NYID Intercultural Collaboration Project', in Hae-kyung Um (ed.), *Diasporas and Interculturalism in Asian Performing Arts*. London: Routledge Curzon.

GOODMAN, David C. 1988. *Drama and Japanese Culture in the 1960s: The Return of the Gods*. Armonk, NY: M. E. Sharpe.

GLUCK, Carol. 1995. 'Rekishi Ishiki wo Kensho suru' ('Interrogating a Historical Consciousness'). *Asahi Shinbun* (Asahi Newspaper), 24 November.

HARDT, Michael and Antonio Negri. 2000. *Empire*. Cambridge: Harvard University Press.

HARVEY, David. 2003. *The New Imperialism*. London: Oxford University Press.

HAROOTUNIAN, H. D. 1993. 'America's Japan/Japan's Japan', in Masao Miyoshi and H. D. Harootunian (eds), *Japan in the World*, Durham: Duke University Press.

HIJIKATA, Tatsumi. 1968. *Hijikata Tatsumi to Nihonjin: nikutai no hanran (Tatsumi Hijikata and the Japanese: Revolt of the Flesh)*. Tokyo: Nihon Seinen-kan Hall.

HIRATA, Oriza. 1995. *Gendai Kogo Engeki no Tameni (For Contemporary Colloquial Theatre)*. Tokyo: Bansei-sha.

HUXLEY, Aldous. 1984 [1932]. *Brave New World*. London: The Hogarth Press.

IBARAGI, Ken. 1973. *Shingeki Sho-shi (A Short History of Shingeki)*. Tokyo: Mirai-sha.

ISHIMITSU, Yasuo. 2000. 'Hisyteric na Shintai no Yume—Shintairon no Yukue' ('The Dream of the Hysteric Body: Whereabouts of Body in Theory'), in Kobayashi Yasuo and Matsuura Hisaki (eds), *Shintai: Hifu no Shuji-gaku (The Body: Rhetoric of the Skin)*, *Volume 3: Hyosho no Disukuru (Discourse of Representation)*. Tokyo: University of Tokyo Press.

IZUMI, Kyoka. 1908. *Kusa meikyu (A Grass Labyrinth)*. Tokyo: Shunyo-do.

JAPAN Playwrights Association (ed.), *Half A Century of Japanese Theatre IX, 1990s*, PART 3 (Tokyo: Kinokuniya, 2007).

KAN Takayuki. 1981a. *Sengo Engeki (Post-war Theatre)*. Tokyo: Asahi Shinbun-Sha.

———. 1981b. *Zoku Kaitaisuru Engeki (Decomposing Theatre 2)*. Tokyo: Renga-shobo Shin-sha.

KAPUR, Anuradha. 2007. 'Uneven Terrain: Mapping Greek Texts Today'. *Performing Women*, Programme Note, p. 20.

KARA, Juro. 1997. *Tokken-teki Nikutai-ron (Theory of Privileged Body)*. Tokyo: Hakuksui-sha.

KAWAMURA, Takeshi. 1984. 'Massara na Basho to Tato no Kaibutsu' ('Tabula Rasa and the Monster with Multiple Heads'), in *Genocide and Nippon Wars: The First Collected Plays of Kawamura Takeshi*. Tokyo: Mirai-sha.

KAYAMA, Rika. 2001. 'Murakami Takashi: Ukete-iru no ha Jun-pu ka Gyaku-fu ka' ('Murakami Takashi: Is the Wind Against Him or For Him?'). *Eureka* 33(12): 114–18.

———. 2002. *Petit-nationalism Shokogun: Wakamono-tachi no Nipponism (Petit-nationalist Sentiments: Nipponism Among the Youth)*. Tokyo: Chuo Koron Shin-sha.

KAZAMA, Ken. 1992. *Sho-gekijo no Fukei (The Landscape of Little Theatres)*. Tokyo: Chuo-koron Sha.

KENG SEN, Ong 2000. 'Notes to Japanese Friends'. Programme Note.

KHOJAKULI, Ovlyakuli. 2007. 'Medea in Relation to World Harmony'. *Performing Women*, Programme Note, p. 7.

KITAMURA, So. 1982. 'Hogi-uta' ('A Celebration Song'), in *Kitamura So no Gyakushu* (*The Revenge of Kitamura So*). Tokyo: Jiritsu-shobo.

KOKAMI, Shoji. 1991. *Asahi no Yona Yuhi o Tsurete* (*With a Rising Sun which Looks Like a Setting Sun*). Tokyo: Kyuritsu-sha.

KONO, Takashi. 1998. 'Brecht Seitan Hyaku-shunen—Gendaisei Minaosu Engekijin' ('Brecht's Centennial—Theatre People are Rethinking Brecht's Contemporaneity'). *Nihon Keizai Shinbun* (The Japan Economy Newspaper), 9 September, p. 40.

KUMAKURA, Takaaki. 2002. 'Mezurashii Kinoko Buyo-dan no Frull (Mini) Wild wo Mite Omotta Koto' ('What I Thought About Watching Strange Mushroom Dance Company's *Frill* (*Mini*) *Wild*'). *Butai Geijutsu* 1: 124–9.

MAROTTI, William. 1997. 'Butoh no Mondaisei to Honshitsu Shugi Wana' ('The Problematics of Butoh and the Essentialist Trap'). *Theatre Arts* 8: 88–96.

MIYADAI, Shinji. 1995. *Owari naki Nichijo o Ikiyo* (*Live and Endure a Neverending Everyday Life*). Tokyo: Chikuma-shobo.

MIYAZAWA, Akio. 2002. 'Program Note' for *Tokyo Body*.

——. 2002–03. *Tokyo Body*, an acting version (unpublished).

——. 2004. 'Press Release' for *Tokyo/Absence/Hamlet*.

——. 2005a. *Fuzai* (Absence). Tokyo: Bungei Shunju-Sha. [Originally published as *The Absence of Akihito*, in *Bungakukai*, August 2004.]

——. 2005b. 'Programme Note' for *Tokyo/Absence/Hamlet*.

——. 2005c. *Tokyo/Absence/Hamlet*, an acting version (unpublished), published in *Teatro* (January 2005): 110–53.

MÜLLER, Heiner. 1977. '*Die Hamletmaschine*' ('*The Hamletmachine*'), in Carl Weber (ed. and trans.), *Hamletmachine and Other Texts for the Stage*. New York: Theatre Communications Group.

MURAKAMI, Takashi. 2000. 'Super Flat Manifesto', in *Super Flat*, Tokyo: Madra Publishing, pp. 4–5.

——. 2005. *Little Boy: The Arts of Japan's Exploding Subculture*. New Haven: Yale University Press.

N.A. 1988 [1984–85] *Daihyakka Jiten* (*World Encyclopaedia*). Tokyo: Heibon-sha.

N.A. 2000. *The American Heritage Dictionary of the English Language*. Boston: Houghton Mifflin.

NAKAJIMA Hiroaki. 1997. 'Brecht to Terayama Shuji' ('Brecht and Terayama Shuji'), in *Doitsu Engeki: Bungaku no Mangekyo (German Theatre—Kaleidoscope of Literature)*. Tokyo: Dogaku-sha.

NISHIDO, Kojin. 1987. *Engeki Shiso no Boken (The Adventures of Theatrical Thoughts)*. Tokyo: Ronso-sha.

———. 1998. 'Mondai to shite no 90 Nendai Engeki' ('Theatre Culture in the 1990s as a Problem'). *Teatro* (August 1998): 25–9.

NODA, Hideki. 2003. 'Engeki moshikuwa Fukushu ni mukawa-nai Chisei' ('Theatre, or Intelligence for Not Going for Revenge'). *Butai Geijutsu* 4: 10–28.

OKADA, Toshiki. 2005. *Sangatsu no Itsukakan (Five Days in March)*. Tokyo: Hakusui-sha.

OOTORI, Hidenaga. 2003. 'Revolt, Dysfunction, Dementia: Toward the Body of "Empire"', in Philippe Vergne (ed.), *How Latitude Become Forms: Art in a Global Age*. Minneapolis: Walker Arts Center.

ORWELL, George. 1949. *Nineteen Eighty-Four*. London: Secker and Warburg.

OTOMO, Katsuhiro. 1984–93. *Akira*, 6 VOLS. Tokyo: Kodan-sha

OZASA, Yoshio. 1985. *Nihon Gendai Engeki-shi (The History of Japanese Contemporary Theatre)*, VOL. 1. Tokyo: Hakusui-sha.

———. 1990. *Nihon Gendai Engeki-shi (The History of Japanese Contemporary Theatre)*, VOL. 3, Tokyo: Hakusui-sha.

PAO KUN, Kuo. 1998. 'The Spirits Play'. Unpublished manuscript. [Later published in *Two Plays by Kuo Pao Kun: Descendants of The Eunuch Admiral and The Spirits Play*. Singapore: SNP Press, 2003.]

PAVIS, Patrice. 1996. 'Toward a Theory of Interculturalism in Theatre', in Patrice Pavis (ed.), *The Intercultural Performance Reader*. London: Routledge.

PHELAN, Peggy. 1993. *Unmarked: The Politics of Performance*. London: Routledge.

PILLAI, Abhilash. 2007. 'An Oil Factory in a Video Game Station'. *Performing Women*, Programme Note, p. 15.

ROLF, Robert T. 1992. 'Japanese Theatre From the 1980s: The Ludic Conspiracy'. *Modern Drama* 34(1): 127–36.

ROY, Arundhati. 2002. *Power Politics*. New York: South End Press.

SAITO, Tamaki. 2006. *Ikinobiru tameno Lacan (Lacan for Survival)*. Tokyo: Bajiriko; for earlier publication see www.shobunsha.co.jp/ [Japanese only].

SAKAI, Takashi. 2001. '"Senso" Jotai no Marx to Foucault' ('Marx and Foucault in the State of "War"' ('Marx and Foucault in the State of "War"). *Jokyo* 2(19): 38–69.

SAKURAI, Keisuke. 2004. 'Kodomo Shintai to wa Nanika: Cotemporary Dance ni okeru "Rekishito Kioku"' ('What Is Child's Body? History and Memory in Contemporary Dance'). *Butai Geijutsu* 5: 11.

SATO, Makoto. 2002. *Zettai Hikoki (An Absolute Plane)*. Unpublished acting script.

SAWARAGI, Noi. 2001. 'Super-flat kara Geisai e' ('From Super-flat to *Geisai*'). *Eureka* (October 2001): 97–8.

SCHECHNER, Richard. 1982. 'Decline and Fall of the American Avant-Garde', in *The End of Humanism: Writings on Performance*. New York: PAJ Publications.

———. 2006. 'Five Avantgardes . . . or None'. In manuscript.

SENDA, Akihiko. 1995. *Nihon no Gendai Engeki (Japan's Contemporary Theatre)*. Tokyo: Iwanami Shinsho.

SENDA, Koreya (ed.). 1961–62. *Collected Plays by Bertolt Brecht* (5 VOLS) (Senda Koreya, Kato Ei, Komiya Kozo, Uchigaki Keiichi, Iwabuchi Tatsuji trans.). Tokyo: Hakusui-sha.

———. 1962. *Konnichi no Sekai ha Engeki-de Saigen dekiruka? Brecht no Engeki-ron shu (Can the Present-day World Be Reproduced by Means of Theatre? Brecht's Theatre Theories)*. Tokyo: Hakusui-sha.

———. 1975. *Mo Hitotsu no Shingeki-shi: Senda Koreya Jiden (An Alternative History of Shingeki: An Autobiography)*. Tokyo: Chikuma-shobo.

———. 1976. *Nijyu-seiki Engeki: Brecht to Watashi (The Twentieth Century Theatre: Brecht and I)*. Tokyo: Yomiuri Sinbun-sha.

———. 1980a. 'Kaisetsu-teki Zuiso 1945–49' ('An Explanatory Essay: 1945–49'), in *Senda Koreya Engeki Ronshu (Collected Theatre Writings of Senda Koreya)*, VOL. 1, Tokyo: Mirai-sha, pp. 343–92.

———. 1980b. 'Kaisetsu-teki Zuiso 1950–54' (An Explanatory Essay: 1950–54), in *Senda Koreya Engeki Ronshu (Collected Theatre Writings of Senda Koreya)*, VOL. 2, Tokyo: Mirai-sha, pp. 329–84.

———. 1985. 'Kaisetsu-teki Zuiso 1955–59' (An Explanatory Essay: 1955–59), in *Senda Koreya Engeki Ronshu (Collected Theatre Writings of Senda Koreya)*, VOL. 3, Tokyo: Mirai-sha, pp. 335–445.

SHIBUYA, Nozomi. 2003. *Tamashii no Rodo—Neoliberaism no Kenryoku ron (Labour of the Soul—Neoliberal Power Structure)*. Tokyo: Seido-sha.

SUZUKI, Tadashi. 1986. *The Way of Acting: Theatre Writings of Tadashi Suzuki*. New York: Theatre Communications Group.

TAN, Marcus. 2000. 'Spirits of Remembrance'. Available at: www.inkpot.com-/theatrelspiritsplay.html

TEZUKA, Osamu. 1984. 'Kanketsu ni atatte' ('In Completing the Work'), in *Buddha*, VOL. 14, Tokyo: Kodan-sha, pp. 2–5.

UCHINO, Tadashi. 1988. 'Suzuki Tadashi no Hoho: *Gekideki naru mono o Megutte* kara *Toroiya no Onna* he' ('Suzuki Tadashi and His Method: From *On Dramatic Passion II* to *The Trojan Women*'). *Littera* 3: 81–123.

———. 1996. *Melorodrama no Gyakushu: Watakushi Engeki no Hachiju-nendai* (*The Melodramatic Revenge: Theatre of the Private in the 1980s*). Tokyo: Keiso-shobo.

———. 2001. *Melodrama kara Performance he: Niju-seiki America Engeki-ron* (*From Melodrama to Performance: The 20th Century American Theatre*). Tokyo: University of Tokyo Press.

———. 2003. 'Pop, Post-postmodernism, and Junk: Murakami Takashi and "J" Theatre'. *Dokkyo International Review* 16: 115–29.

UNAKAMI, Hiromi. 2002. 'Watashi no Tonari ni Iru-nowa Watashitachi da' ('We Are Next to I'). *Butai Geijutsu* 1: 46–53.

WATANABE, Masahiro. 2001–02. *A Historical Bibliography on Western Classical Studies in Japan from Late 16th Century to 1945*, 4 VOLS. Nagoya, Japan: Aichi University of Education.

YASUMI, Akihito. 1995a. 'A Seasonal Review'. *Theatre Arts* 1: 156–67.

———. 1995b. 'A Seasonal Review'. *Theatre Arts* 3: 165–71.

YUNG, Danny. 1997. Interview with NHK Educational Channel.

ŽIŽEK, Slavoj. 2002. *Welcome to the Desert of the Real! Five Essays on September 11 and Related Dates*. London: Verso.

———. 2004. *Iraq: The Borrowed Kettle*. London: Verso.